AF540241

CULTURE, COGNITION AND SCHOOLING
A REASSESSMENT

CULTURE, COGNITION AND SCHOOLING

A REASSESSMENT

Edited by

Dr. B.R. Ghosh
Dr. Nanjunda D.C.
Prof. Annapurna M.
Prof. Rajashekar Reddy
Dr. Subramanay CE
Dr. Bhamini Raghviah
Dr. Mahadeviah V.N.
Dr. Vijaya Kumar B.J.

DISCOVERY PUBLISHING HOUSE PVT. LTD.
NEW DELHI-110 002

Published by:
Tilak Wasan
DISCOVERY PUBLISHING HOUSE PVT. LTD.
4831/24, Ansari Road, Prahlad Street
Darya Ganj, New Delhi-110002 (India)
Phone: +91-11-23279245, 43764432
Fax: +91-11-23253475
E-mail: parul.wasan@gmail.com
discoverypublishinghouse@gmail.com
info@discoverypublishinggroup.com
web: www.discoverypublishinggroup.com

First Edition: **2011**
ISBN: 978-81-8356-761-9

Culture, Cognition and Schooling: ***A Reassessment***

Printed at:
Shree Balaji Art Press
Delhi

Preface

Educational development is a Herculean task to any Government. It would be much more difficult especially to the Indian educational policy makers because more than one fourth of the India's population is still illiterates. The main objective of this book is to improve the quality of teaching and research in educational field. However, the specific objectives of this volume are to prepare policy modules for policy makers on various aspects of education problems, teacher's issue and student reaction.

Editors

Contents

List of Contributors

Prof. S. Venkatesan, Department Psychology, University of Mysore, Mysore-570 006

Nahid Sarikhani Ph.D. Student, Department of Sociology, Mysore University, Mysore-06, Karnataka, India

Ayatollah Karimi, Department Psychology, University of Mysore, Mysore-570006

Afsaneh Khajevand Khoshali Research Scholar Dept. of Psychology, University of Mysore

Dr. K. Yeshodhara *Professor, DOS in Education, University of Mysore, Mysore*

Hadi Mohammad Pour *Research Scholar, DOS in Education, University of Mysore, Mysore*

Dr. Prakash K. Lecturer, National College of Education, Balaraja Urs Road, Shimoga, Karnataka(s), India

Prof. Premalatha Sharma Professor, Department of Education, Regional Institute of Education, Manasagangothri, Mysore, Karnataka(s), India-570 006

Ali Khanekashi Lecturer in Azad University of Behbahan, Khozestan-Iran

Dr. Y.N. Sridhar, Reader in Department of Studies in Education, University of Mysore, Manasagangotri, Mysore-17

Hamid Reza Razavi, Faculty Member of Shomal University in Iran

Mahnoosh Abedini, Research Scholar, Department of Education Mysore University, Mysore

Prof. K. Yeshodhara, Department of Education, University of Mysore

Dr. Ali Khanekashi, Azad University of Behbahan, Khozestan, Iran

Mahvash Ziaeifard, Research Student, Faculty of Education, Mysore University, Mysore

Dr. Lancy D'Souza, Department of Psychology, Maharajas College, University of Mysore, Mysore, India

Jayaraju R., Department of Psychology, Karnataka State Open University, Mysore, India

Venugopal P.N., Anthropological Survey of India, SRC, Mysore, India

Natesha N, Department of Studies in Physiology, University of Mysore, Mysore, India

Dr. Gururaj B. Urs, Asst. Professor and Programme Coordinator, Institute of Health Management Research, Hosur Road, Bangalore, India

Dr. Sudha S.T., Chief Librarian, St. Ann's College, Mangalore-2, India

Dr. Harinarayana N.S. Reader, Department of Library and Information Science, Manasagangothri, Mysore-6, India

Shaban Barimani Varandi, Research Student Islamic Azadi University, Iran

Seyed Younas Mohammadi Yousef Nejad, Research Scholar, Department of Psychology, University of Kerala

Dr. Raju, S. Department of Psychology, University of Kerala

Daryoush Ghasemian, Reserch Scholar, Department of Psychology, University of Mysore, Mysore

Dr. Prabhu Swami, B.S. Lecturer, Mysore

Dr. Ningamma C. Betsur, Reader Department of Studies in Education, University of Mysore, Mysore

Armin Mahmoudi Research Scholar in-Department of Studies in Education University of Mysore, Mysore

Dr. Malli Gandhi, Regional Institute of Education, Mysore-06

Armin Mahmoudi Research Scholar in-Department of Studies in Education University of Mysore, Manasagangothri, Mysore-570 006—India

CHAPTER

1 The Relationship between Mathematics Anxiety, Mathematics Performances and overall Academic Performance of High School Students

— *Ayatollah Karimi and Prof. S. Venkatesan*

INTRODUCTION

Good academic performance is very important not only to students and their parents, but also to institutions of learning, educationists and any progressive. The quality of students' academic performance is influenced by wide range of environmental factors rather simply teacher factors and psychological factors within the learners such as motivation and the self, rather than simply by ability. The test anxiety and Mathematics anxiety are increasingly being seen as factors underpinning levels of motivation for academic performance. Suinn *et al.* (1988), suggested that it affects many people and threatens both performance and participation.

Many learners experience Mathematics anxiety in our schools today. Reported consequences of being anxious toward Mathematics include the avoidance of Mathematics and the decline in Mathematics achievement. This kind of 'anxiety' was first detected in the late 1950s. Dreger and Aiken (1957) noticed undergraduate college students reacting emotionally to arithmetic and Mathematics. Although this reaction appeared to be similar to test anxiety in general; they found that Mathematics anxiety has an existence of its own. They labeled it 'number anxiety'. It is often assumed that high level of anxiety impairs performance. A moderate amount of anxiety may actually facilitate performance. Beyond a certain degree, however, anxiety hinders performance particularly in the case of higher mental activities and conceptual process (Shemp, 1986).

Psychological literature provides a number of conceptualizations of Mathematics anxiety (Rabalise, 1988). Richardson and Suinn (1972) defined Mathematics anxiety in terms of its (debilitating) effect on mathematical performance. They observed that the feeling of tension and anxiety interfere with manipulation and solving of mathematical problems in a wide variety of ordinary life and academic situations. Many students who suffer from Mathematics anxiety have little confidence in their ability to do Mathematics and tend to take the minimum numbers of required Mathematics courses, greatly limiting their career choice options (Garry, 2005).

Mathematics anxiety is an outcome of low self-esteem and fear of failure. It causes problems for processing the next oncoming information as well as in using previously learned information for problem solving. Such students tend to avoid Mathematics whenever or wherever possible (Daane and Tina, 1986). It may be a critical factor in the educational and vocational choices students make and may influence whether or not they achieve their educational or career goals (Betz, 1978). Clute (1984) found that Students who have a high level of Mathematics anxiety have lower levels of Mathematics achievement and Hembree (1990) noted that math's anxiety seriously constrains Performance in mathematical tasks and reduction in anxiety is consistently associated with improvement in achievement.

Despite the many reports on the relationships between test anxiety and academic performance, there is scarce if any documentation of the influence of Mathematics anxiety on academic performance. Secondly, there is need for studies which will address gender differences in the levels of Mathematics anxiety in relation to their overall academic performance. This presents study therefore focuses on these issues.

Goals

The study has two aims:

- To examine the relationship between levels of Mathematics anxiety and Mathematics performances and overall academic performance among high school students in Karnataka
- To examine the effects of gender on students' levels of Mathematics anxiety and Mathematics performances and academic performance.

Clarification of Concepts

Mathematics anxiety: Mathematics anxiety is defined as involving feelings of tension and anxiety that interfere with the manipulating of numbers and the solving of mathematical problems in a wide variety of ordinary life and academic situations (Richardson and Suinn, 1972). In this research, the Mathematics anxiety refers to the scores of Mathematics Anxiety Rating Scale (MARS) by Venkatesan and Karimi (2008).

Hypotheses

1. There are negative significant relationships between Mathematics anxiety, Mathematics performances and overall academic performance in high school students.
2. There are significant differences between boys and girls in Mathematics anxiety, Mathematics performances and overall academic performance in high school students.

METHOD

The Sample

424 of 10 grade high school students (212 males and 212 females) were selected via random sampling from 10 high school in Bangalore, Mysore and Mangalore. The mean age of the students was 14.8.

TOOLS AND MATERIALS

Socio-Demographic Questionnaire

This form contains the information about students background that developed by researcher for this study.

Mathematics Anxiety Rating Scale-India (MARS-I)

This questionnaire was developed by Venkatesan and Karimi (2008) and contains the situations that arouse Mathematics anxiety. The researchers administered the 98 item MARS and found 31 item about Math test/course Anxiety and numerical task anxiety. This version was designed with the belief that "Math anxiety is defined primarily by a Math test anxiety and secondarily by anxiety about executing Math tasks or taking Math courses. The correlation between scores on the 31 item MARS-I and 98 items MARS (Richardson and Suinn 1972), was 0.87. Two-week test-retest reliability of the abbreviated (31-item) scale was 0.85 and internal consistency alpha coefficient for the 31-item MARS–I was computed 0.88. For each item is 5 options (1-not at all anxious, 2-not anxious, 3-slightly anxious, 4-anxious, 5-very much anxious) and the ranges of scores is between 25 to 125.

The instruments were self-administered to the participants in classroom situation in each school on a different day with the help of some teachers from each school used for the study.

RESULTS AND DISCUSSION

Relationship between Mathematics Anxiety (MA), Mathematics Performances (MP) and Overall Academic Performance (OAP)

The correlations between levels of MA, MP, and OAP are presented in the correlation matrix table 1 next page.

It was hypothesized that there are negative significant relationships between Mathematics Anxiety, MP and OAP. Contrary to the hypothesis, negative significant correlations were found between MA with MP [r = –.551, p = .000] and with OAP [r = –.495, P = .000.]

Moreover, there are negative significant relationships between two subscales of Mathematics Anxiety (Math test and Numerical task) with MP and OAP.

These corroborate previous students which reported significant correlations between Mathematics Anxiety and overall academic performance (Clute, 1984 ; Hembree, 1990; Lee, 1996).

Furthermore, there was a high correlations between MP, and AP[r = .909, p = .000].

Table 1.1. Means, Standard Deviations and Correlation Matrix of MA, MP, and OAP

Variables	Math test M=32.17 SD=3.56	Numerical task M=33.99 SD=3.54	Total MA scores M=66.17 SD=7.05	Mathematic performance. M=73.51 SD= 10.75	Academic performance M=73.01S D=10.31
Math test					
-					
Numerical task					
.969(**)	-				
Total MA scores					
.992(**)	.992(**)	-			
Mathematic performance.					
-.551(**)	-.493(**)	-.551(**)	-		
overall academic performance					
-.515(**)	-.466(**)	-.495(**)	.909(**)	-	

N: 424. ** Correlation is significant at the 0.01 level (1-tailed).

The Influence of Gender on Mathematics Anxiety, Mathematics Performances and Overall Academic Performance

Table 1.2 presents the scores of boys and girls in three dependent variables. The results of two independent samples T test are described below.

An inspection of the mean scores of males and females on table 4 below indicates that:

1. Females scored slightly higher on the MA scale (m = 69.41, SD = 9.370) than males (m = 63.81, SD=3.139).

Table 1.2. Means, standard deviations and estimated two independent samples T test of boys and girls in three variables

Dependent Variable	SEX	MEAN	SD	T
Mathematics anxiety	male	63.81	3.139	-4.240**
	female	69.41	9.370	
Mathematics performance	male	72.72	11.052	.270
	female	73.40	9.310	
Academic performance	male	73.75	11.131	-.324
	female	73.16	10.345	

N: 424. ** Correlation is significant at the 0.01 level (1-tailed).

2. There are not significantly differences between males and females on Mathematics performance. (m = 72.72, SD =11.052) for male and (m = 73.40, SD = 9.310) for female
3. In overall academic performance also there is not significantly differences between two gender groups, (m = 73.75, SD =11.131) for male and (m = 73.16, SD = 10.345) for female.

On the whole, it is interpreted that even though the Mathematics anxiety of females is higher than mails, but it hasn't negative effects on their Mathematics performance or overall academic performance.

Discussion and Conclusion

It is hypothesized that there is significant relationship between Mathematics anxiety, Mathematics performances and overall academic performance in high school students. The results of the study reveal significant relationship between Mathematics anxiety, Mathematics performances and overall academic performance in high school students. This means that students who have high Mathematics anxiety tended to perform fewer score in Mathematics and their overall academic performances. However, those who have low Mathematics anxiety tended to perform high score in Mathematics and their overall academic performances. These findings corroborate pervious findings which report significant relationships between Mathematics anxiety, MP and OAP (Clute, 1984; Hembree, 1990 and Lee, 1996).

The results reveal that there is significant gender difference on the scores of Mathematics anxiety. females scored significantly higher than males whereas there is not significant gender difference on the scores of Mathematics and academic performance. These findings are agree with; Lee (1996) and Orenstein (1994), about the role of gender in Mathematics anxiety and performance. In most of these studies the researchers has showed that Mathematics anxiety in females is higher than males (AAUW, 1992).

In support of previous studies this study has established the fact that Mathematics anxiety is a good predictor of Mathematics performances and overall academic performance. It also shows that gender hasn't a moderate's role in the effects of Mathematics anxiety on Mathematics performances and overall academic performance. There is a need for further research with Mathematics anxiety with different stages of academic levels, difference kinds of anxiety and across the other states to further information in this area good.

REFERENCES

American Association of University Women (AAUW). (1992). how schools shortchange girls. Washington, DC: *American Association of University Women Educational Foundation*.

Betz, N.E. (1978). Prevalence, distribution and correlates of math anxiety in college students. *Journal of Counseling Psychology*. 25, 441-448.

Clute, P. (1984). Mathematics anxiety, instructional method, and achievement in a survey course in college Mathematics. *Journal for Research in Mathematics Education*, 5, 50-58.

Daane, C.J., Judy, G., and Tina, S. (1986). "Mathematics Anxiety and learning styles: What is the Relationship in the Elementary pre service Teachers?" *School Science & Mathematics*: 84-88.

Dreger, R. M., and Aiken, L. R. (1957). The identification of number anxiety in a college population. *Journal of Educational Psychology*, 47, 344-351.

Garry, V. S. (2005). The effect of Mathematics anxiety the course and career choice of high school cational-technical education students.

Hembree, R. (1990). The nature, effects, and relief of Mathematics anxiety. *Journal for Research in Mathematics Education*, 21(1):33–46.

Lee, V. E. (1996). The influence of school climate on gender differences in the achievement and engagement of young adolescents (Report No. PS 025 154). Washington, DC.

Orenstein, P. (1994). School girls: Young women, self-esteem, and the confidence gap. New York: Doubleday.

Rabalise, Alien. (1988). Identification of math anxiety subtypes. Thesis submitted for degree master of clinical psychology in West Virginia University.

Richardson, F.C., and Suinn, R.M. (1972). "The Mathematics Anxiety Rating Scale: Psychometric Data". *Journal of Counseling Psychology*, 19, 39-47.

Shemp. R.R (1986). "The psychology of learning" *Mathematics*. Penguin: Harmondsworth. 95-112.

Suinn, Taylor and Edwards (1988). The measurement of Mathematics anxiety: The Mathematics anxiety rating scale for adolescents-MARS-A. *Journal of Clinical Psychology*, 38(3), 576-580.

Venkatesan, S. and Karimi, B.A. (2008). Development of Mathematics anxiety scales in high school students of India and Iran. Thesis submitted for degree Ph.D of clinical psychology in Mysore University.

CHAPTER

2

The Study of Effects of Education on Women's Occupation in India

— Nahid Sarikhani

The present study aims at investigating the study of effects of education on women's occupation in India based on population census in 2001. The researcher has used of descriptive research method. Results indicate the number of workers by sex-ratio, educational level and residential area and states. The results also reveal the age group of working men and women emphasizing their educational level in the country. The researcher compares main and marginal woman workers in different educational levels. Mean while, this study presents the number of main and marginal woman workers by main active at national level, and whether marginal workers of women seeking classified jobs have a suitable educational level, and/or whether non-worker women seeking for a job are mostly illiterate or poorly literate? Moreover, results show households pay more attention to educational males than that of females among household members. In general, it offers suggestions to increase educational level of women so that they can take up suitable and specialized positions in the society.

INTRODUCTION

The role of women in a society is very important and no nation can ignore it. They can affect on economic development. If they improve higher education levels among themselves, they will earn more job opportunities than last time in their communities. Unfortunately, today, data indicate that most of the women have inquired low educational levels and have lost proper job's opportunities in the society. As a result, most of them are faced with unemployment phenomenon. As unemployment has become a vital problem for the women seeking jobs. In this competitive world, it has become more acute. As a matter of fact, in most of the private and government offices men's applications were accepted. Therefore, education has worked as the prime factor to motivate the women to work.

Undoubtedly literate rate of women can be strongly influenced by socio-economic factors. Because they feel that whatever they have acquired through education has to be utilized. It should not be wasted. They should make proper use of their abilities and do something for the service of the society and the nation. They want to use their leisure time in some gainful activity. Again they are fully conscious of their own individuality and they want to maintain the personal status and independent social standing by working and earning for their own needs. They want to be self-sufficient. They understand very well that economic self-sufficiency has improved their social status. They have accomplished more freedom and personal security. They enjoy more rights and if they are questioned they can fight it better. In short, education and self-earnings increased their self-confidence and they are able to come out of the dependency. This is an outstanding achievement of this age (Dak, 1989).

Education has also served as a discriminatory tool to limit work opportunities and wages for women. Since men are better educated, they can use modern technology more efficiently than women. Further, sex-based division of work is imposed in sex stereotyping of "curricula" (i.e. home science for girls), and occupational placements (i.e. nursing or teaching), and it has been reflected in enrolling men and women in different fields of studies and courses as well as in occupational choices.

All these have greatly restricted the areas of employment and work participation of women (Dak, 1989). On the other hand, urbanization has weakened the influence of joint families and the rigidity of social norms affecting women's traditional role has been perpetuated by the system.

In India, formal education of women began a hundred years ago. In spite of this early start, improvement in general literacy was painfully slow especially in the higher educational levels, and it is influenced on the work participation rate. As according to the census in 2001, the work participation rate of women in India is only 25.6 per cent that most of them engage in the informal sector and low levels of economic activities. Mean while studies of professional women elsewhere report discrimination and role conflict as major problems (Kumar and Aknayak.1997).

Early marriage is also very common among the Indian families. This creates problems for the women to acquire education and jobs for themselves. After marriage, they cannot continue their education.

In addition, even when women are professionally trained and aspire to utilize their skills' to produce the best performance and to earn fame and name, their in-laws do not accept their working. In this way, women forget their professional skills and abilities (like doctors, engineers and technicians).

In the study, the author attributes analyzing the study of effects of education on women's occupation in India based on population census in 2001.

FINDINGS

Education is an indispensable means for helping women out of their economic misery because economic dependency is other factor contributing to the low status of women. Educated women everywhere show the tendency towards increasing economic independence. The awareness of the need to become financially independent and to supplement family income, have forced women to accept jobs outside the home.

According to censuses, sex ratio among population of women at the national level has been 934, 927 and 933 during 1981-2001 respectively. It probably presents the position of women has worsened considerably, a decline in the sex ratio due to absolute condition of health and survival for women.

On the other hand, the population of women is steadily increasing as the growth rate is 23.1 per cent in the 2001 census.

As per 2001 census, of the total population of women 84.1 percent consist population aged 7 years and above in India. (Census of India, 2001) literacy rate for women is 53.7 while it is 75.3 per cent for men. In the rural areas, the male and female literacy rates are 86.3 per cent and 72.8 per cent respectively, and in the urban areas, these are 70.7 per cent and 46.1 per cent respectively in country.

According to the 2001 census, the number of literates by completed educational level to total women aged 7 years and above at the national level indicates 3.4 per cent of men and 3.9 per cent of women are categorized as 'Literates without educational level'. Also 24.1 per cent of men and 28.4 per cent of women come in the category 'Below Primary'. More than one-fifth of the men (24.8%) and over one-fourth of women the (28.2%) have completed 'Primary'. Nearly one-sixth of the men (16.6%) and over one-sixth of the women have completed 'Middle level' and more than one-fifth of men the (22.5%) and less than one-fifth of the women (18.4%) have completed the educational level of 'Matric/Secondary' or 'Higher Secondary/Intermediate/Pre-University/Senior Secondary'. Literacy rates of men and women in the category 'Non-technical and technical diploma or certificate not equal to degree' and 'Graduate and above' are less than 10 per cent for men and less 6 per cent for women at the national levels. The proportion of the population with higher level of education is more in urban areas (men 22.5% and women 15.3%) than in rural areas (men 7.6% and women 2.7%). Therefore, there are significant gender differentials among the distribution of the population by educational levels.

The statistics above indicate that women than to men have not been able to take educational advantage special higher educational levels in the society. Because there are several factors such as the governing traditional attitude to women, social structural and institutional factors in communities like early marriage etc.

Also, of the total population aged 7 years and over, 35.2 per cent are illiterate. This rate in rural areas (41.3%) exceeds the urban areas (20.1%). In addition, the data have shown, rate among the women is 46.3 per cent higher than the men (24.7%) and this pattern, similarly blinks among rural areas (male is 29.3 and female is 53.9%) and urban areas (male is 13.7% and female is 27.1%). Then women than men cannot take up suitable opportunities of occupation in society.

As a matter of fact, available literature indicates that there is a close relationship between the spread of female education on the one hand and the development status on the other.

In the other words, literacy rate can affect on the work participation of population special women in societies. The work participation rate is defined as the percentage of the total worker (main and marginal) to the total population. This is often considered as a very crude measure since this does not take into account the age structure of the population. According to the census of 2001, in India, of the total population of 1,028,610,328 the number of populations returned as workers is 402,234,724. In other words, 39.1 per cent of the populations of India constitute workers. That is to say, nearly two fifths of the country's population at the national level, is reported to be participating in economically productive activities. Of these workers, Those workers who had worked for the major part of the reference period (i.e. 6 months or more) were termed as Main Workers and who had not worked for the major part of the reference period (i.e. 6 months or more) were termed as Marginal Workers, 59.5 per cent are literate and 40.5 are illiterate. Sex ratio in between literate population is 234, and among illiterate population is 1008.

A comparative statement of the number of literates among workers by educational levels at the national level, census of 2001, shows that 62.9 per cent of literate workers are categorized as 'Literate but below matric/secondary' while 25.8 per cent, come in the category 'matric/secondary but below graduate'. 1.1 per cent of the literates have completed 'technical diploma or certificate not equal to degree'. Less than one-tenth have completed 'Graduate and above other than technical degree' and 1.5 per cent of the literates have completed the educational level of 'Technical degree or diploma equal to degree or post-graduate degree'. Therefore, the majority of literate workers has fallen in the category 'literate but below matrict/secondary' but could not complete Middle level of education at the national level. Also, more job opportunities are reported in category 'Graduate and above other than technical degree'. There are significant gender differentials among literate workers, and it is reported that participation of men are appreciable higher across all levels of education. The proportion of literate workers with higher level of education is more in urban areas (22.9%) than rural areas (6.1%). Sex ratio of literate workers with higher level of education in rural areas and urban areas are 132 and 209 respectively.

Table 2.1 shows 63.6 per cent of the 'main workers' are 'Literates' at 2001 Census. From among the literate main workers the highest proportion of literacy is reported in the category 'Literate but below matric/secondary', and the second group is level of education 'Matric/secondary but below graduate'. The smallest population group with 1.2 per cent is recorded at 'Technical diploma or certificate not equal to degree' forms. The proportion of literate main workers of Females than males in the all categories is less because men who are heads of families are presented as supplementing family earnings in the society. on the other hands, men, the principle bread-earners, are dominant in all categories of literate main workers. Moreover, illiterate men than illiterate

Total 2.1. Distribution of Main Workers, by Education of Level and Sex in India 2001

	Educational Level	Persons	Females	%
Total (Rural + Urban)	Total	3,130,04,983	72,857,170	23.3
	Illiterate	113,928,238	44,923,253	39.4
	Literate	199,076,745	27,933,917	14.0
	Literate but below matric/secondary	113,911,636	17,327,096	15.2
	Matric/secondary but below graduate	51,015,376	4,657,228	9.1
	Technical diploma or certificate not equal to degree	2,231,975	358,422	16.1
	Graduate and above other than technical degree	18,596,928	2,521,897	13.6
	Technical degree or diploma equal to degree or post-graduate degree	3,314,253	685,868	20.7
Rural	Total	229,186,552	60,085,301	26.2
	Illiterate	98,539,379	40,271,642	40.9
	Literate	130,647,173	19,813,659	15.2
	Literate but below matric/secondary	85,495,660	14,171,354	16.6
	Matric/secondary but below graduate	29,219,970	2,797,562	9.6
	Technical diploma or certificate not equal to degree	933,206	163,205	17.5
	Graduate and above other than technical degree	6,387,642	554,371	8.7
	Technical degree or diploma equal to degree or post-graduate degree	982,173	162,193	16.5
Urban	Total	83,818,431	12771869	15.2
	Illiterate	15,388,859	4,651,611	30.2
	Literate	68,429,572	8,120,258	11.9

Educational Level	Persons	Females	%
Literate but below matric/secondary	28,415,976	3,155,742	11.1
Matric/secondary but below graduate	21,795,406	1,859,666	8.5
Technical diploma or certificate not equal to degree	1,298,769	195,217	15.0
Graduate and above other than technical degree	12,209,286	1,967,526	16.1
Technical degree or diploma equal to degree or post-graduate degree	2,332,080	523,675	22.5

Source: B3 Table, India, Census of India 2001.

women have found more job opportunities in main workers level. Mean while, the proportion of literate main workers of women against men is less in urban areas and rural areas. As a matter of fact, more job opportunities with main workers are allocated to men. Of course, among the literate women, proportion of educated female main workers is higher in the urban areas against rural areas.

Table 2.2 shows that sex ratio of literate population in the age group under 15 years is 452, in the age group 15-19 is between 168 to 264, in the age group 20-24 is between 141 to 437, in the age group 25-29 is between 107 to 332, in the age group30-34 is between 94 to 282, in the age group 35-39 is between 94 to 266, in the age group 40-59 is between 60 to 243, and in the age group 60 year and above is between 32 to 113 at the national level. In general, the level of participation of children in school going age is considerable special girl's children. There are job opportunities for 'working age group 15-59 years' of men against women in level of main workers, and participation rate of females are higher in low literacy levels. Significantly proportion of the elderly persons aged 60years and above is economically active in the national level that a share was allocated to women. Meanwhile the data reveals appreciable rural-urban differentials. In the rural areas the women do most of the work on farms and perform other economic activities of the villages. These activities do not need to high skill and specialism.

Table 2.2. Distribution of Main Workers by Educational Level, Sex Ratio and Age

	Educational Level	-15	15-19	20-24	25-29	30-34
India	Literate but below matric/ secondary	452	264	209	206	196
	Matric/secondary but below graduate	-	219	141	107	94
	Technical diploma or certificate not equal to degree	-	168	213	160	167
	Graduate and above other than technical degree	-	-	284	196	161
	Technical degree or diploma equal to degree or post-graduate degree	-	-	437	332	282
Rural areas	Literate but below matric/ secondary	480	293	245	239	222
	Matric/secondary but below graduate	-	233	157	122	100
	Technical diploma or certificate not equal to degree	-	132	208	183	205
	Graduate and above other than technical degree	-	-	177	127	100
	Technical degree or diploma equal to degree or post-graduate degree	-	-	347	264	218
Urban areas	Literate but below matric/ secondary	354	171	107	117	128
	Matric/secondary but below graduate	-	192	113	85	86
	Technical diploma or certificate not equal to degree	-	219	218	143	141
	Graduate and above other than technical degree	-	-	369	246	202
	Technical degree or diploma equal to degree or post-graduate degree	-	-	476	366	315

	Educational Level	35-39	40-49	50-59	60-69	70+
India	Literate but below matric/ secondary	186	149	104	70	50
	Matric/secondary but below graduate	94	80	60	32	42
	Technical diploma or certificate not equal to degree	196	213	228	100	113
	Graduate and above other than technical degree	157	136	101	54	69
	Technical degree or diploma equal to degree or post-graduate degree	266	243	170	95	113
Rural areas	Literate but below matric/ secondary	203	160	106	66	45
	Matric/secondary but below graduate	91	71	42	21	35
	Technical diploma or certificate not equal to degree	235	238	247	89	94
	Graduate and above other than technical degree	87	70	46	21	39
	Technical degree or diploma equal to degree or post-graduate degree	191	179	110	46	73
Urban areas	Literate but below matric/ secondary	141	120	98	85	72
	Matric/secondary but below graduate	97	91	79	46	50
	Technical diploma or certificate not equal to degree	171	199	217	109	131
	Graduate and above other than technical degree	198	165	124	70	83
	Technical degree or diploma equal to degree or post-graduate degree	303	269	193	114	128

Source: B9 Table, India, Census of India 2001.

On the other hand, part of the employed population consist marginal workers who had not worked for the major part of the reference period (i.e. 6 months or more). Less than one fourth of the employed population is as marginal workers that proportion of women to total marginal workers is 60 (9%) in the 2001 Census at the national level. The proportion of such workers is higher among the 'Illiterate', against 'Literate' section of the population. Female marginal workers are reported to have considerable proportion both among the 'Illiterates' and the overall category of 'Literates'.

Also, of total 89,229,741 the 'marginal workers' 24,923,666 population (27.9%) at national level are reported to be in the category 'Seeking/available for work' who did not have work for major part of the year and were in the look out for work. The proportion of women of seeking for job to total the category 'Seeking/available for work is 37.7 per cent that more than 35 per cent of these workers are reported to be 'literate'. Mean while 1.5 per cent of the female marginal workers 'seeking/available for work' have a Technical diploma/ Degree/Post-graduate degree in the national level.

Table 2.3. Distribution of Marginal workers by Educational Level and Sex in India, 2001

	Educational level	Persons	Females	%
Total	Total	89,229,741	54,363,078	60.9
	Illiterate	49,012,445	36,884,266	75.3
	Literate	40217296	17478812	43.5
	Literate but below matric/ secondary	28654141	13293112	46.4
	Matric/secondary but below graduate	7494972	2426557	32.4
	Technical diploma or certificate not equal to degree	152577	22429	14.7
	Graduate and above other than technical degree	1272495	299479	23.5
	Technical degree or diploma equal to degree or post-graduate degree	116403	30678	26.4

	Educational level	Persons	Females	%
Rural	Total	80769518	51031616	63.2
	Illiterate	45871400	35128855	76.6
	Literate	34898118	15902761	45.6
	Literate but below matric/ secondary	25392057	12274140	48.3
	Matric/secondary but below graduate	6161908	2097074	34.0
	Technical diploma or certificate not equal to degree	107235	15819	14.8
	Graduate and above other than technical degree	882972	181632	20.6
	Technical degree or diploma equal to degree or post-graduate degree	70413	15354	21.8
Urban	Total	8460223	3331462	39.4
	Illiterate	3141045	1755411	55.9
	Literate	5319178	1576051	29.6
	Literate but below matric/ secondary	3262084	1018972	31.2
	Matric/secondary but below graduate	1333064	329483	24.7
	Technical diploma or certificate not equal to degree	45342	6610	14.6
	Graduate and above other than technical degree	389523	117847	30.3
	Technical degree or diploma equal to degree or post-graduate degree	45990	15324	33.3

Source: B3 Table, India,Census of India 2001.

According to data at the 2001 census, 626,375,604 populations are non-workers. In the other hands, more of 60 per cent of the total population of the country are unemployed at the 2001 Census, and the proportion of women non-workers is 58.9 per cent. Proportion of literate female among non-workers is 55.6 per cent. Also, the proportion of higher educational level of female's non-workers to total of higher educational level non-workers is reported to be 57.4 per cent.

Of the total population of non-workers 45,157,896 of them are reported to be 'seeking/available' for work. Interestingly, only about 19 per cent of the non-workers 'seeking/available for work' are 'Illiterate'. Proportion of literate female among non-workers 'seeking/available' for work is 48 per cent, and the proportion of higher educational level of female's non-workers 'seeking/available' for work to total of higher educational level non-workers 'seeking/available' for work is reported to be 42.2 per cent. That is to say, sizeable group of females non-workers 'seeking/available for work' is recorded to be 'Technical diploma/degree/Graduates and above'. Mean while they have not found place in the job market in spite of their educational attainments.

Table 2.4. Distribution of Non-Workers by Educational Level and Sex

	Educational level	Persons	Females	%
Total	Total	626375604	369233308	58.9
	Illiterate	304981848	190491956	62.5
	Literate	321393756	178741352	55.6
	Literate but below matric/ secondary	239232389	130563956	54.6
	Matric/secondary but below graduate	58921734	34291838	58.2
	Technical diploma or certificate not equal to degree	1282128	384990	30.0
	Graduate and above other than technical degree	12746328	7903194	62.0
	Technical degree or diploma equal to degree or post-graduate degree	1623740	695723	42.8
Rural	Total	432534569	249771048	57.7
	Illiterate	236209043	147168292	62.3
	Literate	196325526	102602756	52.3

	Educational level	Persons	Females	%
	Literate but below matric/ secondary	160280903	83739049	52.2
	Matric/secondary but below graduate	26888354	14018041	52.1
	Technical diploma or certificate not equal to degree	559380	152928	27.3
	Graduate and above other than technical degree	3448053	1598581	46.4
	Technical degree or diploma equal to degree or post-graduate degree	389254	132948	34.2
Urban	Total	193841035	119462260	61.6
	Illiterate	68772805	43323664	63.0
	Literate	125068230	76138596	60.9
	Literate but below matric/ secondary	78951486	46824907	59.3
	Matric/secondary but below graduate	32033380	20273797	63.3
	Technical diploma or certificate not equal to degree	722748	232062	32.1
	Graduate and above other than technical degree	9298275	6304613	67.8
	Technical degree or diploma equal to degree or post-graduate degree	1234486	562775	45.6

Source: B3 Table, India,Census of India 2001.

Looking at the distribution of marginal workers 'seeking/ available for work' and non-workers 'seeking/available for work' by broad age-groups, it is seen that majority of the 'seeking/available for work' in the two categories (65.5% for marginal workers and 77.2% for non-workers) have been from the young job seeking age-group 15-34 years. It is interesting to see that where as the proportion 'seeking/available for work' from amongst marginal and non-workers is appreciably higher for those in the age group 35 years and above over the age-group 15-34 years for 'Illiterates', such proportion for the 'Literates' has declined.

Among the illiterates high proportion (43%) of main workers has been reported from rural areas as against 18.4 per cent from the urban areas. In contrast, proportion of main workers reported from among the Literates from urban areas (81.6%) has been more than that reported (57%) from rural areas. The data also reveals significant sex differentials in the proportion of main workers by area of residence. Among the literates, proportion of female main workers is higher in the urban areas. It is more so for literate females with higher levels of education (Technical diploma and above).

DISCUSSION

In general, in India, literacy rate for women is 53.7 while it is 75.3 per cent for men in national level. Illiteracy rate for the women is higher than the men. Sex ratio in between literate population is 234, and among illiterate population is1008. Because there is traditional attitude about women that dominate on community and family structure that men are the head of the family and should supply the income of the household. Also there are other factors such as early marriage, veiling and etc.

In addition, results have indicated there exists a wide gap between the work participation rate of males and females. A majority of women workers are employed as marginal workers. There are traditional attitudes between men, and these attitudes have prevented women from enter to professional training and also professional work markets. Even though women performed best job, and they attained be high educational levels in the office, the management always preferred to use of men. The efficiency of a working woman is always suspected, especially, in the upper cadres.

Besides, in many cases, the women are selected as marginal workers because they can be paid less than men for the same type of work.

The culture of masculism deforms both men and women. As individuals we are all trapped and constrained by gender stereotypes. The way in which sex-typing of jobs has pushed women into inferior places in the hierarchy and into economic dependency, that does not mean that men, too, do not suffer form the pressures of having to live up to ideas of masculine behaviour which may be alien to them as individuals. (Bradley, 1989)

The culture of masculism can get job opportunities of educated women, and they pull toward informal sectors or temporary occupations. Data have indicated that the proportion of women has inquired higher educational levels in the country, but they could not take up suitable job opportunities especially as main workers. Then we can observe clearly that are being equality only on the paper, but not in reality.

Today, various legislations, policies and programmes have been implemented to protect the interests of women and to improve their status especially that of Muslim women. Unfortunately many a times they are not properly implemented or they are not adequate.

According to the social situation of women in India, we should implement proper programmes in related to improve and to increase aware level of women about their equal status with men and this belief should translated into actual practice through several institutions, customs and practices. This can be about a change in men's attitudes towards the women's positions and rights. With use of advertisements, we should create this belief among employers that women like men have abilities and merciless in work's activities. It is essential to implement legislations that protect women's rights by advertisement, plays, films etc.

REFERENCES

Census of India 1991. 1993. Series-1: Social and Cultural Tables-India. New Delhi: Registrar General & Census Commissioner.

Census of India 1981. 1983. Series-1: Social and Cultural Tables-India. New Delhi: Registrar General & Census Commissioner.

Census of India 2001. 2004. C8 Table. New Delhi: Registrar General & Census Commissioner.

Census of India 2001, 2004. B3 Table. New Delhi: Registrar General & Census Commissioner.

Census of India 2001, 2004. B9 Table. New Delhi: Registrar General & Census Commissioner.

Bradley, Harried, 1989. *Men's Work, Women's Work: A Sociological History of the Sexual Division of Labour in Employment*. USA: Polity Press, p. 239.

Dak, T.M. 1989. *Women and Work in Indian Society*. Delhi: Discovery Publishing House, pp. 8,215.

Kumar, Uttam and Singh. Aknayak, 1997. *Recent Trends in Education Series Women Education*. New Delhi: Commonwealth Publishers, p. 267.

CHAPTER

3

Play Peers and Time Involvement in Children with Mental Retardation

— *Dr. Afsaneh Khajevand Khoshali*

ABSTRACT

The present study uses cross-sectional observation and key informant interview techniques to elicit data on play behaviours in a group of 140 children with mild and moderate mental retardation. Their chronological ages ranges between 6-14 years. The sample included 71 males and 69 females. For the purpose of this study, three schedules were used: 'Child Survey Schedule', 'Daily Activity Log Schedule' and 'Play Behaviour Survey Schedule'. In distribution of play peers for children with mental retardation, the results indicate that, the range of play peers for children with mental retardation varies from same age peers (N: 40; 28.6%) to younger age peers (N: 35; 25.0%), senior citizens (N: 27; 19.3%), pets (N: 25; 17.9%) and adults (N: 19; 13.6%). Sizeable segment children with mental retardation in this sample are reported to be without playmates and left to play alone (N: 33; 23.6%). However, these trends appear to be similar irrespective of the age, gender or diagnostic condition of the child (p: >0.05).

But in terms of the actual extent of time involvement by different play peers with these children, it is seen that there are no statistically significant differences (p: >0.05). The involvement of all the peers appears to be more or less similar. The differences emerge only in terms of age, severity or associated condition of mental retardation for the actual amount of time spent by the play peers ($p < 0.05$). On an average, more time is spent by the play peers with younger children (age range 6-11 years) and mild degrees of mental retardation without associated problems than children above 11 years or those with moderate mental retardation having associated problems.

INTRODUCTION

Play is an important medium for social development in young children. It is a 'voluntary activity' engaged for the enjoyment it gives without consideration of the end result (Piaget, 1962). Play is also a medium through which the child is 'instinctively prepared to take up the role of adulthood' (Jeffree *et al.,* 1977). For younger infants and toddlers, play may be simply means of 'expending surplus energy... a method used by children to relieve certain powerful experiences and thus come to terms with them' (Lansdown, 1985). Play activities can serve as recreational as well as propaedeutic task (Peshawaria *et al.,* 1991). There are many types of play observed in children depending on their age/developmental levels (Venkatesan, 2004b).

For the child, the primary goal when playing is to have fun. There is an intrinsic enjoyment derived by the child during play. Besides, it facilitates social adjustment, development and related skills. It improves physical health, language and cognitive development. Participation in play contributes to the overall well-being of the individual or groups of children. For many children with special needs play becomes simply an opportunity to release their unspent or pent up energies in a constructive fashion (Fine, 1982).

The children with special needs are no exception in their penchant for play-even though the nature of their play might be different owing to their primary condition or due to circumstances surrounding them (Venkatesan, 2001). In a related study, it was found that all children with mental retardation showed some form or type of play. No case of child with mental retardation was reported as 'never plays' even though such an item existed in the interview schedule. It was another thing that these children indulged more in solitary than social play and/or toy or pet play like their normal aged peers. The preponderance of solitary play was explained as due to their skill deficits, non-acceptance of these children into play situations by others, non-availability of peers/play fellows, presence of problem behaviors in the child, etc.

Venkatesan (2002) studied a sample of 140 preschool children diagnosed as cases of 'developmental disabilities'. Information on hour wise engagement of each child was undertaken by the investigators. The results showed that the greatest part of the days schedule is spent by this sample of children on 'sleeping' (43.24%), followed by time spent at 'school' (for school going kids only)(14.41%), on 'feeding' activities (10.34%) and 'watching television' (9.61%) respectively. The amount of time spent on needed activity like 'playing with peers' (4.12%) was meager. In the case of autistic children, the amount of time spent on sedentary or exclusion activities like 'watching television' (21.23%) or 'playing alone' (14.6%) almost doubled and 'paying with peers' (1.74%) was almost reduced to half.

In another investigation on activity log of pre-school children diagnosed as 'developmental disabilities' including 'autism spectrum disorders', it was reported that only 4.12 per cent of a day's schedule is spent on playing with peers. This was against 7.9 per cent of the time spent on playing alone and 9.61 per cent of time spent on watching television (Venkatesan, 2004a). These studies have given initial leads into the problem of play behaviors in children with special needs. There is a need to delve into the depths of the problem of play behaviors of children with mental retardation.

AIMS AND OBJECTIVES

It was the aim of this study to

(*i*) discover the nature of play peers for children with mental retardation (*ii*) explore the nature, type, number and amount of time spent by play peers for a typical day in the activity schedule of children with mental retardation

(*iii*) study the relationship of play peers to specific organism variables like age, gender, associated conditions and/or severity of mental retardation and family variables (such as, type of family, socio economic status, parent age and education) as well as their choice of pay peers respectively.

MATERIAL AND METHODS

The study was carried out on a sample of 140 children diagnosed as mental retardation. A part of the sample was taken from various special schools in Mysore and Bengaluru while others were also from the cases routinely seen at All India Institute of Speech and Hearing, under Ministry of Health and Family Welfare, Government of India, located at Mysore. The sample included 71 males and 69 females with mental retardation in the age range of 6-14 years. (Mean Age: 10.43; SD: 3.64). Within the sample, there were 69 cases diagnosed as 'mild mental retardation' and 71 cases with 'moderate mental retardation'. Of the overall sample, 89 children had one or the other associated problems such as epilepsy, hearing or visual difficulties, etc. The remaining 51 children did not have any associated problems.

The procedure for data collection involved use of cross-sectional observation and key informant interview techniques along with two schedules developed exclusively for the purpose of this study. The *'Child Survey Schedule'* covered queries on personal details, diagnostic condition and health status of each child included in this study. Another *'Play Behaviour Survey Schedule'* was used to record details on the 24-hour activity agenda of each child, their types of play activities, play preferences, toys/materials used by them during play, amount of time or money invested on play by significant others and so on. Open ended questions and non-directive interviewing techniques were used to gather as much information about commonly activities and/or situations of play in each child with mental retardation as reported by their parents or teachers. Wherever possible, several examples of reported play were collected to substantiate the declarative statements of parents or caregivers.

A simple *'Daily Activity Log Schedules'* was also designed to elicit information about each child's hourly engagements during a typical day. For every hour in the 24-hour log schedule, data was elicited on the child's and others activities in terms of the time spent on sleeping, ablution, watching television (or playing computer and video games), playing alone, playing with peers, feeding, attending school (if any), home teaching and others. The total time spent by a given child and/or the significant family members under these activity heading were totaled and rounded off to the nearest minute. Wherever information was reported on the child's simultaneous involvement in two or more of the above mentioned activities (such as, feeding while watching television or playing alone while the television is on), they were recorded as such. Thus, there could be less/more than the 24-hour schedule for some children, when totaling the reported activities for a given day or for all the children taken together in this sample. Data were collected and compiled in Microsoft Excel format and subject to statistical analysis by using freely downloadable statistical software/calculators on the web.

HYPOTHESES

Specific Hypotheses Investigated under this theme are:

The volume, variety, duration and length of time spent on play activities, or nature of play peers seen in children with mental retardation differ significantly with respect to child variables (such as, age, gender, presence/ absence of problem behaviors, associated conditions and severity of mental retardation), family variables (such as, type of family, socio economic status, parent age and education) as well as their choice of pay peers respectively.

RESULTS AND DISCUSSION

The results of the study are analyzed and discussed under following headings:

(a) ***Distribution of Play Peers:*** It is seen that the range of play peers for children with mental retardation varies from same age peers (N: 40; 28.6%) to younger age peers (N: 35; 25.0%), senior citizens (N: 27; 19.3%), pets (N: 25; 17.9%) and adults (N: 19; 13.6%). Sizeable segment children with mental retardation in this sample are reported to be without playmates and left to play alone (N: 33; 23.6%) (Table 3.1).

(b) ***Distribution of Time Involvement:*** In terms of the actual extent of time involvement by different play peers with these children, it is seen that there are no statistically significant differences ($p: >0.05$). The involvement of all the peers appears to be more or less similar. The differences emerge only in terms of age, severity or associated condition of mental retardation for the actual amount of time spent by the play peers ($p: < 0.05$). On an average, more time is spent by the play peers with younger children (age range 6-11 years) and mild degrees of mental retardation without associated problems than children above 11 years or those with moderate mental retardation having associated problems (Table 3.2).

The following section highlights the types and distribution of time spent by different play peers for children with mental retardation in terms of gender, age groups, severity and presence or absence of associated conditions and presence or absence of problem behaviors respectively :

(*i*) There are a variety of play peers during play as reported to be available for children with mental retardation. The range of play mates vary from same aged peers (40 out of 140), younger peers (35 out of 140) and others (32 out of 140). Sometimes the child has older peers (27 out of 140) and elderly persons (19 out of 140). There are also instances where these children are left to play with pets (N: 25 out of 140) or all alone by themselves (N: 33 out of 140)

Table 3.1. Distribution by Number of Play Peers of Children with Mental Retardation

Activity	Gender*		Age**			Severity***		Associated Condition****			Total Percentage
	Male	Female	6-8	9-11	12-14	Mild	Moderate	Present	Absent	Total	
N	71	69	34	69	37	69	71	89	51	140	
Same Age Peers	25	15	15	17	8	18	22	27	13	40	28.6
Younger Peers	19	16	14	14	7	14	21	25	10	35	25.0
None	13	20	7	17	9	15	18	24	9	33	23.6
Senior Citizens	13	14	9	11	7	15	12	19	8	27	19.3
Pets	15	10	7	13	5	13	12	16	9	25	17.9
Adults	7	12	7	6	6	12	7	13	6	19	13.6

* X^2: 6.460; df: 5; p: > 0.05; NS

** X^2: 5.426; df: 10; p: > 0.05; NS

*** X^2: 3.625; df: 5; p: > 0.05; NS

**** X^2: 0.669; df: 5; p: > 0.05; NS

Table 3.2. Mean and SD Distribution of Duration of Time Spent by Play Peers and Caregivers of Children with Mental Retardation

Activity	Gender*		Age**			Severity***		Associated Condition****			Total Percentage
	Male	Female	6-8	9-11	12-14	Mild	Moderate	Present	Absent	Total	
N	71	69	34	69	37	69	71	89	51	140	
Same Age Peers	36.9 (24.8)	43.3 (16.0)	40.1 (17.1)	45.0 (26.2)	25.6 (15.0)	54.7 (19.1)	26.7 (15.0)	34.1 (17.0)	50.0 (27.4)	39.3 (21.9)	18.7
Younger Peers	35.5 (20.5)	27.2 (13.8)	26.8 (13.2)	31.1 (16.8)	42.9 (25.5)	27.1 (15.8)	34.8 (20.5)	27.8 (14.2)	41.5 (23.2)	31.7 (18.0)	15.1
None	36.5 (20.5)	26.7 (15.5)	25.0 (13.5)	30.9 (19.3)	34.2 (19.1)	22.9 (16.1)	16.1 (18.0)	33.3 (18.4)	23.1 (15.2)	30.6 (18.0)	14.6
Senior Citizens	29.6 (27.4)	41.1 (21.6)	29.4 (18.3)	44.1 (26.0)	30.0 (29.4)	42.7 (27.8)	26.7 (17.8)	33.7 (21.7)	40.0 (32.3)	36.6 (24.8)	17.4
Pets	46.3 (29.0)	24.0 (22.3)	32.9 (14.1)	40.8 (34.1)	35.0 (30.8)	26.2 (19.0)	50.0 (32.4)	32.2 (27.8)	46.7 (28.4)	37.4 (28.3)	17.8
Adults	35.7 (19.7)	33.5 (26.5)	26.4 (19.7)	55.8 (20.1)	22.0 (17.7)	20.2 (13.8)	58.6 (15.5)	30.8 (18.9)	42.0 (32.4)	34.3 (23.6)	16.4

Note: Figures are expressed in minutes; Figures in parentheses indicate SD values.

* X^2: 10.743; df: 5; p: > 0.05; NS

** X^2: 22.268; df: 10; p: < 0.025; S

*** X^2: 41.098; df: 5; p: < 0.001; VHS

**** X^2: 6.509; df: 5; p: > 0.05; NS

(*ii*) In relation to gender variable, it is seen that there is no statistically significant difference in the choice of play peers for children with mental retardation depending on whether they are males (N: 71) or females (N: 69) (X^2: 0.384; p :> 0.05; NS).

(*iii*) In relation to age variable, however it is seen that there is a statistically significant difference in the distribution of types and duration of time spent by different play peers for children with mental retardation. It is seen that children between 6-8 years (N: 34), 9-12 years (N: 69) and 12-14 years (N: 37) show differences in their types of play peers. (X^2: 6.716; p:<0.05; S).

(*iv*) In relation to severity of mental retardation, there is no difference between the choice of play peers for mild (N:69) and moderate (N:71) cases of the sample included in this study (X^2; 0.384; p :> 0.536; NS).

(*v*) The presence or absence of associated conditions in children with mental retardation influences the choice of play mates .This is evidenced by the observation that children without associated conditions (N:51) have a greater variety of play peers as compared to children with associated conditions along with their primary condition (X^2: 29.578; p :< 0.01; HS).

(*vi*) The presence or absence of problem behaviors in children with mental retardation emerges as a statistically significant variable in influencing the types and duration of time spent by significant others during play (X^2: 5.161; p :> 0.023; S). It appears that children with problem behaviors have fewer companions in the form of same aged or younger aged peers than children without problem behaviors.

The following section highlights the types and distribution of time spent by different play peers for children with mental retardation in relation to various socio-demographic variables:

(*i*) In relation to the type of family, it is seen that there is a statistically significant difference in the choice of play peers for children with mental retardation depending on whether they are hailing from nuclear families (N:89) or joint families (N:51) (X^2: 6.488; p :> 0.01; HS).

(*ii*) In relation to SES, it is seen that there is a statistically significant difference in the choice of play peers for children with mental retardation depending on whether they are hailing from high SES (N:26), middle SES (N:87) or low SES (N:27) (X^2: 11.611 ; p:<0.01; S).

(*iii*) In relation to parent education, there is no difference between the choice of play peers for children whose parents are school educated (N:68) and children whose parents are college educated (N:72) (X^2: 1.923; p :> 0.05; NS).

(*iv*) In relation to parent age, it is seen that there is a statistically significant difference regarding the choice or variety of play peers for various age groups ranging below 29 years (N: 36), between 30-39 years (N:68) and those above 40 years (N: 36) (X^2: 80.654; p :< 0.001; HS).

REFERENCES

Fine, A. (1982). Therapeutic Recreation: An Aspect of Rehabilitation for Exceptional Children. *The Lively Arts*, 4.

Jeffree, D.M., Mc Conkey, R., and Hewson, S. (1977*). Let me play. London: Souvenir*, pp. 17-19.

Lansdown, R. (1985). *Child Development Made Simple.* London: William Heinmann.

Peshawaria, R., Menon, D.K., and Reddi, S. (1991). *Play Activities for Young Children with Special Needs.* Secunderabad: NIMH.

Piaget, J. (1962*). Play, Dreams and Imitation in Childhood*. New York: Norton.

Venkatesan, S. (2001). Parents Opinion on Prevailing Practices in Preschool Education. *Journal of Indian Education*. February, 57-63.

Venkatesan, S. (2002). *Building Bridges: An Analysis of Not for Profits for Disabled in India.*

Venkatesan, S. (2004a). Activity Log of Preschool Children with Developmental Disabilities and Autism Spectrum Disorder. *Asia Pacific Disability Rehabilitation Journal* 16.1.

Venkatesan, S. (2004b). *Children with Developmental Disabilities: A Training Guide for Parents, Teachers and Caregivers.* New Delhi: Sage Publications.

CHAPTER

Teacher Efficacy Among High School Teachers of Mysore (India) and Gonabad (Iran)

—Hadi Mohammad Pour
—Dr. K. Yeshodhara

ABSTRACT

This Chapter aims to investigate the teacher efficacy of teachers in India and Iran. It is an attempt to understand how these perceptions vary by demographic variable such as age and subject taught by teachers. Data were collected from 326 high school teachers in Mysore (India) and Gonabad (Iran). They were asked to respond to the Woolfolk and Hoy (1990) scale. Data were analyzed via SPSS version 16.0. The result revealed that Indian high school teachers tent to personal teacher efficacy when compared with their Iranian counterparts, and it also shows that Iranian high school teachers tent to general teacher efficacy.

This research was limited by the relatively restricted sample of high school teachers in both countries. Further research should test initially confirmed associations in different school contexts with substantially dissimilar teacher demographic, and include consideration of dispositional antecedents that may affect teacher perception. This is the only study comparing Indian and Iranian teacher efficacy of teachers in high schools. The study provides an initial understanding of the possible effect of culture on the teacher efficacy of teachers in two different countries.

Keywords: Teacher efficacy, Teacher, India, Iran.

INTRODUCTION

The construct of teacher efficacy was derived from Bandura's theory of self-efficacy (1977). Applied to the context of education teacher efficacy has been defined as "the extent to which teachers believe they can affect student learning" (Dembo and Gibson, 1985: 173). Teacher efficacy is seen as a multi-dimensional construct with Ashton and Webb (1982), for example, identifying two dimensions as "teaching efficacy" and "personal efficacy". The first factor represents a teacher's sense of teaching efficacy or belief that teachers can overcome factors external to the teacher such as the background of students. The second dimension, personal efficacy, is the belief of an individual teacher in their own personal capacity to deliver the necessary teaching behaviors to influence student learning. Studies have shown that these two dimensions are independent (Woolfolk and Hoy, 1990: 82). Ross (1992) found little correlation between teaching efficacy and personal efficacy. This means that individual teachers could believe, for example, that teaching can significantly determine what students learn but that they are not capable of having much of an effect on the learning of their own students.

Researchers have also questioned whether there are three rather than two dimensions to the construct of teacher efficacy. For example Guskey (1988) suggested the possibility of a third dimension following his study of elementary and high school teachers' sense of responsibility for positive and negative student outcomes. In their study of prospective teachers using a revised version of the sixteen-item Gibson and Dembo Teacher Efficacy Scale (1984), Woolfolk and Hoy (1990) concluded from the factor loadings that the construct of teacher efficacy consisted of three dimensions: teaching efficacy; and, two dimensions of personal efficacy. These two related dimensions were teachers' sense of personal responsibility for positive student outcomes and their personal responsibility for negative outcomes.

Research suggests that teacher efficacy may underlie critical instructional decisions including the use of time, classroom management strategies and questioning techniques (Gibson and Dembo 1984; Saklofske, *et al.*, 1988; Woolfolk, *et al.*, 1990). Teacher efficacy has also been shown to be a strong predictor of commitment to teaching (Coladarci, 1992), adoption of innovations (Midgley *et al.*, 1989) and higher levels of planning and organization (Allinder, 1994). Teachers with a higher sense of efficacy are less critical of students when they make mistakes (Ashton and Webb, 1986) and exhibit more enthusiasm about teaching (Allinder, 1994).

Theoretical Framework

Efficacy is the belief in one's capabilities to achieve a goal. Teacher efficacy is how teachers feels about their own capability in teaching all types of students (Coladarci and Brenton, 1997). Many studies have noted that a teacher's sense of efficacy can directly affect student achievement (Coladarci and Brenton, 1997). There is little research to indicate how a teacher's sense of efficacy influences his or her teaching of students with disabilities within an inclusion setting. Parker (2006) noted that many teachers reported feeling confused and unprepared to make the necessary accommodations needed to individualize the education so students with disabilities could learn successfully. Teachers' confusion and lack of confidence also affected their attitudes towards teaching students with disabilities. Some studies have found that teachers' attitudes towards inclusion can also influence the success of students with disabilities (Burke and Sutherland, 2004). There is limited research linking teacher efficacy and their attitudes towards inclusion. Many studies have found that teacher efficacy and teachers' attitudes can influence student achievement, but there are few studies that show the relationship between efficacy and their subject taught. More information regarding the relationship between teacher efficacy and their subject taught towards inclusion is necessary so specific information and training can be provided to teachers so they can feel more confident and successful in teaching students with disabilities within their classroom.

There are a number of factors which affect teachers' efficacy and their attitudes towards inclusion. Parker (2006) noted that teachers seemed to benefit from in service training that showed them how to use specific teaching strategies. In other studies, teachers reported that training influenced their attitudes and willingness to accommodate special education students, but little was done to give details regarding this training (*et al.*, 2000; Burke and Sutherland, 2004; Jobb, *et al.*, 1996; Leyser and Tappendorf, 2001). One study was conducted which demonstrated the benefits of teacher training. Parker (2006) noted that when teachers received training on specific instructional strategies, or accommodations, they were more willing to use them in their classroom. When teachers received training, several educators used the strategies taught and reported that they felt more confident in their teaching and the strategies facilitated student learning.

Sutherland, *et al.*, (2005) noted that professional development needs must be examined with teachers that are working with special education students. In order to increase their confidence, teachers need to be trained sufficiently on how to work, manage, and provide high-quality instruction to special education students. Information on training is needed for educators because providing more training to regular education teachers can directly affect their work with special education students (Parker, 2006).

A prevalent classification of teachers' efficacy was developed by Gibson and Dembo (1984), who identified two SE factors. The first is *general teacher efficacy* (GTE), which addresses a teacher's general feeling that teaching and the educational system are capable of fostering student academic achievement despite negative influences external to the teacher. A second factor is *personal teaching efficacy* (PTE), which reflects a belief in the teacher's own ability to advance significantly the learning and achievements of his or her students.

METHOD

Objectives

The following objectives guided the present study:

1. To study the level of teacher efficacy in terms of general teacher efficacy (GTE) and personal teaching efficacy of high school teachers in Mysore (India) and Gonabad (Iran).
2. To study the difference in teacher efficacy in terms of general teacher efficacy (GTE) and personal teaching efficacy of high school teachers in Mysore (India) and Gonabad (Iran).
3. To study the relationship between age and teacher efficacy in terms of general teacher efficacy (GTE) and personal teaching efficacy of high school teachers in Mysore (India) and Gonabad (Iran).
4. To study the influence of subject taught by high school teachers in terms of general teacher efficacy (GTE) and personal teaching efficacy in Mysore (India) and Gonabad (Iran).

Hypotheses

H1. There is no significant difference in teacher efficacy (in total and its components) of high school teachers in Mysore city (India) and Gonabad city (Iran).

H2. There is no significance difference in teacher efficacy (in total and its components) of high school teachers of different age groups in Mysore city (India) and Gonabad (Iran).

H3. There is no significance difference in teacher efficacy (in total and its components) of high school teachers teaching arts and science subjects in Mysore and Mysore city (India) and Gonabad city (Iran).

Sample

A total of 326 teachers selected from India and Iran. In India the data were collected in Mysore city in the southern part of the country, in Iran data were collected in Gonabad city in the East of country that teachers were randomly selected. The details of selection are as follows. This sample of study consists of two stage sampling:

- Selection of schools
- Selection of teachers

1. ***Selection of Schools:*** Schools were selected randomly 16 from Mysore city in India and 17 from Gonabad city in Iran. Therefore, a total of 33 schools were selected for the study. In India there are several types of high schools such as government, private aided, private unaided, central, and public, etc, but in Iran there are only the government and private aided schools. For the purpose of valid comparison, only government and private aided high schools in both countries were included in the present study.

2. ***Selection of Teachers:*** All the teachers of the subjects (Science, Arts) teaching in each secondary school were considered as sample for the study. Thus the sample of study consisted of 326 teachers of secondary schools (156 from Mysore 103 male + 53 female (India) and 170 from Gonabad 124 male + 46 female (Iran). In the selecting teachers consideration was given to their age and subject taught such as science or arts group subjects (Table I). In each school selected for the study, all teachers of all the subjects (languages, social science, science and math) were considered (about ten teachers in each school) for the sample.

Tools Used for Data Collection

Teacher Efficacy Scale (TES) used for this study was designed by Woolfolk and Hoy (1990) to measure two dimensions of teacher efficacy. The instrument includes 12 statements to measure personal teacher efficacy (PTE) and 10 statements to measure general teacher efficacy (GTE). Teachers were asked to rate the statements on a 6-point scale. The rating was scored on *Likert-type scale.* The scale ranges from 1 for "strongly disagree" to 6 for "strongly agree". The Teacher Efficacy scale developed originally in English, was translated by the investigator into Persian language for Iranian teachers, so two versions (English, and Persian) have been used in this study.

Table 4.1 Details for the Sample Selected for the Study

	Subject groups			Age groups (years)				
Country	Arts	Science	Total	20-29	30-39	40-49	50+	Total
Iran	96	74	170	21	66	58	25	170
India	89	67	156	24	69	44	19	156

PROCEDURE

Both in India and Iran, the investigators personally visited all the selected schools and teachers. Then teachers were met individually for explaining the purpose of the study and were instructed how to respond to the tool namely Teacher Efficacy scale (TES). Further clarifications were offered on the questions raised by them and they were requested to cooperate with the investigators for successful completion of the research.

The questionnaires that were personally distributed to more than 250 teachers each in the selected schools of Mysore city and Gonabad city. Finally 156 useable questionnaire sets were returned in Mysore city and 170 useable were returned in Gonabad city. The response rates were 62 per cent for the former and 68 per cent for the latter. Completed data sheets were scored according to the manual provided.

Descriptive Statistics

Multi-variate Analysis of Variance (MANOVA) was employed to test for the differences in teacher efficacy according to country, age group and subject. In the present investigation countries (India and Iran) age groups (20-29, 30-39, 40-49, 50+ years) and subjects taught (arts and science) are identified as independent variables; teacher efficacy and its

Table 4.2. Distribution of Teachers in Mysore (India) and Gonabad City on Different Level of Teacher Efficacy (GTE and PTE)

Country		India				Iran			
		Low	Moderate	High	Total	Low	Moderate	High	Total
GTE	No.	9	17	22	48	8	39	58	105
	%	18.75	35.41	45.84	30.76	7.62	37.14	55.24	61.76
PTE	No.	8	36	64	108	11	23	31	65
	%	7.40	33.34	59.26	69.24	16.92	35.39	47.69	37.64
Total	No.	17	53	86	156	19	62	89	170
TE	%	10.89	40.39	48.72	100	11.17	36.47	52.36	100

components as dependent variables. SPSS for Windows (version 16.0 was used for statistical analysis.

RESULTS

A. Differences Between two countries : In the PTE component a significant difference was identified between teachers of Mysore and Gonabad city (F= 10.51; P< 0.010), where teachers of Mysore had significantly higher teacher efficacy than teachers of Gonabad city (means 46.92 and 40.22 respectively). Whereas, the GTE component Iranian teachers scored significantly higher perceived than Indian counterparts (mean 41.86 and 39.72 respectively) and this difference was statistically different (F= 13.76; P< 0.000) (Table 4.3). In the total teacher efficacy teachers both Indian and Iranian more or had equal mean scores.

B. Differences age groups and teachers of different : Age groups did not have any influence on any sub- component or the total scores as the obtained "F" values for all the sub-component and the teacher efficacy scores were found to be non-significant.

C. Differences Between teachers of different subject taught : As in the case of age groups, in subject also none of the sub-component and teacher efficacy scores "F" values reached the significant level criterion. In other words, subject backgrounds did not have any influence over teacher efficacy.

DISCUSSION

The main findings of the present study:

- Teachers of Mysore (India) and Gonabad (Iran) did not differ in their teacher efficacy in total.
- Teachers of Mysore (India) displayed better perceived teacher efficacy in the personal teacher efficacy (PTE).
- Teachers of Gonabad (Iran) displayed better perceived teacher efficacy in the general teacher efficacy (GTE).
- Age and subject taught (arts and science) were not related to teacher efficacy in total or its components.

Table 4.3. Mean Scores forVarious Components of Teacher Efficacy and Total Teacher with Reference to Countries and Age Groups

Country	Age groups	PTE		GTE		Total teacher efficacy	
		Mean	SD	Mean	SD	Mean	SD
India	20-29	48.12	7.11	38.25	6.32	86.37	15.20
	30-39	47.38	6.92	37.20	6.85	84.58	14.19
	40-49	47.11	7.63	37.11	7.11	84.22	15.92
	50+	46.53	6.55	36.12	6.68	82.35	14.81
	Total	46.92	6.99	39.72	7.19	86.64	17.25
Iran	20-29	42.31	7.19	39.32	6.12	81.36	18.25
	30-39	43.80	7.22	41.19	6.98	84.99	16.91
	40-49	44.32	7.98	40.92	6.42	85.24	15.51
	50+	41.29	7.33	38.22	7.17	79.51	17.81
	Total	40.22	7.15	41.86	6.47	82.08	15.28
F(country) A		F= 10.51 P<0.010 (HS)		F= 13.76 P<0.000 (HS)		F= 1.62 P<0.19 (NS)	
F (age groups) B		F= 0.551 P<0.241 (NS)		F= 1.612 P<0.318 (NS)		F= 1.402 P<0.309 (NS)	

Note: HS – highly significant; S – significant; NS – non-significant

Table 4.4. Mean scores for various components of teacher efficacy and total teacher with reference to countries and subject taught

Country	Subject	PTE		GTE		Total teacher efficacy	
		Mean	SD	Mean	SD	Mean	SD
India	Arts	47.18	7.11	36.21	6.32	83.39	17.21
	Science	48.31	7.91	38.22	6.41	86.53	15.11
	Total	48.94	7.19	38.39	6.74	87.33	16.29
Iran	Arts	46.32	7.44	39.12	6.14	85.44	17.25
	Science	46.80	6.29	40.17	6.99	86.97	16.17
	Total	46.92	6.11	40.86	6.47	87.78	15.27
Total	Arts	46.40	7.14	39.17	7.21	85.57	16.25
	Science	45.16	7.16	39.11	6.81	84.27	16.88
	Total	45.11	7.29	39.98	7.91	85.09	16.89
F(country) A		F= 12.51 P<0.000 (HS)		F= 16.61 P<0.000 (HS)		F= 1.76 P<0.17 (NS)	
F (subject taught) B		F= 0.147 P<0.416 (NS)		F= 1.612 P<0.411 (NS)		F= 1.102 P<0.129 (NS)	

Note: HS – highly significant; NS – non-significant

Conclusion

To conclude, educational organizations, such as schools, colleges and universities should have individuals who are committed to their organization, profession and well- being of their students. The vitality of all educational organizations lies in the willingness of teacher to contribute to the development of their organizations. In the process, there will be all round development of the institution, teachers and students, if teachers working in schools seriously consider efficacy factors.

The literature reveals that most research shows there is a positive relationship between age, experience and teacher efficacy. Goddatd *et al.*, (2004) argued "teachers' sense of efficacy is a significant predicator of productive teaching". Moreover, when considering teacher's sense of efficacy and its impact on student learning, Milner and Hoy (2002) determined the importance of context and its impact on teacher's experiences and teacher efficacy. Teachers' sense of efficacy related to the context of available support was investigated by Tschannen-Moran and Hoy (2002).

Tschannen- Moran and Hoy (2002) conducted a study involving a group of 155 in-service teachers including novice and experienced teachers. Their finding indicated no significant differences in teacher efficacy beliefs between groups related to age, gender, and race or teaching context. However teaching level and number of years of experience did seem to influence efficacy with elementary teachers exhibiting significantly higher overall efficacy than either middle or high school teachers. Teachers with five or more years of experience showed a higher overall sense of efficacy than novice teachers. Further, perceived support was correlated to efficacy for novice teachers rather than experienced teachers, which according to the researchers, seemed to emphasize the importance of the beginning years of teaching in developing teacher efficacy.

The result reported herein show that Indian high school teachers tent to personal teacher efficacy when compared with their Iranian counterparts, and also it shows that Iranian high school teachers tent to general teacher efficacy.

REFERENCES

Allinder, R.M. 1994. The relationship between efficacy and the instructional practices of special education teachers and consultants. *Teacher Education and Special Education*, 17, pp. 86-95.

Ashton, P.T. and Webb, R. 1982. *Teachers' sense of efficacy: Toward an ecological model*. Paper presented at the Annual Meeting of the American Educational research Association, New York.

Ashton, P. T., & Webb, R. B. (1986). *Making a difference: Teachers' sense of efficacy and student achievement*. New York: Longman.

Bandura, A. 1977. Self-efficacy: Toward a unifying theory of behavioral change. *Psychological Review*, 84, pp. 191-215.

Burke, K., & Sutherland, C. (2004). Attitudes toward inclusion: Knowledge vs. experience. *Education, 125(2),* 163-174.

Coladarci, T. (1992). Teachers' sense of efficacy and commitment to teaching. *Journal of Experimental Education, 60*(4), 323–337.

Coladarci, T., & Breton, W.A. (1997). Teacher efficacy, supervision, and the special education resource-room teacher. *Journal of Educational Research, 90(4),* 230-240.

Dembo, M.H., & Gibson, S. (1985). Teachers' sense of efficacy: An important factor in school improvement. *The Elementary School Journal, 86,* 173-184.

Gibson, S., & Dembo, M. (1984). Teacher efficacy: A construct validation. *Journal of Educational Research, 76*(6), 569–582.

Goddard, Roger D., Hoy, Wayne K. and Hoy Woolfolk, Anita. 2000. Collective Teacher Efficacy: Its Meaning, Measure, and Impact on Student Achievement. *American Educational Research Journal,* 37 (2), pp. 479-507.

Guskey, T.R. 1988. Teacher efficacy, self-concept, and attitudes toward the implementation of instructional innovation. *Teaching and Teacher Education*, 4, 63-69.

Jobb, D., Rust, J.O., & Brissie, J. (1996). Teacher attitudes toward inclusion of students with disabilities into regular classrooms. *Education, 117(1),* 148-153.

Leyser, Y., & Tappendorf, K. (2001). Are attitudes and practices regarding mainstreaming changing? A case of teachers in two rural school districts. *Education, 121(4),* 751-761.

Midgley, C., Feldlaufer, H., & Eccles, J. S. (1989). Change in teacher efficacy and student self and task related beliefs in mathematics during the transition to junior high school. *Journal of Educational Psychology, 81*(2), 247–258.

Milner, H.R., & Hoy, A.W. (2002, April). *Respect, social support, and teacher efficacy: A case study.* paper presented at the annual meeting of the American Educational Research Association, New Orleans, LA. Retrieved February 7, 2002.

Parker, B. (2006). Instructional adaptations for students with learning disabilities: An action research project. *Intervention in School and Clinic, 42(1)*, 56-58.

Ross, J. A. (1992). Strategies for enhancing teachers' beliefs in their effectiveness: Research on school improvement hypothesis.*Teacher College Record, 97*(2), 227–251.

Saklofske, D.H., Michayluk, J.O. and Randhawa, B.S. 1988. Teachers' efficacy and teaching behaviors. *Psychological Reports*, 63, 407-414.

Sutherland K.S., Denny, R.K., & Gunter, P.L. (2005). Teachers of students with emotional and behavioral disorders reported professional development needs: Differences between fully licensed and emergency-licensed teachers. *Preventing School Failure, 49(2)*, 41-47.

Tschannen-Moran, M.,& Hoy, W. K. (2002, April). *The influence of resources and support on teachers' efficacy beliefs.* Paper presented at the annual meeting of the American Educational Research Association, New Orleans, LA.

Woolfolk, A. E., Rosoff, B., & Hoy, W. K. (1990). Teachers' sense of efficacy and their beliefs about managing students. *Teaching and Teacher Education, 6*(2), 137–148.

Woolfolk, A.E. and Hoy, W.K. 1990. Prospective teachers' sense of efficacy and beliefs about control. *Journal of Educational Psychology*, 82, 81-91.

CHAPTER

5 Assessment of MLL Attainment Levels in Mathematics among V Standard Students in Shimoga District: Influence of Secondary Variables

—*Prakash, K and Premalatha Sharma*

Present study is aimed to assess the mastery levels in mathematics on MLL attainment in mathematics among V standard students of Shimoga district of Karnataka State. A total of 1457 students of 166 government primary schools from 7 taluks of Shimoga constituted the sample for the study, of which 704 were boys and remaining 753 were girls. They were selected from both urban and rural areas of Shimoga district. MLL based test developed by Kashinath (2005), which had seven competencies was administered to all the selected sample of Shimoga district. On the whole it was found that only 24.6 per cent of the sample attained mastery as against a large majority of the sample of 75.4 per cent did not attain the mastery. Taluk-wise comparison revealed that only students from Hosanagara taluk had at least 50 per cent mastery compared to students from other taluks. Further analysis revealed that students from rural taluks had higher levels of mastery than students of urban areas and gender-wise comparison revealed that girls had higher levels of mastery compared to boys.

Universalisation of Elementary Education (UEE) has been recognised as a one of the important pre-conditions to socio-economic and political development of any society. Particularly so if it is a developing society. The Government of India, recognising UEE as a goal of national importance has been every effort making to achieve it. The provisions contained in the Article 45 of the Constitution of India insist on providing Free and Compulsory Elementary Education to all children.

The National Policy on Education (1986) has also considered the importance of mathematics in general education and suggests that mathematics should be visualized as the vehicle to train a child to think, reason, analysis and articulate logically apart from being a specific subject it should be treated as concomitant to any subject involving analysis and reasoning.

At the primary stage, learning of mathematics is supposed to lay foundation for mathematical thinking about the numerical and special aspects of the objects and activities which the children at this stage are required to deal with. Learning by doing with concrete material is the expected main method of learning at this stage. But unfortunately mathematics is being taught in a mechanical way by chalk and talk method. Students are cramming the formulae for passing the examination as routine. It is sad to observe that even today, after 63 years of Independence, the education system in India remained essentially examination-oriented. Under this system learners do not receive mathematics education. They mostly prepare themselves for preparing examinations. Such a situation not only damages the purpose of all education but also proves ruinous for mathematics education. Learners memorize important results in order to be able to reproduce them in the examinations has become the all important objective of mathematical education.

Mathematics education at the elementary school level is the first basic step or foundation towards mathematics education as a whole. It has often been found that students who have not fare well in their elementary schools are destined to have unsuccessful and frustrating experience to their school career. Also one cannot deny the fact that the achievement in mathematics relates to other achievements of a person in different fields. Therefore one must keep in mind that the foundations of mathematics should be laid at this level but often it is found that mathematics through the foundation is laid at this level. Yet, often it is found that mathematics remains as a difficult subject for majority of students. Opinions regarding the cause are poor quality of instruction.

In the past, there have tremendous developments in theories of learning and science of teaching. Though mathematics occupies a place of importance, the researchers in this area have been scanty.

Mathematics, by and large, is taught in a stereotyped and mechanical way in schools "Experience has shown that the majority of students normally fail in Mathematics at the end of class X (NCERT, 2000). A mid term National survey on learning Achievement of class V Children (2008) states that: (*i*) National average in Mathematics was 48.46%;indicating an increase of 1.95% from Base Line Achievement measured in year 2001-02. (*ii*) There was no significant difference between boys and girls. In achievement however, rural children scored significantly better than their urban counterparts. Urban girls scored significantly better than urban boys. (*iii*) The performance of children is the poorest in Mathematics and better in Language.

The National Resource Group of SSA (2008) advised Central and State Governments on all aspects of quality improvement in elementary education, through SSA and related programmes, with special reference to Laying down of minimum levels of learning and their incorporation in curricula, textbooks and teaching process and Monitoring learner achievement *vis-à-vis* MLL's and action for improving attainment levels.

Learning of mathematics is very essential to develop life skills but as stated earlier, the achievement level of students from primary schools and particularly of female students are very poor. Hence, it becomes more essential to explore the attainment levels of MLL competencies in mathematics and to over come these difficulties with appropriate remedial strategies. This study came in this response. Following null hypotheses were formulated for the present investigation.

Following null hypotheses were formulated for the present investigation:

H1: There is no significant difference in the competency levels of the students studying in different taluks.

H2: Students studying in urban and rural areas do not differ significantly in their competency levels.

H3: Male and female students do not differ significantly in their competency levels.

Sample

The sample of the study included 1457 students from 166 schools of 7 Blocks of Shimoga district in Karnataka State. All the Government Primary schools of Shimoga district formed the units of the study. 10 per cent of students selected from each block. This sample was stratified on the basis of rural and urban locale. All the Vth standard students studying in these schools initially formed sample of the study. Following table illustrates the distribution of the sample by gender and locale.

Table 5.1. Distribution of the Sample by Gender and Locale

Area	Gender		Total
	Male	Female	
Urban	124	135	259
Rural	580	618	1198
Total	704	753	1457

Tools

MLL Competency Based Test in Mathematics:

For assessing, MLL competencies taught in first semester were made as base for adapting the test which was developed by Kashinath (2005). The investigator confined to the competencies taught only in Ist semester to Vth standard students.

Competencies Covered by the Test were :

1. Numbers,
2. Different numerals,
3. Fundamental operations,
4. Fractions,
5. Decimals fundamental operations,
6. Decimals addition and subtraction with mixed operations,
7. Angles.

Reliability of the Achievement Test

"The reliability of a test or any measuring instrument depends upon the consistency with which it gauges the ability to which it is applied" (Garret, 196). There are number of approaches to assess the reliability of a test. The choice of approach depends on the type of information one is seeking. As a test score is only interpretable when the test possesses substantial internal consistency, that is, all the items in the test measure the same construct, the coefficient of internal consisting would be interest (Coronbach, 1954). In this study the coefficient of internal consistency has been obtained by using the split-half method.

Reliability refers to the consistency with which a test measures whatever it measures. There are a number of approaches to assess the reliability of test. The choice of approach depends on the type of information one is seeking. The test scores can be interpreted when it possesses substantial internal consistency. In this study the coefficient of internal consistency was obtained by Kashinath, the author of original test but investigator also found out internal consistency through using the split half method. A test is said to be internally consistent if all its items measures the same thing. To estimate the internal consistency of the test the split half method has been used. The coefficient of internal consistency has been computed for the test by finding the product moment correlation between the score on odd and even numbered sub-competencies and then self-correlation coefficient of the whole test has been estimated by using Spearman-Brown prophecy formula.

$$rtt = \frac{Nrt/2t/2}{1+ (n.1)\ rt/2t/2}$$

The reliability was found as 0.77. Thus the test has a high reliability

Validation of the Test

The test is valid if the scores it assigns to examinees are free from constant and systematic errors and hence the interference based on these scores were justified. The content validity of the test refers to the extent to which the test contains a representatative sample of items, which define the content domain of interest.

Copies of the this test were distributed, along with the copies of the list of competencies selected to six content specialists in mathematics education and mathematics teachers of Regional Institute of Education and Subject Inspector and experts in mathematics in Shimoga district. The experts are requested to judge the relevance of each item in the test and to critically examine them to ascertain the adequacy and clarity of the items. Based on the opinion of the content experts, suitable modifications were made in the test.

PROCEDURE

Selection of the Sample

To select the sample the investigator visited schools to gather the data regarding the students' background information from selected schools. The investigator conducted on all the students of 166 schools to diagnose non masters in mathematics to form sample of the study for selecting sample to represent the total population of non-masters based on pre-test in mathematics, the investigator selected 10 per cent of total population on random basis from Vth standard students from the selected schools of Shimoga district. Investigator selected carefully the 10 per cent of students from rural, urban schools and also from boys and girls from the toal selected sample. Investigator maintained the same 10 per cent representation in selection of gender. Total 197 schools randomly selected from the all 7 blocks for meeting 10 per cent representation of the sample selected. Information regarding type of school, infrastructure etc., was obtained from *Sarva Shiksha Abhiyan* (SSA) office, Shimoga district of Karnataka State. After selection of 10 per cent of students from 166 Government primary schools of 7 blocks of Shimoga district, researcher visited all the Block Education officers and Block Resource Persons to get the permission for collecting data needed for the study. Number of sub-competencies answered correctly on the test was obtained for each student on each competency. Students obtaining 80 percent or more on a competency were designated as the masters of the competency. Those who mastered 80 percent or more of the competencies were considered as the overall master of competencies.

Administration of the Tool

The researchers visited all the schools in person and administered the test himself with the help of BRC's and teachers and assured the confidentiality of the data. At the end of first semester the students were given test to assess their attainments on the MLL competencies taught in Mathematics.

Statistical Methods Applied

To find out the levels of mastery frequency and percentages were applied. To see the association between taluks and mastery level, area and mastery level, gender and mastery level, contingency coefficient tests were applied. All the statistical operations were done through SPSS for windows (version 16.0)

Results

Tables 5.2, 5.3 and 5.4 present the distribution of the sample by taluks, area and gender along with results of Independent samples 't' test.

Table 5.2. Distribution of the Sample by Mastery Level and Taluks

Taluks		Students		Total
		Non masters	Masters	
Soraba	Frequency	123	17	140
	%	11.2%	4.7%	9.6%
Thirthahalli	Frequency	147	15	162
	%	13.4%	4.2%	11.1%
Hosanagara	Frequency	78	78	156
	%	7.1%	21.7%	10.7%
Bhadravathi	Frequency	200	57	257
	%	18.2%	15.9%	17.6%
Shimoga	Frequency	197	64	261
	%	17.9%	17.8%	17.9%
Sagar	Frequency	180	53	233
	%	16.4%	14.8%	16.0%
Shikaripura	Frequency	173	75	248
	%	15.8%	20.9%	17.0%
Total	Frequency	1098	359	1457
	%	100.0%	100.0%	100.0%
	CC=0.244; P<.000 (HS)			

On the whole we find of the 1457 students selected, 1098 did not attain mastery and 359 of them had mastery. Though we find less number of masters, the pattern was not found to be similar for different blocks. In the case of Hosanagara block we find 50 per cent of each was masters and non-masters. In all other blocks we find more students who did not attain mastery and only few of them attained mastery. Further, contingency coefficient test revealed a significant association between blocks and mastery, where CC value of .244 was found to be significant at .000 level (Table 5.2).

Table 5.3. Distribution of the Sample by Mastery Level and Area

Area		Mastery		Total
		Non-masters	Masters	
Urban	Frequency	208	51	259
	%	80.3%	19.7%	100.0%
Rural	Frequency	890	308	1198
	%	74.3%	25.7%	100.0%
Total	Frequency	1098	359	1457
	%	75.4%	24.6%	100.0%
CC=0.053; P<.042 (S)				

Area-wise comparison revealed a significant association between area and mastery where contingency coefficient of .053 was found to be signfiant at .003 level. From the table we find more students who attained mastery in rural area compared to urban area (25.7% vs 19.7%) (Table 5.3).

Table 5.4. Distribution of the Sample by Mastery Level and Gender

Gender		Mastery		Total
		Non masters	Masters	
Male	Frequency	549	155	704
	%	78.0%	22.0%	100.0%
Female	Frequency	549	204	753
	%	72.9%	27.1%	100.0%
Total	Frequency	1098	359	1457
	%	75.4%	24.6%	100.0%
CC=0.059; P<.025 (S)				

A significant association was observed between gender and level of mastery. Contingency coefficient of .059 was found to be significant at .025 level. From the table we find female students had attained more mastery than male students (27.1% vs 22.0%) (Table 5.4).

DISCUSSION

Main findings of the study are :

- Only 24.6 per cent of the sample attained mastry level in MLL competencies in mathematics.
- Students of Hosanagara Taluk was found to have higher mastery levels compared to other taluks of Shimoga.
- Rural area students had higher levels of mastry in mathematics than students of urban area
- As expected girl students excelled boys in attaining mastery levels.

Hypothesis 1

There is no significant difference in the competency levels of the students studying in different blocks (taluks).

In the case of Hosanagara taluk we find 50 per cent of each was masters and non-masters. In all other blocks we find more students who did not attain mastery and only few of them attained mastery. Further, contingency coefficient test revealed a significant association between blocks and mastery, where CC value of .244 was found to be significant at .000 level. Hence hypothesis 1 is rejected as the test statistics showed significant difference in the competency levels of students studying in different blocks.

It is quite evident that differences in geographical reasons and heterogeneity of the population influences over the attainment levels so this we can see in the case of Hosanagara taluk. Some of the studies revealed the reasons of the non attainment of competency levels in mathematics. Van de Walle (2005), "the very fact that many students in grades 4 and 5 have not mastered addition and subtraction and students in the middle and upper grades do not have good command of their multiplication facts suggest that this method simply does not work well." It is concluded that children develop a variety of different thought processes for basic facts regardless of the amount of drill they undergo (Van de Walle, 2005). They also found that children create and hold on to procedures that develop from their own conception of numbers and that drill does not help students develop any new or more efficient strategies (Van de Walle, 2005). However, drill can be used once a student has acquired an efficient strategy. Premature drill (using drill before a student develops their own understanding of numbers), will certainly be ineffective, waste valuable time, and for many students contribute to a strong dislike and a faulty view of learning mathematics (Van de Walle, 2005). Overall, Van de Walle (2005) suggest that drill can provide four things: an increased facility with a strategy but only with a strategy already learned; a focus on a singular method and an exclusion of flexible alternatives; a false appearance of understanding; a rule-oriented view of what mathematics is about. In conclusion, drill can only help students get faster at what they already know. We feel that manipulatives have a place in the classroom but that children learn through reflective thought and not through the manipulation of objects (Colgan, 2007). We agree with Jon Van de Walle's statement that you 'cannot judge the value of an activity by the presence or absence of a physical model' and we feel that some problems are best solved without the assistance of a manipulative (Colgan, 2007). Proof is and has been for long a problematic area in the teaching of mathematics at the school level. While proof remains central to the discipline of mathematics (like Horgan, 1993, its pedagogic role at the school level remains unclear.

A major contributory factor to this problem is surely that we introduce proofs at too late a stage. Moreover, it is done in too abrupt, too formal, and too stylized a manner. This results in a feeling of alienation for the child, who finds proofs unmotivated and unnatural. This feeling is added to if what is being proved looks obvious. And a majority of the early results encountered in geometry do indeed look obvious. (Recall some of the results we meet early in the study of geometry; e.g., the bridge of asses theorem.) Whatever be the cause, the problem challenges us to respond with some effective pedagogy. The cost of not doing so is considerable. A child reaching the senior grades without a significant exposure to the culture of proof has lost a valuable opportunity to experience a central component of the discipline of mathematics.

Learning achievement surveys undertaken by National Council of Education Research and Training (NCERT) and other agencies show that mathematics pedagogy calls for more attention to help children acquire the basic skills in mathematics. At present the attempt is to strengthen the early reading and mathematics skill development programmes at the Primary level and Mathematics teaching at Upper Primary level to prepare the students in a better manner.

National Knowledge Commission (2008) on attracting students to maths and science revealed that curriculum reform remains an important issue in almost all schools. School education must be made more relevant to the lives of children. There is need to move away from rote-learning to understanding concepts, good comprehension and communication skills and learning how to access knowledge independently.

The main educational implication of this study is that one cannot be rigid in the use of teaching methods. All teaching methods are effective in certain situations and not so effective in other situations. Content and objectives determine the methods to be used

Hypothesis 2

Male and female students do not differ significantly in their competency levels

A significant association was observed between gender and level of mastery. Contingency coefficient of .059 was found to be significant at .025 level. From the table we find female students had attained more mastery than male students (27.1% vs 22.0%).

Hence hypothesis 2 is rejected as we find that female students excelled male students in their competency level.

Research evidence has consistently shown that female students in Hawai'i outperform males in mathematics. The data from the 1982 and 1983 mathematics Stanford Achievement Test (SAT) administered to Hawai'i public school students in grades four, six, eight, and ten, found that overall, females consistently outperformed males across these grade levels. The 1991 SAT mathematics results for tenth graders in Hawai'i and confirmed that girls performed better than boys. A majority of studies found that females perform better than males (DeMars 2000, Garner & Engelhard, 1999; Myerberg, 1996; Zhang & Manon, 2000).

Rastogi, (1983) attempted a study on diagnosis of weaknesses in arithmetic as related to the basic arithmetic skills and their remedial measures and he revealed that one of the important causes of backwardness in mathematics was the poor command over basic arithmetic skills.

On delay of feedback and retention in rational understanding in mathematicsand he found that the retentive capacity of the girls was more than that of the boys, in the following order, namely, decimals, arithmetic, numerals and geometry. The girls possessed better understanding factors than boys in long-term retention. In memory ability there was a small but consistent sex difference, the girls being higher than the boys over the entire range in all the three standards.

Chitkara (1985) studied on the effectiveness of different strategies of teaching on achievement in mathematics and she found that girls of average ability scored significantly higher in mathematics than boys of average ability

Gupta (2004) studied gender disparity in madhyamik examination result and he revealed that difference in overall achievements i.e., average percentage of pass of boys and girls of West Bengal is small. Marginally higher percentage of girls passed the Madhyamik Examination than the boys.

Basic literary skills (reading and writing) are prerequisites to mathematics achievement. For instructional and learning purposes, increasing students' verbal scores might assist in increasing their performance on mathematics assessments. This is especially important for boys, whose lower linguistic skills negatively influence their mathematics assessment.

Because gender differences exist in early literacy skills, mathematics educators may need to consider gender-appropriate pedagogical approaches for boys and girls. To benefit males and females, the instruction for males and females might need to be differentiated. As Gambell and Hunter (2000: 712) stated, "Males are in trouble in literacy!". And as a result, boys are in trouble with mathematics as well. While mathematics performance of males might be improved by focusing on linguistic skills, for females beneficial outcomes might be obtained by focusing on mathematics. Boys might benefit from additional guidance in reading comprehension and verbalization along with quantitative reasoning, whereas for girls the benefit might accrue from focused practice with mathematics-specific semiotics, e.g., symbols, formulas, and algorithms.

Hypothesis 3

Students studying in urban and rural areas do not differ significantly in their competency scores.

Area-wise comparison revealed a significant association between area and mastery where contingency coefficient of

.053 was found to be significant at .003 level. From the table we find more students from rural area attained mastery than students in urban area (25.7% vs 19.7%).

Hence, hypothesis 3 is rejected, since we find that students from rural area were found to be better than urban area students in the mastery of competencies.

In this study sample included only government primary schools of Shimoga district. The students in the rural sample were selected from government schools. Usually students of all levels of mathematical ability have no option, but to enroll themselves in government schools. Thus, the students from rural areas present a more heterogeneous nature in mathematical ability than urban students. Usually in urban areas, children of well to do families are enrolled in private schools, which are perceived to be, and to an extent in actual sense qualitatively better than government schools. Naturally in urban areas, majority of students belong to the higher ability group. In addition, in urban areas many of the children studying in private institutions opt for additional tuition classes than rural students. It is quite surprising that rural students outshined urban students and hence shown better performance in mathematics compare to rural students. In urban government schools almost all students enrolled come from lower economic levels and impoverished environment. Hence it is likely that they tend to be lower in their performance in mathematics competencies. Many studies quoted above reported lower mathematics achievement by urban students from government schools. In the present study the sample from urban and rural area was drawn only from government schools. As a result the rural sample becomes more heterogeneous having many higher ability students as well as lower ability students for the reason mentioned above. But the urban sample becomes more homogeneous which consisting students from first generation learners and poor family support. This difference between rural and urban students is due to these reasons.

REFERENCES

Chitkara, M. (1985), To Study the Effectiveness of Different Strategies of Teaching on Achievement in Mathematics in Relation to Intelligence, Sex and Personality, Ph.D. Edu., Pan. U Sastri, S.M., A Study of Delay of Feedback and Retention in Rational Understanding in Mathematics, Ph.D. Edu., And. U.

Colgan, Lynda. (2007). Mathematics Education Loses a Giant: Van de Walle Tribute *OAME/AOEM Gazette*, 7-11.

Coronbach, L.J.(1954). *Educational Psychology*. New York, Horcourt, Brace Javanovich.

DeMars, C.E. (2000). Test stakes and item format interactions. *Applied Measurement in Education, 13*(1), 55-77.

Gambell, T., and Hunter, D. (2000). Surveying gender differences in Canadian school literacy. *Journal of Curriculum Studies, 32*(5), 689-719.

Garner, M., & Engelhard, G. J. (1999). Gender differences in performance on multiple-choice and constructed response mathematics items. *Applied Measurement in Education, 12*(1), 29-51.

Garrett, H.E. Statistics in Psychology and Education. David Mckay Company, Inc., New York, 1986.

Gupta Rumki (2004). Empowerment of Women in Terms of Education and their Deprivation. In: *Issues on empowerment of Women*, Utpal Kumar De and Bhola Nath Ghosh (Eds.). Mohit Publications, New Delhi.

Horgan, J. (1993). The Death of Proof. *Scientific American*, 269(4), 93-103

Kashinath, H.M.(2005), Construction and validation of battery of tests in mathematics for II,V and VII standard based on KSQAO Competencies. Report of Karnataka School Quality assessment organization (KSQAO) Karnataka State Education Examination Board, Bengaluru.

Myerberg, N. J. (1996). *Performance on different test types by racial/ethnic group and gender.* Paper presented at the Annual Meeting of the American Educational Research Association, New York.

NCERT (2008). Baseline Achievement Survey, Learning Achievement of class V. children, New Delhi

RASTOGI, S. (1983), Dignosis of Weaknesses in Arithmetic as Related to the Basic Arithmetic Skills and Their Remedial Measures, Ph.D. Edu., Gau. U.

Van de Walle, J. A. (2005). *Elementary and Middle School Mathematics.* Toronto: Pearson Allyn and Bacon.

Zhang, L. & Manon, J. (2000). *Gender and achievement - understanding gender differences and similarities in mathematics assessment*. Retrieved July 24, 2004.

CHAPTER

6

Social Adjustment Problems, Academic Performance and Academic Hardiness in High School Students

—*Ali Khanekashi*

ABSTRACT

This Chapter examined the relationship between social adjustment problems, academic performance and academic hardiness of high school students. The sample contained of 212 (105 males and 107 females) 10 grade of high school students from Iran. Bill's Adjustment Inventory (BAI) and Academic Hardiness Scale *(AHS)*, carried out on the group sample and data analyzed by Pearson correlation and two independent samples T test.

The results revealed that social adjustment problems significantly have negative correlation with academic performance but it has positive correlation with Academic Hardiness. Moreover, there is no significant differences between boys and girls in three variables

INTRODUCTION

The quality of students' academic performance is influenced by wide range of environmental factors rather simply teacher factors and psychological factors within the learners such as motivation and the self, rather than simply by ability. School as a social environment is not only the places in which many students spend most of their day, it also is where they engage in the important activities of learning academic knowledge; acquiring and practising more generalized skills, such as solving problems, being on time, and following directions; and developing formative relationships with peers and adults. Moreover, the consequences of their behaviour at school can be powerful. As noted, students' inappropriate behaviour at school can distract both the students themselves and those around them from their learning tasks. In addition, research has shown that teachers' evaluation of students' academic performance is influenced by the students' behaviour in the classroom (Minuchin & Piro, 1983). Adjustment is one of the factors which can even be influential on pedagogical achievement. In other words, adjustment is a person's ability in establishing relationship with the environment, and a person cannot expect optimum results until he/she bridges between environment and the situation in a curriculum atmosphere (Erica, 1996).

The term 'adjustment' means a state of harmonious relationship between a person and his environment. It also refers to a continuous process by which a person changes his own behaviour or tries to change the environment or brings change in both to produce satisfactory relationship with his environment. It also means how efficiently an individual performs his duties in different circumstances. It is concerned with the individual's ability to cope effectively with his environment. According to Parameswaran and Beena (2004) adjustment is a process by which a living organism acquires a particular way of acting or behaving or changes an existing form of behavior or action.

Since school is a communal location, it is fundamental that every single individual keeps in touch with his/her peer groups. Besides, the adjustment conflict can be posited in terms of the manner of adjustment to the school atmosphere, principals, teachers and subject matters is incorrect behaviours and will be pessimist to the future (Douglas, 1968). Moreover, there is some other school variables related to learning. Academic hardiness is one of the important variables not only so students and their parents, but also to institutions of learning, educationists and any progressive. The quality of students' academic hardiness is influenced by wide range of environmental factors. Despite the many reports on the relationships between variety of variables and adjustment, there is scarce if any documentation of the influence of adjustment problems on academic variables. Secondly, there is need for studies which will address gender differences in the levels of adjustment in relation to their academic performance and academic hardiness. This presents study therefore focuses on these issues.

Goals

The study has two aims:

- To examine the relationship between levels of social adjustment problems, academic performance and academic hardiness among high school students in IRAN.
- To examine the effects of gender on students' levels of social adjustment problems, Academic performance and Academic Hardiness.

METHOD

Sample

The sample contained 212 students of tenth grade high school (105 males and 107 females), were selected via random sampling in Behbahan High Schools. The mean age of the students was 15.4 and they were selected from two kinds of Iranian schools (government and private).

Tools and Materials

Social adjustment problems: In the study we used of 35 items developed by Bell's Adjustment Inventory – BAI. The whole of inventory comprises of 140 items in relation to four areas of adjustment (School, Health, Social and Emotional) with 35 items in each factors. The test is helpful in screening the poorly adjusted students who may need further psycho-diagnostic study and counseling for their adjustment problems.

This scale possesses high reliability by split half method (for social subscale it was 0.87) and concurrent validity also commuted 0.82 for this subscale.

Academic Hardiness Scale (AHS)

This Scale created by Benishek and Lopez (2001) with 18-item self-report instrument in a four-response Likert format. This instrument was designed to gather information about student attitudes regarding academic success. The four response options range from 1 = completely false to 4 = completely true. The psychometric properties of this scale has shown that internal consistency alpha coefficient was computed 0.86.

Academic Performance

Average of marks obtained by students in the last class examination in the school was collected.

RESULTS AND DISCUSSION

Results

According to the hypothesis of the current investigation, the analysis of data divided in two parts: At first part we have evaluated the relationship between three variables and in the second part we analyzed the gender differences in three variables.

Relationship between Social Adjustment Problems (SAP), Academic Performance (AP) and Academic Hardiness (AH)

The correlations between levels of social adjustment problems, academic performance, and academic hardiness are presented in Table 6.1.

It was hypothesized that there are significant relationships between social adjustment problems, academic performance and academic hardiness. Contrary to the hypothesis, positive significant correlations were found between SAP with AP [r= 0.19, p = .05] and also there was negative significant correlation between SAP with AH [r = 0.30, P <.01].

Table 6.1. Means, standard deviations and correlation matrix of SAP, AP, and AH

Variables	Social adjustment problems M=9.75 SD=3.81	Academic performance M=14.30 SD= 1.35	Academic Hardiness M=50.81 SD=8.24
Social adjustment problems	-		
Academic performance	0.19 (*)	-	
Academic Hardiness	-0.30(**)	0.15 (*)	-

N: 284.** Correlation is significant at the 0.01 level (2-tailed).
* Correlation is significant at the 0.05 level (2-tailed).

These corroborate previous studies which reported significant correlations between adjustment problems and Academic performance (Sroufeet *et al.*, 1999).

Furthermore there was a significant correlations between SAP, and AH [r = .15 (*), p = .05].

The Influence of Gender on Social Adjustment Problems, Academic Performance and Academic Hardiness

Table 6.2 presents the scores of boys and girls in three dependent variables. The results of two independent T test are described below.

Table 6.2. Means, SD and estimated two independent samples T test of boys and girls in three variables

Dependent Variable	SEX	MEAN	SD	T
Social adjustment problems	male	9.98	3.79	1.65
	female	9.46	3.83	
Academic performance	male	14.46	1.26	.82
	female	14.16	1.42	
Academic Hardiness	male	50.46	8.02	1.24
	female	51.12	8.48	

N: 212

An inspection of the mean scores of males and females on Table 6.2 below indicates that:

1. Males scored slightly higher on the SAP scale (m = 9.98, SD = 3.79) than females (m = 9.46, SD=3.83). But this difference is not significant.
2. There are not significantly differences between males and females on AP, (m = 14.46, SD =1.26) for male and (m = 14.16, SD = 1.42) for female.
3. In Academic Hardiness also there is not significantly differences between two gender groups, (m = 50.46, SD =8.02) for male and (m = 51.12, SD = 8.48) for female.

DISCUSSION AND CONCLUSION

The first hypothesis of the current investigation suggested that there is significant relationship between social adjustment problems, academic performance and academic hardiness in high school students. The results of the study reveal significant relationship between Social adjustment problems and academic performance(r = -.21, p < .01). This means that students who have high social adjustment problems tended to perform fewer scores in Academic performance. However, those who have low social adjustment problems tended to perform high scores in Academic performance. These findings corroborate pervious findings which report significant relationships between SAP and AP (Bjorklund & Green, 1992). More over there was significant relationship between SAP and AH (r = 0.33, p <0.01).

The second hypothesis suggested that there is no significant difference between boys and girls three variables. These findings are not agree with; Lee (Ackerman *et al.*, 2004), about the role of gender in social adjustment problems and academic performance.

In support of previous studies this study has established the fact that adjustment is a good predictor of academic performance and Academic Hardiness. It also shows that gender hasn't a moderate's role in the effects of Social adjustment problems on academic performance and academic hardiness.

REFERENCES

Ackerman, B., Brown, E., & C. Izard, (2004). The relations between contextual risk, earned income, and the school adjustment of children from economically disadvantaged families. *Developmental Psychology, 40,* 204-216.

Bjorklund, D. F., & (1992). Child development and evolutionary psychology. *Child Development, 71,* 1687-1708.

Benishek, L. A., & Lopez, F. G. (2001). Development and initial validation of a measure of academic hardiness. *Journal of Career Assessment, 9 (4),* 333-352.

Douglas, C. Kimmel Irving, B. Weiner (1968). Adolescence development transition.

Erica, F. (1996). Adolescent coping theatrical and research perspectives.

Parameswaran, EG and Beena, C. (2004) *An in vitiation to psychology,* Hyderabad, Nelakamal Publications Pvt. Ltd., reprint 618-621.

Minuchin, P., & SSAPiro, E. (1983). The school as a context for social development. In: E. M. Hetherington (Ed.) *Manual of Child Psychology, Vol. 4.* (pp. 197-274). New York: Wiley.

Sroufe, L.A., Egelund, B., & Carlson, E.A. (1999). One social world: The integrated development of parent-child and peer relationships. In: W.A. Collins & B. Laursen (Eds.), *Relationships as developmental contexts. The Minnesota Symposia on Child Psychology,* Vol. 30 (pp. 241-261). Mahwah, NJ: Erlbaum.

CHAPTER

7

School Organizational Climate in Secondary Schools of India and Iran : A Comparative Study

—Dr. Y.N. Sridhar and Hamid Reza Razavi

The studies on school climate, both past and present, emphasize "shared perceptions" about policies, practices, and procedures used in school, research in the area of school climate continues today because of its significant impact on those learning and working within a school. School climate can be defined as the learning environment created through the interaction of human relation, physical setting, and psychological atmosphere (Perkins, 2006).

Research randomly selected Iranian and Indian secondary school teachers to identify that there is no significant difference in school organizational climate as measured by SOCQ and significant level between Government (public) secondary schools with Private secondary schools in Iran and India. For each participant school, secondary teachers were asked to complete Sharma's (1978) School Organizational Climate Questionnaire. This instrument includes 64 items and 8 dimensions (4 dimensions refer to teacher, 4 dimensions refer to principal) that have been identified by the research on school climate.

Two research questions and sub-questions were analyzed. Distribution of central tendency and dispersion statistics were computed for each subscales on each instrument. Coefficient contingency and MANOVA were used to determine the relationships among the variables. According to tree group toward to school climate of teachers' perception indicate that,

36.4 per cent of secondary school teachers have high teacher moral, 45.4 per cent only satisfactory teacher moral and 18.2 per cent low teacher moral in government and private environments of secondary schools in Iran. Teachers' perceptions toward school climate are 25.3 per cent high teacher moral, 47.6 per cent only satisfactory teacher moral and 27 per cent low teacher moral in government and private environments of secondary schools in India. Finding in this study indicate that there is a difference between types of school organizational climate in both countries.

Definitions and Concept of School Organizational Climate

Within the first five minutes of walking into a school, one can often determine the climate. John and Taylor (2002) state that school climate is: the feel of a school (Halpin & Croft, 1963), as its 'collective personality' (Norton, 1984). Climate is the human environment within which the teachers of a school do their work. Like the air in a room, climate surrounds and affects everything that happens in an organization (Friedberg, 1983:5). As one moves from school to school, it is possible to note that one school feels different from another. This is primarily the result of school climate.

The Denver Public Schools Teacher Association (2003:5) defines climate as

> "...the atmosphere in an organization. Climate affects the morale, productivity, and satisfaction of all persons involved in the organization. It reflects how staff, students and the community feels about a school and/or the District whether it is a positive place to work and learn or one that is full of problems").

The Ciruli Study shows a correlation between a poor work environment and teacher recruitment and retention problems. Teachers identify a "good" principal as critically important to a good work environment (cited in Denver Public, 2003).

Teacher retention is not the only outcome of positive school climate. The other outcomes include higher student test scores, strong employee morale, and a positive community relationship with the school (Denver Public, 2003). lithe Denver Colorado

Task Force found that five factors are essential to positive school climate: respect, responsiveness, relationships, and rites and responsibilities". Plucker (1998) showed a correlation between school climate and student aspirations. The outcome of the study showed that schools that want to improve student aspiration should also work on fostering a positive school climate. The importance of a positive connection between the community and school climate was also shown through the Higher Inspiration test scores of students who felt they were valuable members of the school community.

Climate can also be defined in six different ways: open, autonomous, controlled, familiar, paternal, and closed (Halpin and Croft, 1963). These climates are based on four teacher-related factors: hindrance, intimacy, disengagement, and esprit; and on four principal-teacher relations factors: production emphasis, aloofness, consideration, and trust. These climate factors are also supported in the use of the Organizational Climate Description Questionnaire for Secondary Schools (OCDQ-RS), which focuses on supportive principal behavior, directive principal, behavior, restrictive principal behavior, collegial teacher behavior, committed teacher behavior, and disengaged teacher behavior. Halpin and Croft recognize the importance of focusing on principal and teacher factors. Other school related factors can be involved when looking at school climate. John and Taylor (2002) state that: In prior research, an analysis of the perceptions of parents, teachers, and students regarding the climate of their schools was conducted biannually in the United States from 1979 to 1982 and discovered that the climate of the School was a function of several school-related factors (Freidberg, 1983:5). These factors included leadership qualities of principals, teacher-colleague relations, parent-teacher relations, students-teacher interpersonal relations, student-teacher instruction-related interaction, school buildings and facilities, and student-peer relations. These indicators were the degree of respect, trust, opportunity for input, cohesiveness, caring, high morale, and school renewal.

The Influences of Principals/headmaster on School Climate

Many studies have looked at the relationship between teacher commitment and school climate. "Strong associations have been reported between organizational commitment and climate openness (McDaniel, 1992), collegiality (Combs, 1995; Firestone & Pennell, 1993), collaboration (Gibson, 1996; Hatton, 1996 and teacher empowerment (Hornung, 1995). Overall these studies make a strong case for a relationship between the climate of a school and the level of teacher commitment" (John and Taylor, 2002: 6).

A relationship between leadership style and school climate has also been drawn. John and Taylor (2002) cited the following studies: Al-Gasim (1991), for example, found a strong relationship between an open climate and principals who were high in both consideration and initiating structure dimensions. Similarly, Bailey (1988) concluded that school principals who, desire to improve their school climate need to exhibit both high task-oriented behaviors and high relationship behaviors with their teachers. Other studies have likewise underscored the importance of the leadership style of principals to the development of a positive school climate (e.g., Bancroft, 1986; Bishop, 1991; Chen, 1990; Hayes, 1994; Marschilok, 1993).

Prior studies have similarly found significant relationships between leadership style and climate. Holley (1995), for example concluded from her study of high school administrators and staff members of an urban school district that leadership style of the administrators can create a climate that is conducive and supportive of the instructional emphases in the school. Bailey (1988) found that high school teachers in West Virginia perceived a positive relationship between their principals' leadership styles and the school climate. The findings indicated that high school principals who desire to improve their school climate need to exhibit high task and high relationship behaviors with their teachers.

When looking at school climate, one finds that the building principal is extremely important. Not only does the principal affect how the school runs, but also the morale of the teachers and the students is highly affected by the type of relationships the principal fosters. The Ciruli Study (2002) findings states that:

> Teachers uniformly believe the principal is the most "important" person at the school. Principals are important in setting expectations for teachers and in boosting morale through positive feedback. The main complaint about less effective principals is that they *offer* no positive feedback. Whether teachers get along with and/or respect their principal seems key whether the teacher will stay at the school. This factor overrides other issues such as teaching environment and whether the school is rated satisfactory or unsatisfactory.

The building principal sets the climate of the school as measured by staff productivity, student productivity, and creative thought. The principal must demonstrate a set of attributes that are a combination of manager and instructional leader. One of the primary responsibilities of the principal is to support and encourage teachers to embrace new and innovative strategies of instruction.

"Administrators can improve school climate and student achievement by understanding their role in the school environment and working to improve them. Successful principals encourage risk-taking and support good tries. When principals back teachers, when they are fair and trust-worthy, and genuinely concerned about teacher growth, teachers go the extra milen. (Winter & Sweeney, 1994: 12)." School leaders shape school climate by the things they pay attention to in the day-to-day life of the school. Principals need to be aware of and attend to the factors of respect, responsiveness, recognition, relationships, and rites and responsibilities. For example, giving positive feedback to staff promotes an achievement-oriented culture by reinforcing behavior that should be encouraged and focusing on the good things that are happening at school. (Cited in Denver Public, 2003: 13)

As shown, research has been done on the principal's effect on school climate and the ways a principals can enhance school climate. However, only limited research shows the effect principals have on the climate in rural schools.

METHOD

Sample

The sample population for the study included teachers working in secondary schools in Mysore city (India). Around 300 secondary teachers on the basis of the number of schools and teachers (separately government and private schools) were selected in two stages were using stratified random sampling technique as sample and care would be taken to see that is representative both in Mysore (India). In this case, the sample of the present study consisted of 300 secondary school teachers in Mysore (India). Site Selection the participants in this study were from secondary schools through grade 8, 9 and 10 in Mysore (India) area school district. The selected participants were classroom teachers (specialized teachers assigned to a school) within the school district.

In order to collect data about school organizational climate, It was decide to select 300 teachers using simple random sampling technique from the selected 63 schools in Mysore city. Even though, 300 questionnaires were given to selected teachers, the researcher could get only 262 questionnaires from India (87.3%).

Procedure of Collecting Data

The researchers used written consent and explained the purpose of the study and the instrument that was, used to collect the data. A consent form was attached to the set of *questionnaires* Teachers were, requested to complete' and return the questionnaire if they wished to participate. If they choose not to participate, they returned the questionnaire unanswered. Participants were, informed by the headmaster or headmistress and principals and they provided consent for this study. Teachers were able to withdraw from participation without prejudice or reprisal. To ensure no information would identify participants and/or building principals, demographic data was limited to the following: age, gender, qualification, total years experience, and type of school. To ensure anonymity participants were, instructed not to put their names on the inventory, demographic data sheet or the return envelope. The self-sealing envelope further protected confidentiality.

The researchers informed the participants that the findings of this study would be, made available to the district for review. It is, expected that the district would benefit from the study, providing data on desirable leadership traits and behaviors of principals, as perceived by teachers.

The method in which the inventory was distributed, completed, and collected, guarded against identification of the participants. This information will be, kept in a file cabinet at the researchers' home office for one year.

Coded data were analyzed with the help of SPSS software. MANOVA and coefficient contingency was used to compare the school organizational climate with government and private schools in India and in Iran.

Research Hypotheses

The fallowing two hypotheses are put in the present research study:

1. There is no significant difference in school organizational climate of secondary schools as measured by SOCI in Mysore and in Amol.
2. There is no significant difference between government and private secondary schools in Mysore and in Amol in terms of dimensions of school organizational climate as measured by SOCI.

Instrument

The tool used in the present investigation was School Organizational Climate Description Questionnaire by Sharma (1978). Sharma's study is one of the pioneer works in the field of organizational climate conducted in India. He translated Halpin's test (OCQD) into Hindi and standardized it over a large sample in the state of Rajasthan. This scale consisted of

64 items distributed over eight dimensions of organizational climate of which four refer to the characteristics of the teachers as a group and other four refer to the characteristics are: (I) Disengagement, (II) Alienation, (III) Esprit and (IV) Intimacy and four dimensions of leader behavior are (I) Psychophysical hindrance, (II) Control, (III) Production emphasis, and (IV) Humanized trust. Each item is to be answered on a scale of 4 alternatives i.e., RO - Rarely occurs, SO - Sometimes occurs, OF - Often occurs, and VO - Very Often occurs. To score the items on the scale measures of 4, 3, 2 and 1 are given in the case of positive statement, and 1, 2, 3 and 4 scoring in the case of negative statements. Thus a range of scores on the scale for each area varies from 8 to 32. The total score of the entire scale varies from 64 to 256. The scale was found to have a reliability ranging from .34 to .81 and a validity of .63 (Sharma, 1978).

RESULTS

FINDINGS

There is no Significant Difference in School Organizational Climate of Secondary Schools as Measured by SOCI in Mysore and in Amol

As already described, SSOCDQ was used to determine the school organizational climate of selected secondary schools. To classify the selected schools on the organizational climate in both the countries, the profile of the climate of each school was prepared using the scores obtained by the teachers. For this purpose, the scores on each subtest of SSOCDQ of all the teachers selected from a particular school were added separately and means were calculated separately for each subset. Then the mean obtained on all of the eight subset of SSOCDQ were converted in to standardized scores. From these doubly standardized scores the profiles of the climate of all the schools selected for the study were obtained and the schools the schools were categorized under different climates. The results obtained are presented in Tables 7.1 to 7.3.

Result from Table 7.1 and 7.2 reveals that there is a significant difference between type of climate in government and private schools in India. In fact, more number of government schools fall under "Familiar" type of climate and more number of private schools also fall under "familiar" type of climate. In total more number of schools comes under" Familiar" and less numbers of the schools under "closed" type of climate.

Table 7.1. Classification of Indian secondary schools on school organizational climate (Number of schools and percentage)

	Climate						
Type of school	Open	Autonomous	Familiar	Controlled	Paternal	Closed	total
Government	2	3	6	3	4	1	19
	(10.5%)	(15.8%)	(31.6%)	(15.8%)	(21.05%)	(5.25%)	(100%)
Private	2	9	11	10	10	2	44
	(4.5%)	(20%)	(25%)	(23%)	(23%)	(4.5%)	(100%)
Total	4	12	17	13	14	3	63
	(6.4%)	(19.2%)	(26.9%)	(20.6%)	(22.2%)	(4.7%)	(100%)

By examining Table 7.1, it is noticed that there is a significant difference between type of climate in government and private schools in Iran more number of government schools fall under "Familiar" type of climate and more number of private schools also fall under "familiar" type of climate. In total more number of schools comes under" Familiar" and none of the schools come under "closed" type of climate.

Table 7.2. Classification of Iranian secondary schools on school organizational climate (Number of schools and percentage)

	Climate						
Type of school	Open	Autonomous	Familiar	Controlled	Paternal	Closed	total
Government	3	3	5	2	4	17	-
	(17.6%)	(17.6%)	(29.5%)	(11.8%)	(23.5%)	(100%)	
Private	1	1	3	-	-	-	5
	(20%)	(20%)	(60%)	(100%)			
Total	4	4	8	2	4	-	22
	(18.2%)	(18.2%)	(36.4%)	(9%)	(18.2%)		(100%)

As it is shown in Table 7.3 respect to subset of school climate at 85 schools in India (63 schools) and Iran (22, schools).

The table below revealed that most of type of school is "Controlled" in Iran and "familiar" type of school in India. Also the research result distinctive that least number is relation with "closed" type of school in Iran and "closed" type of school in India. Totally in the both country result show that most of school have "controlled" type of school and least number is "closed" type of school in India and Iran. *F ratio of the 8 dimensions was calculated based on the mean scores obtained in three levels.* Tables 7.4 to 7.12 precent results related to Iran and India respectively.

Table 7.3. Overall classifications of Iranian and Indian secondary schools on school organizational climate (Number of schools and percentage)

Type of school		Climate						
		Open	Autonomous	Familiar	Controlled	Paternal	Closed	total
IRAN	No	4	4	2	8	4	0	22
	%	18.2%	18.2%	9.1%	36.4%	18.2%	%	100.0%
INDIA	No	4	12	17	13	14	3	63
	%	6.3%	19.0%	27.0%	20.6%	22.2%	4.8%	100.0%
Overall	No	8	16	19	21	18	3	85
	%	9.4%	18.8%	22.4%	24.7%	21.2%	3.5%	100.0%

There is no Significant difference between Government and Private Secondary Schools in Mysore and in Amol in Terms of Dimensions of School Organizational Climate as Measured by SOCI

Table 7.4 indicated that the critical value of F table at the .05 level of significance. The derived value of F were Country Groups (F=1.60; P<.206), Type of School (F=0.096; P<0.755) and Type & Country (F=1.548; P<0.213) which fallen to exceed the critical value of F. As a result Hypothesis was accepted for the Government and private variables schools in India and Iran. The results tended to show that disengagement of teachers' behaviour was not affected significantly and relation by teachers behaviour at government and private secondary school in both countries.

Table 7.4. Mean scores, S.D, result of MANOVA and significant level for 'DISENGAGEMENT' of SOCDQ with reference to Country and Type of School

Country	Government school			Private school			Overall		
	Mean	S.D	N	Mean	S.D	N	Mean	S.D	N
Iran	19.7731	5.1903	216	19.0351	4.0221	57	19.6190	4.9714	273
India	18.5825	4.3103	103	19.0252	4.9860	159	18.8511	4.7283	262
Total	19.3887	4.9481	319	19.0278	4.7416	216	19.2430	4.8645	535
F (country groups)	F=1.60; P<.206 (NS)								
F (type of school)	F=0.096; P<0.755 (NS)								
F (type & country)	F=1.548; P<0.213 (NS)								

Alienation of sub-scale SOCDQ and the three categories ranging from country group, type of school and over were compared using Multiple Analysis of Variance (MANOVA). Table 7.5 revealed the data regarding alienation of teacher behaviour versus two countries and private and government secondary schools of perception teachers in India and Iran.

Table 7.5. Mean scores, S.D, result of MANOVA and significant level for 'ALIENATION' of SOCDQ with reference to Country and Type of School

Country	Government school			Private school			Overall		
	Mean	S.D	N	Mean	S.D	N	Mean	S.D	N
Iran	10.3611	1.9069	216	10.4561	2.0448	57	10.3810	1.9331	273
India	9.8932	2.2092	103	9.3082	2.5106	159	9.5382	2.4094	262
Total	10.2100	2.0179	319	9.6111	2.445	216	9.9682	2.2177	535
F (country groups)	F=14.473; P<.000 (S)								
F (type of school)	F=1.331; P<0.249 (NS)								
F (type & country)	F=2.563; P<0.110 (NS)								

The analysis F ratio of country groups (F=14.473; P<.000) which exceeded the critical table value at the .05 level is significance. Thus, the alienation variable with government and private teachers' secondary school in both countries were rejected. This finding tended to provide evidence that perception teachers respect alienation at private and government secondary school in Iran is more than in Indian country.

At the .05 level of significance, the critical test statistic table. The F ratio of type of school (F=1.331; P<0.249) and over variables (F=2.563; P<0.110), derived from the MANOVA did not exceed the critical value. Based on the finding the Alienation variable for Hypothesis was accepted.

The analysis F ratio of between Esprit and country groups (F=31.67; P<.000) and also type of school, country (F=7.15; P<0.008) which exceeded the critical table value at the .05 level are significance (Table 7.6). Thus, the Esprit variable with government and private teachers' secondary school in both countries were rejected. This finding tended to provide evidence that perception teachers respect Esprit teachers' behavior at private and government secondary school in Iran is more than in Indian country.

Table 7.6. Mean scores, S.D, result of MANOVA and significant level for 'ESPRIT' of SOCDQ with reference to Country and Type of School

Country	Government school			Private school			Overall		
	Mean	S.D	N	Mean	S.D	N	Mean	S.D	N
Iran	24.8148	3.9015	216	26.3509	5.3402	57	25.135	4.2771	273
India	23.4951	5.3886	103	22.9771	4.5539	159	22.9770	4.9067	262
Total	24.3887	4.4706	319	23.6203	5.0351	216	24.0785	4.7172	535
F (country groups)	F=31.67; P<.000 (S)								
F (type of school)	F=0.58; P<0.445 (NS)								
F (type & country)	F=7.15; P<0.008 (S)								

At the .05 level of significance, the critical test statistic table. The F ratio of type of school (F=0.58; P<0.445), derived from the MANOVA did not exceed the critical value. Based on the finding the Esprit variable for Hypothesis was accepted.

A score for Intimacy teacher behaviour was computed using the SOCDQ scores for this subscale range from 1 to 4 representing the highest level of Intimacy teacher behaviour on the subscale (Table 7.7). Referral rates for each participant were determined based on the perception of secondary teachers' schools and the districts record in India and Iran. The analysis F ratio of between Intimacy and country groups (F=20.635; P<.000) and also type of school (F=2.913; P<0.088) which exceeded the critical table value at the .05 level are significance. Thus, the Intimacy variable with government and private teachers' secondary school in both countries were rejected. This finding tended to provide evidence that perception teachers respect Intimacy teachers' behavior at private and government secondary school in Iran is more than in Indian country (Table 7.7).

Table 7.7. Mean scores, S.D, result of MANOVA and significant level for 'INTIMACY' of SOCDQ with reference to Country and Type of School

Country	Government school			Private school			Overall		
	Mean	S.D	N	Mean	S.D	N	Mean	S.D	N
Iran	20.7269	4.1095	216	19.8947	2.9682	57	20.5531	3.9086	273
India	18.7573	4.0836	103	18.2201	4.4489	159	18.431	4.309	262
Total	20.0909	4.1973	319	18.6620	4.1698	216	19.514	4.2408	535
F (country groups)	F=20.635; P<.000 (S)								
F (type of school)	F=2.913; P<0.088(S)								
F (type & country)	F=.135; P<0.713 (NS)								

At the .05 level of significance, the critical test statistic table. The F ratio of over variables (F=.135; P<0.713), derived from the MANOVA did not exceed the critical value. Based on the finding the Intimacy variable for Hypothesis was accepted.

The analysis F ratio of type of school (F=2.749; P<0.098) which exceeded the critical table value at the .05 level is significance. Thus, the Psychophysical Hindrance variable with secondary school in both countries was rejected (Table 7.8).

At the .05 level of significance, the critical test statistic table. The F ratio of country groups (F=0.035; P<.852) and over variables (F=1.417; P<0.234), derived from the MANOVA did not exceed the critical value. Based on the finding the Control variable for Hypothesis was accepted.

Table 7.8. Mean scores, S.D, result of MANOVA and significant level for 'PSYCHOPHYSICAL HINDRANCE' of SOCDQ with reference to Country and Type of School

Country	Government school			Private school			Overall		
	Mean	S.D	N	Mean	S.D	N	Mean	S.D	N
Iran	13.8750	2.8265	216	13.7368	2.4751	57	13.8462	2.7530	273
India	14.2816	3.3502	103	13.4403	3.3502	159	13.7710	3.2977	262
Total	14.0063	3.0063	319	13.5185	3.0469	216	13.8093	3.0294	535
F (country groups)	F=0.035; P<.852 (NS)								
F (type of school)	F=2.749; P<0.098(S)								
F (type & country)	F=1.417; P<0.234 (NS)								

Table 7.9 revealed the data regarding Control of Principal's/Headmasters' Behavior versus two countries and private and government secondary schools of perception teachers in India and Iran.

Table 7.9. Mean scores, S.D, result of MANOVA and significant level for 'CONTROL' of SOCDQ with reference to Country and Type of School

Country	Government school			Private school			Overall		
	Mean	S.D	N	Mean	S.D	N	Mean	S.D	N
Iran	17.4722	3.1311	216	17.4211	2.6319	57	17.4615	3.0292	273
India	16.5631	3.7460	103	16.6289	3.4006	159	16.6031	3.5335	262
Total	17.1787	3.3631	319	16.8380	3.2287	216	17.0411	3.3107	535
F (country groups)	F=6.997; P<.008 (S)								
F (type of school)	F=0.001; P<0.982(NS)								
F (type & country)	F=0.033; P<0.856 (NS)								

The analysis F ratio of country groups (F=6.997; P<.008) which exceeded the critical table value at the .05 level is significance. Thus, the Control variable with government and private teachers' secondary school in both countries were rejected. This finding tended to provide evidence that perception teachers respect Control at private and government secondary school in Iran is more than in Indian country.

At the .05 level of significance, the critical test statistic table. The F ratio of type of school (F=0.001; P<0.982) and over variables (F=0.033; P<0.856), derived from the MANOVA did not exceed the critical value. Based on the finding the Control variable for Hypothesis was accepted.

Table 7.10 indicated that the critical value of F table at the .05 level of significance. The derived value of F were Country Groups (F = 0.402; P<0.526), Type of School (F=0.021; P<0.884) and Type & Country (F=1.161; P<0.282) which fallen to exceed the critical value of F. as a result Hypothesis was accepted for the Government and private variables schools in India and Iran. The results tended to show that production emphasis of Principal's/Headmasters' behavior was not affected significantly and relation by Principal's/Headmasters' at government and private secondary school as teachers' perception in both countries.

Table 7.10. Mean scores, S.D, result of MANOVA and significant level for 'PRODUCTION EMPHASIS' of SOCDQ with reference to Country and Type of School

Country	Government school			Private school			Overall		
	Mean	S.D	N	Mean	S.D	N	Mean	S.D	N
Iran	18.4815	3.8591	216	18.9474	2.9545	57	18.5788	3.6885	273
India	18.6505	3.7644	103	18.2956	4.3086	159	18.4351	4.0995	262
Total	18.5361	3.8237	319	18.4676	3.9999	216	18.5084	3.8922	535
F (country groups)	F=o.402; P<0.526 (NS)								
F (type of school)	F=0.021; P<0.884(NS)								
F (type & country)	F=1.161; P<0.282 (NS)								

Table 7.11 revealed the data regarding Humanized Trust of Principal's/Headmasters' Behavior versus two countries and private and government secondary schools of perception teachers in India and Iran.

The analysis F ratio of country groups (F=31.742; P<.000) which exceeded the critical table value at the .05 level is significance. Thus, the Humanized Trust variable with government and private teachers' secondary school in both countries were rejected. This finding tended to provide evidence that perception teachers respect Humanized Trust at private and government secondary school in Iran is more than in Indian country.

At the .05 level of significance, the critical test statistic table. The F ratio of type of school (F=0.121; P<0.728) and over variables (F=0.904; P<0.342), derived from the MANOVA did not exceed the critical value. Based on the finding the Humanized Trust variable for Hypothesis was accepted.

Table 7.11. Mean scores, S.D, result of MANOVA and significant level for 'HUMANIZED TRUST' of SOCDQ with reference to Country and Type of School

Country	Government school			Private school			Overall		
	Mean	S.D	N	Mean	S.D	N	Mean	S.D	N
Iran	39.9398	7.1294	216	40.3860	6.4718	57	40.0330	6.9881	273
India	36.4757	7.7255	103	35.5157	8.3741	159	35.8931	8.1238	262
Total	38.8213	7.4927	319	36.8009	8.1897	216	38.0056	7.8372	535
F (country groups)	F=31.742; P<.000 (S)								
F (type of school)	F=0.121; P<0.728(NS)								
F (type & country)	F=0.904; P<0.342 (NS)								

Table 7.12 revealed the data regarding All Dimensions Behavioral versus two countries and private and government secondary schools of perception teachers in India and Iran.

The analysis F ratio of country groups (F=22.547; P<.000) which exceeded the critical table value at the .05 level is significance. Thus, the All Dimensions Behavioural variables with government and private teachers' secondary school in both countries were rejected. This finding tended to provide evidence that perception teachers respect All Dimensions Behavioral at private and government secondary school in Iran is more than in Indian country.

At the .05 level of significance, the critical test statistic table. The F ratio of type of school (F=0.483; P<0.488) and over variables (F=1.224; P<0.269), derived from the MANOVA did not exceed the critical value. Based on the finding the All Dimensions Behavioral variable for Hypothesis was accepted.

Table 7.12. Mean scores, S.D, result of MANOVA and significant level for 'Total of dimensions' of SOCDQ with reference to Country and Type of School

Country	Government school			Private school			Overall		
	Mean	S.D	N	Mean	S.D	N	Mean	S.D	N
Iran	164.2500	20.3651	216	165.1228	18.7236	57	164.4322	20.0032	273
India	156.5243	23.1186	103	152.7044	23.4714	159	154.2061	23.3637	262
Total	161.7554	21.5621	319	155.9814	22.9403	216	159.42429	22.2888	535
F (country groups)	F=22.547; P<.000 (S)								
F (type of school)	F=0.483; P<0.488(NS)								
F (type & country)	F=1.224; P<0.269 (NS)								

Discussion

According to tree group toward to school climate of teachers' perception indicate that, numbers of 36.4 per cent have high teacher moral, 45.4 per cent only satisfactory teacher moral and 18.2 per cent low teacher morale in government and private environments of secondary schools in Iran.

Teachers perception toward school climate are 25.3% high teacher moral, 47.6 per cent only satisfactory teacher moral and 27 per cent low teacher morale in government and private environments of secondary schools in India.

Finding of tables 7.1 to 7.3 indicate that there is a difference between types of school organizational climate in both countries. The findings of the study are:

- The number of school with percentage of familiar climates is more in Iran than in India. But highest numbers of schools with familiar and controlled climate are more in India.
- The percentage number of schools with close (none) and controlled climate are less in Iran than in India. But the least number of schools in India are closed and open climate.
- The private school have not controlled, paternal and closed climate but versus there are open and closed climate at private schools in India and familiar climate in both country is more.
- The government schools has not closed climate and controlled is less in Iran, but same result shows that closed, controlled and autonomous climate are less in India familiar climate in both country is more at secondary government school.
- The overall Table 7.3 revealed that familiar climate is more in India and controlled climate is more in Iran.
- The overall Table 7.3 revealed that none of Iranian schools come under closed climate and same like close climate is less in India, which both country are same like together.
- The result also shown that the perceptions of secondary teachers, in both countries are very close respect school climate together.
- School climate in the both countries shown that most of teachers have high teachers moral and satisfy in Iranian teachers and only satisfactory teacher moral and satisfy concerning to environment in secondary school and least numbers teacher perceived respect to low teacher morale in government and private environments of secondary schools in the both countries.

Finding of the present study are table 7.1, 7.2 shown that most of schools climate are familiar and least if school climate are closed climate in the both countries. Comparative of previous studies shows that Government schools climate in India and private schools climate in Iran are similarly climate. The supports of the research confirm that most of school climate were controlled in India and Iran. Cited of the finding of Arani (2003) reported that the government schools paternal climate is more as familiar and open are less, on the private schools familiar is more, such that no exist closed climate in Iran. The government school has not paternal climate as autonomous is more such that the private school has not paternal climate as controlled climate is more in India.

James (1997) who found more number of private schools with controlled climate. This is contrary with finding of study by Natrajan (2001) who reported that in India open climate exists in greater number of private schools.

As already mentioned regard to School Organizational Climate Description Questionnaire (SOCDQ) has 8 dimensions. These dimensions have further been grouped under two categories '*Principal* Behavior' and '*Teachers'* Behavior'. Therefore, it is possible to find similarities and differences between two countries in terms of two categories.

As attempt, has been made to finding the differences in teachers rating to two categories as mentioned above for each of the eight dimensions of the School Organizational Climate Description Questionnaire (SSOCDQ) in both countries.

Research conducted by Stone (2003) using the Leadership Practices Inventory (Kouzes & Posner, 2003) found significant relationships among all five leadership practices and the school culture, as perceived by teachers in public (government) schools. However, no difference was found in the leadership practice of the principal based upon school level (e.g., elementary, middle or high school).

Stone (2003) did not find a significant difference in leadership practices of the principal within public (government) schools based upon teacher's instructional level.

However, the findings mentioned above indicate that teachers who are working in government and private schools do not have same perceptions about their school organizational climate. This finding in support with the finding of Louw (1989), Sharma (1989) and McGrath (1991) who found that there is no statistically significant relationship between the type of school and organizational climate. Ross (1995), too, noted that collaboration with other teachers, a variable under the control of the school, affected teacher efficacy. Ross further discusses the notion that collaboration is relate to teacher and school variables and that teacher efficacy is effect-not cause-of collaboration.

Sofford (1995) examined "the direct influence of social systems dimensions of climate on teachers' perceptions of their own sense of efficacy". Sofford found that supportive principal behavior and directive principal behavior were significantly correlated with personal teacher efficacy and school climate.

SUMMARY

This study has focused on two major topics: instructional leadership, and school organizational climate. In order to improve the school climate in smaller schools, research must be done on what affects the climate in small schools by starting with a study of the principals'/headmasters' instructional leadership and the effectiveness of these principals'/headmasters' behavior on the climate.

By having the teachers complete a survey that details their view of the principal and a survey that details the view of school climate, it will be determined if the teachers' view of the principal's leadership style matches the type of school climate that that type of leadership style strives to create. Due to the focus on small rural school districts, the teachers' view of the principal will have a great impact on the school climate. The view of the principal will be connected to the type of leadership style the principal uses, thus affecting the type of climate that is created in the school. "I feel that this kind of knowledge [how the staff perceived the principal] is very important for our advancement to being a better and more reflective educational leader. I would argue that it is indeed crucial for our survival as educational leaders" (Pashiardis, 2001: 22).

REFERENCES

Al. Gasim, S.S. (1991). *The relationship between principal leader behavior and middle school climate in Hail District, Saudi Arabia* [CD-ROM]. Abstract from: ProQuest: Dissertation Abstract International Item: 53/01.

Arani, M.A. (2003). A comparative study of secondary school teachers' job satisfaction in relation to their value orientation and school organizational climate in Iran and India. PhD thesis. University of Mysore

Bailey, S.S. (1988). The relationship between leadership styles of high school principals and school climate as perceived by teachers [CD-ROM]. Abstract from: ProQuest File: Dissertation Abstracts International Item, 50(09).

Bancroft, R.M. (1986). Principal's leadership style and school climate [CD-ROM]. Abstract from: ProQuest: *Dissertation Abstracts International Item,* 47(07).

Bishop, H., & Dagley, D. (1991). The relationship between leadership or principals and organizational climate within selected middle schools [CD ROM]. Abstract from: ProQuest File: *Dissertation Abstracts International Item 52(03).*

Chen, M.T. (1990). Relationship between principals' leadership styles and school climate in senior industrial high schools in Taiwan, the Republic of China [CD-ROM]. Abstract from: ProQuest File: *Dissertation Abstracts.*

Ciruli Associates. (2002). *Recruitment and retention* of *new teachers: focus groups and surveys* of *current and retired teachers.* Denver, Colorado: Author.

Combs, J.R. (1995). *Teacher* commitment to change. A case study of elementary school [CD-ROM]. Abstract from: ProQuest File: *Dissertation Abstracts International Item,* 56(09).

Denver Public Schools-Denver Classroom Teacher Association. (2003, March, *20). Report on task force on school and district climate.* Retrieved December 1, 2004.

Firestone, W.A., & Pennell, J.R. (1993). Teacher commitment, working conditions, and differential incentive policies. *Review of Educational Research,* 63(4), 489-525.

Freiberg, J.H. (1983). *Improving school climate-A facilitative process.* Paper presented at the Seminar in Organizational Development in Schools, University of La Verne, La Verne, CA.

Gibson, N.C. (1996). A state mandated initiative and the role of the high school principal as a change agent: A case study of quality review in five Illinois high schools [CD-ROM]. Abstract from: ProQuest File: *Dissertation Abstracts International Item:* 57(06).

Halpin, A. W. & Croft, (1963). *The organizational climate* of *schools.* Chicago: Midwest Administrative Center, The University of Chicago.

Hatton, S.A. (1996). Teacher organizational commitment in high performing, low socio-economic status, border elementary schools [CD-ROM]. Abstract from: ProQuestFile: *Dissertation Abstracts International/tern,* 58(01).

Hayes, C.A. (1994). An analysis of the relationship between participative decision making practice and school climates in elementary schools of the Elk Grove Unified School District [CD-ROM]. Abstract from: ProQuestFile: *Dissertation Abstracts International Item,* 57(02).

James, M, S (1997). Teachers' attitudes, morale and job satisfaction in relation to their personality factors and school organizational climate. PhD thesis. University of Mysore.

John, C. M, & Taylor, J.W. (2002). *Leadership Style, School Climate, and the Institutional Commitment* of *Teachers.* Retrieved July 9, 2004, from Adventist International of Advanced Studies.

Kouzes, J., & Posner, B. (2003). *Leadership practices inventory.* San Francisco: Jossey-Bass.

Louw, D, C(1989). Organizational climate and desegregation in South African Schools. Thesis (ED.D.)—University of Virginia. *Dissertation Abstracts International.* V.50-07, Section: A,P. 1876.

Marschilok, E.S. (1993). A study of relationship between leadership behavior of high school principals and selected areas of educational achievement [CD-ROM]. Abstract from: ProQuest File: *Dissertation Abstracts International Item,* 54(06).

McDaniel, A. K. (1992). A comparison of elementary and secondary schools with respect to levels of conflict, conflict resolution behaviors, teacher commitment and organizational climate [CD-ROM]. Abstract from: ProQuest File: *Dissertation Abstracts International Item 53(07).*

McGrath, T, (1991). The associations between students' perceptions of school organizational climate, self-concept, and attendance in Connecticute Middle Schools. Thesis (ED.D.)—University of Bridgeport. *Dissertation Abstracts International.* 52-02 Section: A, 0371.

Natarajan, R (2001). School organizational climate and job satisfaction of teachers. *Journal of Indian Education.* XXVII (2).

Norton, M.S. (1984). What's so important about school climate? *Contemporary Education,* 56(1), 43-45.

Pashiardis, P. (2001). Secondary principals in Cyprus: The views of the principal versus the views of the teachers-A case study. *Leadership and Learning,* 29(3): 11-23.

Perkins, B.K. (2006). *Where we learn: The CUBE Survey of Urban School Climate.* Alexandria, VA: National School Board Association.

Plucker, J. A., (1998, March/April). The relationship between school climate 104 conditions and student aspirations. *Journal of Educational Research.* 91(4): 240-253.

Ross, J. (1995). Strategies for enhancing teachers' beliefs in their effectiveness: Research on a school improvement hypothesis. *Teachers College Record,* 97 (2), 227-251.

Sharma, I. P (1989). Organizational climate of government and privately managed higher secondary schools: A comparative study. *Journal of Educational planning & Adminstration.*3, (3&4): 147

Sharma, M. (1978). *Technical handbook for school organizational climate description questionnaire.* South Gujarat University.

Sofford, S.A. (1995). *Teachers' sense of efficacy and social systems dimensions of school climate.* Unpublished doctoral dissertation, University of New Orleans, New Orleans, Louisiana.

Stone, C. M. (2003). *A study of the relationship between principal's leadership behavior and the school culture as perceived by teachers.* Unpublished doctoral dissertation, University of Mississippi. Retrieved February 9, 2005 from www.theleadershipchallenge.com.

Winter, J.S., & Sweeney, J. (1994, October). *Improving School Climate: Administrators are Key.* NASSP Bulletin.

CHAPTER

A Study of Participation in Decision - making (PDM) among High School Teachers in India and Iran: A Comparative Study

(Influence of Age and Subject Taught)

—Mahnoosh Abedini and K. Yeshodhara

In the present study participation in decision-making of high schools teachers in India and Iran was investigated. Three hundred were selected from fifty high school in Mysore city (India), and Bandar Abbas city (Iran). They were assessed using the decision participation analysis survey (DPA) developed by Theirbach (1980) and Biziorek (1998). Findings indicated that between PDM of subject taught (art and science) Iran, India and both countries there was no significant difference even the findings indicated that between PDM of age group teachers high schools there was no significant difference in both countries. But the result shows that PDM for India and Iran between PDM of teachers in different of age group so, there was significant different for India and Iran.

INTRODUCTION

Teachers' participation in the School Decision-making process has been a topic of concern and discussion since the beginning of the twentieth century. Participation in Decision-making of an organization, often called Participatory Decision-making, is a term used to describe a style of organizational management. It is more than just allowing employees to make some decisions.

Participation in Decision making (PDM) has received intense theoretical consideration from writers who have studied the industrial setting. In the early fifties; participation in decision making was examined within the context of schools. Even in the eighties, participation in decision making was viewed as resting on substantial theoretical base, while the empirical base was less substantial. Researchers reported that teachers wanted to have more chances to participate in the decision-making process in the public school system. Reforms often adopted what we now call 'school-based management' as the means for teacher participation in the decision making process and democratization of schools.

The surest way to reform education is to give schools and their leaders the freedom and authority to make important decisions on what happens, while being held accountable for making well-conceived efforts at improvement and for achieving the desired results. Generally, participants in the decision-making process in organizations gain a sense of ownership in decision-making and more likely to carry them out. They also can be held accountable for what they decide to and not to do. Teacher participation in the decision-making process is aimed at giving the teachers more authority and power in the domain of their daily professional activities related to their school life and teaching. Involving teachers in decision-making is believed to add value and help everyone in the school setting.

Meaningful involvement in the decision-making process makes teachers committed to work towards the achievement of the system's goals, thereby, boosting their morale and leading to a positive work environment that allows the workers to initiate and implement new ideas, resulting in enhanced learning opportunities and outcomes for all. Actively participating in the decision-making process is thought to heighten an employee's involvement in work and to increase satisfaction, loyalty and motivation. It is reported that teachers who have the opportunity to participate regularly and actively in making school policies are far more likely to exhibit enthusiasm and support for their system than teachers who report limited opportunities to participate. Participatory decision-making also shifts authority closer to the classroom. This means that the professionals who know the students best, share values and beliefs with colleagues, and understand that the curriculum can better influence key policies, procedures and programmed implementation.

Review of Related Literature

A brief review of literature in this case of the research studies are related to Participation Decision-making of teachers on the influence of different factors on this variable. The details of certain relevant studies are reviewed and presented here.

In an educational setting, Belasco & Alutto (1972) used a Porter type discrepancy model to indicate the difference between teachers' actual and desired decision participation levels. Teachers were asked their actual and desired levels of participation in twelve decision areas and for overall level of job satisfaction. They were placed in one of the following three conditions: decisional deprivation (participating less than desired), equilibrium (participating as much as desired), and saturation (participating more than desired) on the basis of their responses. The teachers from two school districts in New York in the decisionally deprived conditions were the most militant and were the lowest in satisfaction.

Thierbach (1980) made use of the Belasco and Alutto's framework to investigate the relationship between decision conditions (deprivation, equilibrium, and saturation) and job satisfaction. Using data from 266 middle and junior high school teachers, she found that teachers perceived a general condition of decision deprivation and determined a significant relationship between the variables, by the discrepancy between actual and desired participation. The teachers' perceived levels of influence in the decision-making process were positively related to their level of job satisfaction. She, however, did not find significant relationships between the desired level of participation, expertise and interest and job satisfaction.

Rice (1993) replicated Thierbach's study and also reported the teachers' general condition of decision deprivation in the school decision making process. She found significant relationships between job satisfaction and actual participation, influence, and interest in decision issues. In the comparison of Thierbach's study, it was reported that respondents perceived increased actual participation, increased desired participation, reduced deprivation, and increased expertise in decision issues.

Biziorek (1998) studied 217 elementary teachers in Michigan and found significant, positive relationships between actual levels of participation, levels of influence in the decision making processes and job satisfaction. No significant relationships were found between teachers' expertise level, desired level of participation and job satisfaction. Biziorek reported that teachers desired a higher level of participation than they were actually experiencing.

Investigators who have examined the impact of personal and demographic characteristic variables such as gender, age, marital status, teaching experience and school/district location have found that they significantly effect teacher participation. Several studies have shown that gender, age and marital status are related to participation.

Belasco & Alutto (1972) found that younger male secondary school teachers tended to expect to participate more in decision making at the school and district level than did older female teachers. They also tended to experience more frustration, greater role conflict and lower levels of job satisfaction than their female counterparts.

Bloland & Selby (1980) found that male teachers were also more prone to leave the profession than female teachers. After their review of literature they also found support for the statement that school size is positively associated with teacher decisions to leave the school. Riley claimed that larger school districts tend to be complex hierarchies. Their decision- making processes have more bureaucratic obstructions; they distance teachers from policy-making bodies and dilute their influence. Their leadership tends to rely more on a command one, than on a participative structure and negatively impact teachers' job satisfaction by stifling autonomy and initiative.

Lortie (1975) concluded that married women were more satisfied with teaching than single women. School/district size was found to be a factor affecting decision participation. As Lortie pointed out, the larger the school, the more complex the organization, and the greater the teachers' distance from decision making, also, the larger the school, the greater the level of bureaucratic impediments; therefore, there was a lower level of job satisfaction.

In contrast, Niadozie (1993) found no significant relationship between teacher participation in decision making, teachers' perception of job satisfaction, and the teacher demographic factors, such as, teacher's race, sex, teaching experience, academic preparation, school size and class size.

Historical Roots of Teacher Participation in Decision-making

Teacher participation in school decision-making has its roots in organizational and management literature. Though the rationale has changed somewhat, the notion of workers participating in the management of their organizations has existed since the early twentieth century. In 1938, Chester Barnard suggested that workers could be induced to cooperate with management if offered incentives to do so. One such incentive was the opportunity of enlarged participation (Barnard 1938: 94). Barnard and his contemporaries believed that, by allowing workers to think they had more control and authority in the workplace, they could eventually improve production and efficiency. The idea of worker participation gained some credence, but it remained a component of the centralized, top-down structure of scientific management (Taylor, 1911) that was the dominant paradigm of the day.

Around 1950, theorists began to criticize the traditional organizational structure, arguing that it had negative effects on workers' morale, motivation and productivity (Lawler, 1986). One well-known study by Coch and French, in 1948, of employees in a manufacturing company, set up experimental groups of employees who were then involved in varying levels of participation in designing job changes. The study found significant evidence that participation in considering changes to their jobs led to higher productivity, lower turnover, less aggression toward management, and faster learning of new job procedures (Coch & French, 1948).

In addition to acknowledging the potential benefits to the organization of participation, during the 1950s, worker participation also was increasingly viewed through a human relations lens (Bolman & Deal, 1997) as a way to actually help employees reach their full potential and feel fulfilled by their work (Lawler, 1986). In 1957, for example, McGregor wrote that, "the essential task of management is to arrange organizational conditions and methods of operation so that people can achieve their own goals best by directing their own efforts toward organizational objectives" (McGregor, 1957: 183).

Over the next twenty years, companies experimented with employee participation models, and research showed that the approach did result in increased productivity and financial gains (Lawler, 1986). The popularity of the theory ebbed and flowed, however, until in the mid-1980s, competition from other countries threatened the American economy, which sparked an interest in progressive, alternative organizational models. In 1986, Lawler presented his High Involvement Model (Lawler, 1986), which laid out in detail the rationale and process for worker participation. Since then, participative management and employee participation have become common in American industry and other organizations (Bacharach *et al.*, 1990).

Hypotheses of the Study

In the absence of a strong theoretical base and consistent findings of the research studies on different variables selected for the study, the following null hypotheses were formulated for the present study :

H1: There is no significant difference in the **Participation Decision Making (PDM)** of high school teachers of different age group in Mysore City (India) and Bandar Abbas (Iran).

H2: There is no significant difference in the **Participation Decision Making (PDM)** of high school teachers teaching different subjects taught in Mysore City (India) and Bandar Abbas (Iran).

Design and Methodology

Sample of Study : In India, data were collected in Mysore City in south India and Iranian data in Bandarabbas city in south part of Iran. A sample of 50(25 Indian and 25 Iranian) high school were selected randomly for the research work 243 teachers (119 teachers from India and 124 teachers from Iran) were selected using stratified random sampling technique. While selecting teachers, consideration was given to their different age groups and subject taught by them that is, science or arts group subjects.

Procedures: In India and Iran, the investigator personally visited all the selected schools after getting prior approval from principals or vice-principals of the concerned schools for collecting data. Questionnaires were distributed to the teachers selected as described above. These teachers responded to the teachers' version of the survey. Over 150 sets of Questionnaires were personally delivered to 50 randomly selected schools spread over the Bandarabbas city (Iran) and 150 sets of Questionnaires were personally delivered to 50 Randomly selected over the Mysore city (India). A total 124 useable Questionnaires sets were returned in Bandarabbas city (Iran) and 119 useable Questionnaires sets were returned in Mysore city (India), at a response rate of 82.67 per cent for

Iran and 79.34 per cent for India. Completed data sheets were collected they were scored according to the manual provided. Later a master chart was prepared and fed into the computer for further statistical analysis.

Tools used for Data Collection : Survey instruments were developed to examine the teacher decision making participation concept. They were modified based on the Decision Participation Analysis (DPA) developed by Thierbach (1980) to study the decision participation for a group of middle and junior high school teachers in Wisconsin. More than a decade later, Rice (1993) replicated and expanded Thierbach's study to test whether teacher perceptions of participation had changed as emphasis on shared decision making in schools increased. Biziorek (1998) conducted a study similar to Thierbach's and Rice's using the same instruments on a sample of public elementary school teachers in Michigan.

The original decision participation analysis survey developed by Theirbach (1980) was used by several other researchers in their studies (for example, Lipham *et al.*, 1981, Schneider, 1986; Rice, 1993; Biziorek, 1998). The decision participation questions (actual participation) for each of the 20 decision-related issues have a forced choice four-point Likert type scale that varies from a low of 1 to a high of 4 with: None = 1. Little = 2, Some = 3 and Great - = 4. Teachers were asked to rate the actual extent of their participation in making decisions pertaining to the 20 selected issues. Bass categorizes these 20 items in two dimensions, namely, instructional/technical area and school wide/managerial (2 items). In India, the English version of the questionnaire was administered for collecting data from the teachers. However, for administering the tool in Iran, the questioner was translated into Persian language and given to experts, two professors of education. The reliability coefficient calculated for the Persian version was 86.86% and for English version 87.61%, indicating that it was reliable for the purpose of the study.

Methods of Statistical Analysis : The SSPS for windows (version 16.0) was used for statistical analysis. In this study simple statistical techniques, such as, mean, standard deviation, t-test and F-test, were employed to find out the significant difference between countries, Age and Subjects taught for PDM.In the present investigation, countries (India and Iran), Age (25-34, 35-44, 45-54 years and 55 year above) and Subjects taught (Art and Science) were taken as independent variables and PDM was taken as dependent variables.

Results of the Study

Result of the Teacher Demographic Factors (Descriptive) : Among 300 questionnaires sent to the teachers, 243 questionnaires were returned a return rate of 81 per cent that 119 (79.34%) was returned for India and for Iran was returned 124 (82.67%). All demographic data of respondents are presented in the forms of individual frequencies and percentages in Table 8.1.

The data show that the teacher respondents consisting of 36 or 30.3 per cent of the teacher respondents were 25-34 years, 60 or 50.4 per cent of the teacher respondents were 35-44 years, 17 or 14.3 per cent of the teacher respondents were 45-54 years and 6 or 5 per cent of the teacher respondents were 55 above in India.

The data also indicated that 30 or 24.2 per cent of the teacher respondents were 25-34 years, 60 or 48.4 per cent of the teacher respondents were 35-44 years, 30 or 24.2 per cent of the teacher respondents were 45-54 years and 4 or 3.2 per cent of the teacher respondents were 55 above in Iran.

Table 8.1 also reveals that both countries (India and Iran) for 25-34 years 66 (27.2%), for 35-44 years 120 (49.4%), for 45-54 years 47(19.3%) and for 55above years 10(4.1%).

The data also indicated that in India 66 (55.5%) of the teacher respondents were art teachers and 53 (44.5%) were science teachers. In Iran 59 (47.6%) of them were art teachers and 65 (52.4%) were science teachers.

Table 8.1 also reveals that both countries (India and Iran) art teachers 125 (51.4%) and science teachers 118 (48.6%).

Table 8.1. Descriptive Demography Characteristics of Respondent (India and Iran)

Variable	Category	Countries					
		India	(N=119)	Iran	(N=124)	Total	(N=243)
		N	Percent	N	Percent	N	Percent
Age	25-34	36	30.3	30	24.2	66	27.2
	35-44	60	50.4	60	48.4	120	49.4
	45-54	17	14.3	30	24.2	47	19.3
	55 above	6	5.0	4	3.2	10	4.1
Subjects	Art	66	55.5	59	47.6	125	51.4
taught	Science	53	44.5	65	52.4	118	48.6

Discussion based on Table 8.2 only for India: From Table 8.2, it is clear that art and science teachers have no significant difference between subjects taught (art-science) in PDM. Null Hypothesis (H_0) formulated for PDM for art and science high school teachers in India is accepted.

Discussion based on Table 8.2 only for Iran: From Table 8.2, it can be seen that there is no significant difference for art and science teachers in PDM as the obtained (t = 0.186, P=0.732) was found to be less than table value (1.96 at 0.05 level of significant). The observation of means indicates that mean score of science teachers (mean = 3.111) is higher than mean score of art teachers (mean = 3.107). In PDM, art and science teachers have no significant difference as the obtained (t = 0.186, P=0.732) null hypothesis 1 formulated for PDM of art and science in Iran is accepted.

Discussion based on Table 8.2 for both countries: For Table 8.2, it is observed that art and science teachers in PDM have no significant difference as the obtained (t = 0.279, P=0.780) was found to be less than table value, (1.96 at 0.05 level of significant). The observation of means indicates that the mean score of science teachers (mean = 2.945). There is no significant difference in PDM between art and science teachers.

Table 8.2. Descriptive Mean Scores for PDM with Reference to Subjects Taught and Results of t-test in Mysore (India) and Bandar Abbas (Iran) Separately and Together

Variable	Category	Countries											
		India				Iran				Total			
		Mean	St.D	T-test	sig-value	Mean	St.D	T-test	sig - value	Mean	St.D	T-test	sig – value
Subjects taught	Art	3.107	0.531		0.774	2.753	0.478		0.732	2.942	0.534		0.780
				0.288				0.186				0.279	
	Science	3.111	0.509		H_0=A	2.750	0.501		H_0=A	2.945	0.538		H_0=A

NOTE: If $p<\alpha$ ($\alpha=0.05$) so null hypothesis is rejected.

•R= Reject, A :=Accept, H_0= Null hypothesis

Null hypothesis 1 formulated for PDM art and science high school teachers in India and Iran is accepted for PDM.

Discussion based on Table 8.3 only for India: From Table 8.3, it is clear that age groups teachers have significant difference between age groups (25-34, 35-44, 45-54, 55 above) in PDM. Null Hypothesis (H_0) formulated for PDM for age group high school teachers in India is rejected.

Discussion based on Table 8.3 only for Iran: From Table 8.3, it can be seen that there is significant difference for age groups teachers in PDM as the obtained (f = 1.99, p = 0.048.) was found to be more than table value, (1.96 at 0.05 level of significant). The observation of means indicates that there is significant different between mean score all of age group teachers. In PDM, age groups teachers have significant difference as the obtained (f = 1.99, P = 0.048) Null hypothesis 2 formulated for PDM of age groups teachers in Iran is rejected.

Discussion based on Table 8.3 for both countries: For Table 8.3, it is observed that age groups teachers in PDM have no significant difference as the obtained (f = 0.151, P = 0.929) was found to be less than table value, (1.96 at 0.05 level of significant).The observation of means indicates that there is no significant different between mean score all of age group teachers. Null hypothesis 2 formulated for PDM of age groups high school teachers in India and Iran is accepted for PDM.

Conclusion

The main findings of the present study are:

- Different Subject Taught of teachers do not have significant influence on their PDM of the high school in Mysore (India).
- Different Subject Taught of teachers does not have a significant influence on their PDM of the high school in Bandar abbas (Iran).
- The art and science high school teachers in Mysore (India) and Bandarabbas (Iran) have no significant difference on their perception about PDM.

Table 8.3. Descriptive Mean Scores for PDM with Reference to Age and Results of F-test in Mysore (India) and Bandar Abbas (Iran) Separately and Together

Variable	Category	Countries											
		India				Iran				Total			
		Mean	St.D	F-test	sig - value	Mean	St.D	F-test	sig - value	Mean	St.D	F-test	sig – value
Age	25-34	2.950	0.610			2.870	0.508			2.913	0.563		
	35-44	3.187	0.480	2.056		2.717	0.483	1.99	0.048	2.936	0.534	0.151	
	45-54	3.164	0.347		0.01 H_0=R	2.785	0.467			2.929	0.468		
	55 above	3.333	0.581			2.437	0.548		H_0=R	2.951	0.708		0.929 H_0=A

NOTE: If $p < \alpha$ ($\alpha = 0.05$) so null hypothesis is rejected.
•R= Reject, A :=Accept, H0 = Null hypothesis

- The mean score of art teachers are almost equal mean score of science teachers in Mysore (India) and Bandar abbas (Iran).
- Different age group of teachers has significant influence on their PDM of the high school in Mysore (India)
- Different age group of teachers has significant influence on their PDM of the high school in Bandar abbas (Iran).
- The age group high school teachers in Mysore (India) and Bandarabbas (Iran) do not have significant difference on their perception about PDM.

It should be noted that the purpose of this study was not to report the evaluations of teachers by comparing Indian and Iranian teachers of high schools. The main purpose of this study is to identify conceptions and possible differences in conceptions about participation decision making (PDM) in Indian and Iranian high schools.

REFERENCES

Bacharach, S.B., Bamberger, P., Conley, S.C., & Bauer, S. (1990), The dimensionality of decision participation in educational organizations: the value of a multi-domain evaluative approach, *Educational Administration Quarterly*, 26(2), 126-167.

Barnard, C.I. (1938). The economy of incentives. In Shafritz, J.M and Ott, J.S (Eds) Classics of organization theory (5th ed. pp. 93-102).Fort Worth, TX: Harcourt College.

Belasco, J.A. & Alutto, J.A. (1972), Decisional participation and teacher satisfaction, *Educational Administration Quarterly*, 8(44-58).

Biziorek, M.K. (1998), School-based decision making: the relationship between teachers' decision involvement and their job satisfaction, unpublished doctoral dissertation, Michigan State University.

Bloland, P.A., & selby, T.J. (1980), Factors associated with career change among secondary school teachers: a review of the literature, *Educational Research Quarterly*, 5(3), 13-24.

Bolman, L, G. and Deal, T.E. (1997). *Reframing organization: Artistry, Choice and Leadership* (2th ed) San Francisco: Jossey-Bass.

Coch, L, and French.J.R.P. (1948). Overcoming resistance to change: *Human Relations*, 4(1), 512-532.

Conley, S.C., & Bacharach, S.B. (1990), from school-site management to participatory school-site management, Phi Delta Kappan, 71(7), 539-544.

Lawler, E.E. (1986). *High-involvement Management*. San Francisco: Jossey-Bass.

Lortie, D.C. (1975), *School teacher: a sociological study*, Chicago, IL: University of Chicago Press.

Lipham, J.M., Dunstan, J., & Rankin, R. (1981). The relationship of decision involvement and principals' leadership to teacher job satisfaction in selected secondary schools. Wisconsin Research and development Center for Individualized Schooling at the University of Wisconsin-Madison, WI. ED 207 129.

McGregor, D.M. (1957).The human side of enterprise. In Shafritz, J.M and Ott, J.S (Eds) *Classics of organization theory* (5th ed.pp. 179-184).Fort Worth, TX: Harcourt College.

Ninadozie, C.A. (1993), A study of the relation between participation in decision making and school culture and perception of job satisfaction among teachers, Unpublished doctoral dissertation, Morgan State University.

Rice, E.M. (1939). Teacher involvement in decision making: relationships to job satisfaction, unpublished doctoral dissertation, University of Wisconsin-Madison.

Schneider, G.T. (1986). The myth of Curvilinearity: an Analysis of Decision-Making Involvement and Job Satisfaction. *Planning & Changing*. 17(3), 146-158.

Taylor, F.W. (1911). *The Principles of Scientific management*. New York: Harper and Row.

Thierbach, G.L. (1980), Decision Involvement and Job Satisfaction in Middle and Junior High Schools, Unpublished Doctoral Dissertation, University of Wisconsin-Madison.

CHAPTER

Academic Standards and Rules of Schools for Talented Students in Asian Countries: A Comparative Study

—*Mahvash Ziaeifard*

This study has been performed regarding the Academic Standards and rules of Schools for Talented Students in Asian countries. By reviewing the educational system for the gifted it was evident that Asian countries such as Iran and India are trying their best for achieving higher standard in their gifted Educational system. This strategy is properly managed by both countries educational ministration although some private sectors are active in Iran in this field. But it is noteworthy that many Iranian gifted students may be under diagnosed in this system because of only one method of general testing in the country. Since there are many high level students in Iranian regular schools, a more perfect system is needed for better diagnosis and selection of the gifted in the country.

Introduction

The Merriam *Webster's Collegiate Dictionary* defines the term "gifted" as: (1) Having great natural ability and (2) Revealing a special gift.

"Gifted" children have been defined as those "who by nature of outstanding abilities are capable of high performance". The term "outstanding abilities" refers to general intellectual ability, specific academic aptitude, leadership ability, ability in the visual or performing arts, creative thinking, or athletic ability.

Most gifted children display a higher rate of concentration and memory capacity. There is no typical gifted child, for particular talents and social environments give rise to varying personality patterns. Achievement patterns also vary. Differences among them will be found, even when they are grouped together. Some are very strong in one subject and weak in others. The gifted mathematician may be an average reader, the gifted artist may be poor in mathematic and the early reader may lack the ability to organize time and materials.

Statement of the Problem

In the business world, many management studies attempt to find the traits and characteristics of the successful company leaders, with believes that leaders can be nurtured and trained. Likewise, there are also qualities and characteristics that are frequently found among gifted children, although no child will possess them all. One way that parents can tell if their children might be gifted is to focus on a range of behaviours that occur in the daily conversations, activities, and responses to learning opportunities. A list of characteristics common in gifted four-, five-, and six-year olds includes abilities such as Express curiosity about many things, Ask thoughtful questions, Have extensive vocabularies and use complex sentence structure, Are able to express themselves well, Solve problems in unique ways, Have good memories, Exhibit unusual talent in art, music, or creative dramatics, Exhibit especially original imaginations, Use previously learned things in new contexts, Are unusually able to order things in logical sequence, Discuss and elaborate on ideas, Are fast learners, Desire to work independently and take initiative, Exhibit wit and humor, Have sustained attention spans and are willing to persist on challenging tasks, Are very observant, Show talent in making up stories and telling them, Are interested in reading.

A gifted child might not show all of the above characteristics all the time, but parents and professionals will generally see a pattern when observing over an extended period of time.

Many parents feel that there is little practical value to get their 'potential' gifted child tested. But there are potential risks with putting off the testing. Knowing the pattern of cognitive strengths and weaknesses can help parents to plan the best learning experience. Also waiting till the school tests the child can risk a ceiling effect on the tests, one that gets more pronounced each and every year. Many gifted students often appear to be troublemakers and often challenge authority figures by questioning classroom rules. Are interested in reading. At the present time,in all over the world, there have been different methods and programmes for a better selection and education of the gifted students based on the original educational situation of the country. Some countries are following high standards in their educational centers and this policy has led them to better utilization of gifted students and graduate. This study will compare Iran and India according t their educational system for gifted students.

Significance of the Study

The behaviour of a gifted child is sometimes confused with attention disorders such as ADD (Attention Deficit Disorder) and ADHD (Attention Deficit Hyperactivity Disorder). Hence, the test would identify between a gifted child and a possible learning disorders kid such as ADHD, Asperger's Syndrome, and other problems as early as possible. Children who are gifted are more comfortable with children and classes that deal with them at their own level. Research has shown that gifted students thrive when placed with students of similar ability. In the wrong learning setting, giftedness can be as paralyzing as a learning handicap. Unfortunately, these gifted children are terrible introverts, misunderstood by peers and parents, with their undiscovered exceptionality leading to a dead end. Bored and unchallenged at school, they may drop out and choose a direction that will never make use of their exceptional abilities. Know in the most practical standard regarding the education for the gifted is very important and this will lead us to gain more profit from gifted students. This study will evaluate the current educational system in Asian counties.

Aims of the Study

- To evaluate the educational system for the gifted in India
- To evaluate the educational system for the gifted in Iran
- To compare evaluation in Iran and India

Literature Review

Now-a-days, identification and programming for gifted and talented (GT) students is not only a part of School and universities curriculum in developed countries,[1] but also is accounted as a model of progress for developing countries.[2] Although the best time for identification of GT students is at childhood,[3] but several investigators have developed methods for identification of GTs before entering colleges.[4] Then, they have proposed special measures for those identified, for example, acceleration or compacting the usual curriculum content, training the managers and teachers of GTs about the concept and needs of GTs, and annual evaluation of these programs[5]. In regards to GT education, schools play two roles: (1) Conducting programs to educate GTs from elementary to high school: examples are Colorado University training program for students of elementary and middle schools (GTs go to some classes at the university on Saturday afternoons)[6] and Georgia University program for high school GTs[7] . Such programs are also found in other countries such as UK. (2) Designing and conducting programs for their own GT students. Examples are Johns Hopkins University program (provision of financial aids, accelerated programs and Early Entrance Program for GTs)[9] and Brazil universities programmes.

In the following parts a review will be dome regarding the Indian and Iranian gifted students educational systems.

India

India is the second most populous country in the world with a population of 1.08 billion. The UN predicts that by 2025 India will have surpassed China as the most populous nation. Life expectancy is 64 years. The country is divided into 28 States and seven Union Territories, each with their own elected or appointed governments. The following religions are practised:

- Hindu (80.5%)
- Muslim (13.4%)
- Christian (2.3%)
- Sikh (1.9%).

About 70 per cent of Indians live in rural villages, which are often very remote; 64.8 per cent of adults are literate, 75.3 per cent of males, and 53.7 per cent of females. Kerala is the only State that is completely literate. Officially, 23 languages are recognized by the Constitution but over 840 dialects are spoken. Hindi and English are the national languages used by the Central Government.[10]

There are approximately 888,000 educational institutions in India enrolling around 189.2 million students.[11]

In its commitment to raise the quality of education, the central government has been steadily increasing the education budget since Independence in 1947. The goal is to allocate to it at least 6 per cent of GDP (currently approximately 4 per cent of GDP makes up the education budget). From this budget, 86 per cent goes to support higher education explaining in part India's world-class management and IT institutes. As a result India produces an elite number of highly educated graduates, but at the same time is struggling to meet basic educational goals including universal primary education, the total eradication of illiteracy and improving access and the quality of education in rural areas.

In accordance with the National Policy of Education (1986), the Central Government envisaged a scheme in which intellectually gifted and talented rural students would be provided with quality residential education free of cost. The government made the decision to invest in gifted children because they are viewed as crucial to the social and economic development of India. One anticipated outcome of this scheme is that students will return to their rural villages in the future as professionals (for example teachers and doctors) and thereby help to raise the overall standard of living in their communities. The scheme was started in 1986 with the opening of the first two Jawahar Navodaya Vidyalaya (JNV) schools. This has grown to 515 schools at present serving 158,897 gifted and talented students. The goal is to have at least one JNV in each district of India.[12]

The JNV schools are co-educational residential schools for students aged 11–17. Education is free for all enrolled students including all residential care, uniforms, textbooks, medical care, and travel fares home. Many of the students come from uneducated and illiterate families, a trend which has never before occurred in Indian education. Admission of the 80 new students to each school each year is made on the basis of a selection test administered by the Central Board of Secondary Education (CBSE). It aims to be an objective, class-neutral test designed to ensure fairness regardless of prior educational attainment and is offered in 20 languages. It includes three sections covering mental ability, arithmetic and language, consisting of a total of 100 multiple-choice questions. Admission is extremely competitive, the national acceptance rate being roughly four per cent.[13]

The JNV head office in New Delhi provided the following list of JNV key objectives:[14]

- *Quality education:* to provide a quality education including a strong component of culture, societal values, awareness of the environment and extra-curricular activities to intellectually talented students from predominantly rural areas.

- *Language skills:* to ensure that all students attain a reasonable level of competency in three languages (i.e. Hindi, English and one regional language).
- *National integration:* to promote national integration through the migration programme, a one-year exchange program in which students from Hindi speaking districts attend a JNV in a non-Hindi speaking district and vice-versa.
- *Social responsibility:* to improve the quality of education in all schools in each district by sharing JNV facilities, programmes and expertise.

All JNV schools follow the standard national CBSE curriculum which includes at least two languages, general studies, work experience, physical and health education and three of the following; mathematics, physics, chemistry, biology, biotechnology, economics, political science, history, geography, business studies, accountancy, fine arts, agriculture, computer science, multimedia and web technology, sociology, psychology, philosophy, physical education, music and dance, entrepreneurship or fashion studies. The curriculum is not accelerated, but students are provided with enrichment opportunities. These are:[15]

- *Three languages:* students will have been educated in their mother tongue/regional language in their village school and at secondary level at a JNV school they are instructed in English for maths and science, and Hindi for social studies. As a result students are fluent in at least three languages.
- *Computer education:* each JNV school has a computer lab to which all students have access and all students take computer classes. In addition there is at least one JNV 'Smart School' in each state with additional IT resources and expertise including teacher training for the staff of other schools.
- *Migration programme:* this exchange programme promotes national integration.

- *Extracurricular activities:* sport plays an important role in schools. Each morning consists of an hour of yoga and a wide range of other sports are offered. The JNV head office organises regional and national sports meetings which also provide an extended community for JNV students. An 'Art in Education' programme is also offered which is led by invited guests and other extracurricular activities include Boy Scouts and Girl Guides, debating clubs, traditional dance, speech and song competitions, and a youth parliament.

All students sit exams at the end of Class X (age 15) and Class XII (age 17), which are extremely rigorous and competitive and they have been criticized for promoting rote-learning in Indian schools. The JNV students have successively scored much higher than the national averages in these exams.[16]

Teaching staff at JNV schools live on the rural campus with the students which facilitates a close-knit community. Incentives are provided to encourage good applicants to apply for the teaching posts, such as rent-free housing at the school and the enrolment of two sons/daughters without having to sit the entrance test. The JNV head office organises extensive teacher training and workshops to upgrade skills and identify teacher needs. In addition staff receive extensive computer training in collaboration with IT organisations.[17]

The JNV schools also provide educational opportunities to students attending local schools in the district as the goal is to raise the overall quality of rural education by extending JNV services and facilities to local teachers and students. For example, JNV 'Smart Schools' are part of a computer literacy programme that have been given the responsibility of providing computer training to students at 10 local schools. To date over 9000 rural students have benefited from this programme. The JNV schools also support their local communities by providing free access to their libraries, by allowing local teachers to participate in the workshops and seminars organised by JNV, and also by providing health and hygiene services to local residents. The JNV students are also encouraged to use their strengths and skills to contribute to their local communities and teaching staff expressed the view that these students were part of a unique community that would open the door to many future possibilities. They encouraged the students to recognise this opportunity they were given and to search for ways in which they could help those less fortunate. A key feature of the model of gifted and talented education in India is that it is a holistic one, uniting academic development with character formation and the development of social responsibility, and viewing the individual as first and foremost a part of society. However this should not be divorced from the contextual issues of Indian society and the views presented by government officials, teachers and students alike that education was crucial to social and economic change. Schools dedicated to the education of gifted and talented students are seen not only as a means of educating an elite group of gifted individuals who will go on to improve the quality of life in their communities, but centres of excellence from which the local community can draw on in a wide variety of ways.

Gifted Education Programme (Singapore)

The Gifted Education Programme (GEP) is a Singaporean academic program designed for the top one per cent of pupils, identified in two rounds of tests at the end of Primary 3. The Gifted Education Program was first implemented in Singapore in 1984 amid some public concern. It was initiated by the Ministry of Education (MOE) in line with its policy under the New Education System to allow each pupil to learn at his/her own pace. The MOE has a commitment to ensure that the potential of each pupil is recognized, nurtured and developed. It was recognized that there are pupils who are intellectually gifted and that there should be provisions to meet their needs. It actually began with two primary centres and two secondary centers but it has currently expanded to nine primary centers (as at October 2004) and was at its peak before the introduction of the Integrated Program.

As of 2007, nine primary schools and two secondary schools offer GEP.

In 2004, with the first five secondary schools implementing their own Integrated Programs with their affiliated Junior Colleges, they are officially no longer under the GEP. However, they still have their own programs within their respective Integrated Programmes to cater to these gifted students, who still retain their "gifted" status. Despite all the changes, there have not been any major changes to the program, and this is basically just a change of name.

However, the Integrated Program proved so popular that in 2004, the remaining schools officially in the program (Dunman High School and Victoria School) saw a drastic decrease in enrolment. Dunman High School had to cut down on the number of GEP classes from the usual 2 to 1 while Victoria School had to totally suspend GEP classes.

As of 2005, four of the secondary schools officially offer only the Integrated Programme (Hwa Chong Institution, Raffles Institution, Raffles Girls' School (Secondary), Nanyang Girls' High School.

Anglo-Chinese School (Independent) and Dunman High School are exceptions: it offers both the GEP and IP to its students. There are also two GE-IP classes in the school who are offered both the programs of the GEP and the IP.

From 2008 year-end, the MOE will phase out the secondary GEP due to the impact of the IP. The severity of the situation is apparent in the fact that there are only 13 pupils enrolled in the entire Secondary One GEP as of 2006. However, GEP pupils who do not wish to take up the Integrated Program after 2008 can enroll in schools with school-based special programmes at Secondary 1. Examples of such schools are Anglo-Chinese School (Independent), Catholic High School, Methodist Girls' School and St. Joseph's Institution.

The mission statement of the Gifted Education Programme is to provide leadership in the education of the intellectually gifted. The programme is committed to nurturing gifted individuals to their full potential for the fulfilment of self and the betterment of society. Their vision is to make the Gifted Education Programme a model of excellence in the education of the intellectually gifted. They will achieve this vision by providing professional expertise and exemplary resources to develop intellectual rigor, humane values and creativity in gifted youths to prepare them for responsible leadership and service to country and society.

All Primary three students, at the age of nine, can choose to take 2 rounds of tests, the first round being the Screening Test, and the second round being the Selection Test. The 2 GEP tests allows the top one per cent pupils to enter GEP.

During the Screening Test, English and Mathematics are tested. After the Screening Test, a certain number of pupils are eliminated. The remaining will go through the Selection Test.

During the Selection Test, English, Mathematics and IQ will be tested. Those who get through the second round will be identified as the top one per cent pupils. Before 2003, there was a third round of testing to allow entry for pupils who missed the chance in P3, after the PSLE. This last round of testing was offered to students who achieved 3 or more A*s for the examination. Students who got in at this round were referred to as being Supplementary Intake students. However, this practice was discontinued as of 2003 as statistics showed that it was too difficult for the Supplementary Intake students to catch up and excel in the programme.

The pupils will have to study in this program from Primary 4 to 6, and after that, the pupils can choose to continue studying in the program only, in the Integrated Programme, or in the mainstream. Some parents and pupils have argued that the stress in the program is too great.

Schools in the program set separate (sometimes jointly set with other GEP schools) test papers and generally hold more enrichment activities for the students in the program.

In GEP, pupils in Primary 4 Chinese (not Higher Chinese) attend a program which includes content like Chinese poetry, comics, riddles etc. The program is called Chinese Language Appreciation (CLA) and is to be attended once a week. Individualized Research Study (IRS) is compulsory for pupils in Primary 4 or 5, wherein pupils do research on a specific topic. At the end of P4, the teachers would select approximately half the pupils to do the Innovation Program (IvP), where pupils invent items to solve real-life problems. Other pupils will have the option to do the Future Problem Solving (FPS), or continue staying in IRS.

Pupils in the GEP have to take Social Studies as a graded subject. They will study textbook based content more in-depth. Overall, lessons in the GEP are conducted with fewer textbooks and workbooks; lessons are more discussion worksheet- and project-based.

Pupils in GEP learn poetry and literature (Charlotte's Web in Primary 4, A Wrinkle in Time in Primary 5, and Friedrich in Primary 6) as part of the Concept Unit under the English Language subject. Charlotte's Web will be tested under the Miscellaneous section during the end-of-year-examination for P4. A project on A Wrinkle in Time and a Reading Journal will have to be completed in Term 4 at P5. These books replace the English textbook.

The GEP and its students has been criticized by many, the program as elitist and the students as arrogant nerds. The issue of the GEP has been raised many times in Singapore, both online in blogs and in the mainstream media. GEP students are sometimes prejudiced against and insulted by others and portrayed as nerds who spend large amounts of time studying and have no interests in sports or other non-academic activities. While this perception may ring true for some GEP individuals, as a blanket stereotype of all GEP students it does not hold true as there have been and still are GEP students who have been and/or are good in sports and have taken part in numerous sports competitions, both at Inter-School and National levels. The GEP is often criticized to be elitist, as highlighted by the Wee Shu Min elitism scandal, in which the 18-year old Raffles Junior College and GEP alumus student caused public outcry in November 2006 for making insensitive and judgemental remarks against others. There was a similar controversy a year before, whereby a Primary Six GEP student wrote a letter to Today openly declaring that non-GEP students (referred to as "mainstreamers") were immature, and that she preferred to mix with "(similar) people like us".[23]

In an article in The Straits Times on 3 November 2007, the MOE announced its new scheme to "encourage" greater integration between GEP and mainstream students, to combat elitism and encourage socialization. GEP students in the nine primary GEP centers would spend up to 50% of their lesson time with the top 2% to 5% of the cohort, or the top mainstream students. They would do activities such as building structures with plastic blocks. The announcement of the integration provoked much buzz on the blogosphere. While some felt that this might alleviate some of the stereotypes and prejudice and relieve the generally bad press that GEP students and the GEP had gotten over the past few years, others raised objections such as the fact that the only mainstream pupils affected were the top students, which in their view did not eradicate elitism. Gifted scheme kids to mix more with others.

Iran

In I.R. of Iran: development of rules and regulations is done by the IslamicParliament, Higher Council of Education and the Cabinet.[19]

According to the article 30 of the IRI Constitution the government is obliged to provide all citizens with free education up to the end of secondary school and must expand free higher education to the extent required by the country for attaining self-sufficiency under article education should be gratuitous.

Some of the rules and regulations approved by the authorized bodies in this regard are presented in the appendix. Compulsory schooling is 5 years at present which covers 6 to 10 year old children. According to the Third Five Year Development Plan it will cover 6to 13 year old children which will improve compulsory schooling to 8 years.[20]

In order to improve the quality of educational activities, the assessment system which is one of the effective factors in teaching/learning process has been revised. There are many reasons why this reform was made, some of which are outlined as: the previous system was based on traditional, non scientific and ineffective methods. The actual usage of the finding in the real life was neglected and there was overemphasis on a great deal of knowledge. In the reform process some objectives like, matching the assessment methods with scientific findings, increasing the efficiency and effectiveness of school teachings and students active participation in teaching -learning process were taken into consideration. The I.R. of Iran has been trying hard, during the recent years, to increase the enrollment rate, in other words, to increase schooling chances for various groups of people regardless of their gender, age, tribal and ethnic diversities, In this regard the priority has been focused on the education of school age (6-10 year old) children. It has taken efficient measures and practical strategies in the framework of the country's second development plan to achieve this main objective. According to the CIA World Factbook, from information collected in 2003, 85.6 per cent of males and 73 per cent of females over the age of 15 are literate, Thus 79.4 per cent of the population is literate.

Literacy training has been a prime concern in Iran. For the year 2000, adult illiteracy rates were estimated at 23.1% (males, 16.3%; females, 30.0%). A literacy corps was established in

1963 to send educated conscripts to villages. During its first 10 years, the corps helped 2.2 million urban children and 600,000 adults become literate. In 1997, there were 9,238,393 pupils enrolled in 63,101 primary schools, with 298,755 teachers. The student-to-teacher ratio stood at 31 to 1. In that same year, secondary schools had 8,776,792 students and 280,309 teachers. The pupil-teacher ratio at the primary level was 26 to 1 in 1999. In the same year, 83 per cent of primary-school-age children were enrolled in school. As of 1999, public expenditure on education was estimated at 4.6 per cent of GDP.

The National Organization for Development of Exceptional Talents (NODET), also known as SAMPAD, maintains Middle and High Schools in Iran. These schools were shut down for a few years after the revolution, but later re-opened. Admittance is based on an entrance examination, and is very competitive, especially in Tehran.(school names: Allameh helli for boys and farzanegan for girls). Their tuition is similar to private schools, but may be partially or fully waived off depending on the students financial condition. Some nodet alumni are world leading scientists.

Gifted Students education in Iran is under supervision of Iranian Ministry of Education and this ministration manages and controls all Gifted students centers all over the country.

The central headquarters located in Tehran and approves all disciplinary terms and condition for these schools in nearly 500 towns and cities in the country. Teachers and principals are selected and admitted through the yearly evaluation and assessment program and a close investigation is held on t their yearly activities. These teachers are paid a considerable salary most of them are dedicated themselves for serve gifted students of their city. Most of the teacher in gifted high school system are in post graduate levels.

For Admission in these schools a yearly examination is held in all over the country for elementary and secondary levels and students who passed such exam are eligible for enrolling in the schools. But this does not guaranty their whole enrolment for all three years in each elementary level. Each student is closely monitored and evaluated by his/her teacher and all his/her activities are monitored in the system. If any weakness or failure are noted,students are referred to psychological consultants and monitored for their mental and emotional condition and it is tried to find out the predisposing or causing factors. It is possible that a student may be rejected from the school because of law adaptation ability.

All schools of gifted and talented students in Iran are supported completely by Iranian Ministry of Education and there is a special budget for these educational centers.

Educational material and curriculum are much different from ordinary education in t he country and gifted students are supposed to pass many laboratory And theoretical subjects in school.

At the end of each year more than 90% of Ir5anian talented students are enrolled in high level public universities and continue their study under the supervision of Talented Students System there.

Conclusion

As it is evident from the above detail, Asian countries such as Iran and India are trying their best for achieving higher standard in their gifted Educational system. This strategy is properly managed by both countries educational ministration although some private sectors are active in Iran in this field. But it is noteworthy that many Iranian gifted students may be under diagnosed in this system because of only one method of general testing in the country. since there are many high level students in Iranian regular schools, a more perfect system is needed for better diagnosis and selection of the gifted in the country.

REFERENCES

1. Brody L.E., The talent searches: A catalyst for change in higher education. *J of Secondary Gifted Education* 1998; 9(3): 124-33.

2. Harris CR. Talent development: potential for developing nations. *Gifted Education International* 1993; 9(1): 48-52.
3. Damiani VB. Young gifted children in research and practice: the need for early childhood programs. *Gifted Child Today Magazine* 1997; 20(3): 18-23.
4. Rosenthal R. *An honors program for an open dimensions community college. Metropolitan Universities: An International Forum* 1998; 9(2): 47-56.
5. Texas Education Agency Division of Advanced Academic Services. Texas state plan for the education of the gifted/talented students. Austin: The Agency. Nov 1996.
6. Flack J, Friedberg J. When children go to college on Saturday. *Teaching Pre* 1997; 27(6): 44-46.K-8,
7. Boothe D, Sethna B. The advanced academy of Georgia: A unique collaboration of high school with college. *NCSSSMST Journal* 1996; 2(2): 3-6.
8. Williams M, Dodds P, Koshy V, Cole L. College for kids—what higher education can do to improve the educational opportunities for the exceptionally able—A review of the approaches in the United Kingdom and the United States. *Gifted Education International* 1997; 12(1).
9. Brody LE, *et al.* Five years of early entrants: predicting successful achievement in college. *Gifted Child Quarterly* 1990; 34(4): 138-42.
10. Proulx Kerrie, 2005, Comparative Study Strand 2:,Summary of Gifted and Talented Education in India, NAGTY Research Programme Archive.
11. *Ibid.*
12. National Policy of Education Centre (1986), General background, India.
13. Indian Central Board of Secondary Education (CBSE), 2005, Year-book.
14. JNV head office in New Delhi, 2007.
15. *Ibid.*
16. Proulx Kerrie, 2005, *op. cit.*
19. *Ibid.*
18. Singapore Examinations and Assessment Board.
19. Education System at the End of the Twentieth Century in the of I.R of IRAN, 2007, Iran Ministry of Eduction, yearly report.
20. *Ibid.*

CHAPTER

10

Assessment of Shyness among Adolescent Students Studying in Rural and Urban Areas: Influences of Gender and Age

—Gururaj B. Urs

The present study reports assessment of shyness among students studying in urban and rural areas of Mysore district. A total of 751 students studying in urban (n = 335) and rural areas (n = 416) were randomly selected for the study. They were administered Shyness scale (Crozier, 1995) and their gender and age were also recorded. Students studying in rural area had significantly higher shyness compared to students studying in urban areas. Female students were found to be shyer than male students; shyest were rural female students. Though, statistically non-significant, comparatively as the age increased, shyness also increased linearly.

Introduction

Shyness may be defined experientially as discomfort and/ or inhibition in interpersonal situations that interferes with pursuing one's interpersonal or professional goals. The reactions for shyness can occur at any or all of the following levels: cognitive, affective, physiological and behavioural, and may be triggered by a wide variety of arousal cues. (Henderson and Zimbardo, 1996). Shyness expresses itself as poverty in the quality of life. It can be observed in many social situations. Examples: difficulty, but not impossibility, in participating in group activities, in practicing group sports, in speaking in public, in asking questions in class, in asking somebody for a date or intimate relation, in writing what he thinks, in speaking to someone in an authority position, or in entertaining in public.

Many pre-school, school going children and adolescents, show initial wariness on meeting a stranger, have doubts about one's ability to contribute effectively to social encounters and the belief that others will negatively evaluate one's action/behavior may contribute to the withdrawal behavior and social anxieties that characterize shyness or social phobia (Crozier, 1995). About 13 per cent of the general population actually withdraws from daily life experiences in order to avoid the social interactions they dread (Anonymous, 2000). According to recent estimates, approximately 40 to 50 per cent of American college students and in India, 26.2 per cent of the children showed high levels of shyness, followed by 36.6 per cent moderate and remaining 37.3 per cent of the children showed low levels of anxiety (Natesha & D'Souza, 2007).

A common observation in most of the shyness research is that the consequences of shyness are deeply troubling.

The authors are grateful to management and students of various high schools and pre-university colleges of Mysore district with which data have been gathered.

Shyness leads to higher levels of anxiety (D'Souza, 2003), decreased levels of happiness (Sreeshakumar, *et al.*, 2007), neurotic tendency and lower academic performance (D'Souza, *et al.*, 2000), lowered performance in physical education students (D'Souza, *et al.*, 1999), lowered self-esteem and decreased self concept (D'Souza, *et al.*, 2003), increased fear reactions (D'Souza, *et al.*, 2006) and social and emotional maladjustment (D'Souza and Urs, 2001).

A degree of shyness is normal whenever social expectations are new or ambiguous. Shyness begins to emerge as a problem if it becomes not merely situational but dispositional, so that the child is labeled as shy. The studies related to shyness and its prevalence in India is not very much promising. This study aims to study the extent of shyness among adolescents in urban and rural areas along with the influence of gender and age. It was hypothesized that students studying in rural area express more shyness than students of urban area.

Sample

High school and pre-university students studying in few of the urban and rural areas of Mysore district were randomly selected for the present study. Of the total 751 students included in the study 335 (209 male + 126 female) were from urban area and remaining 358 (184 male + 232 female) from rural areas. Stratified Random sampling technique was used to select the sample. The sample involved students studying in both Kannada and English medium. Their age varied from 11 to 19 years.

Shyness Questionnaire

This questionnaire was developed by Crozier (1995) of University' College of Cardiff. It consists of 26 items and requires the subject to indicate his/her response by ticking "YES\ 'NO" OR 'DON'T KNOW". The items of the questionnaire are based on situations or interactions like performing in front of the class, being made fun of, being told off, having one's photograph taken, novel situations involving teachers, school-friends interaction and so on. Of the 26 items, shyness is indicated by a 'YES' response for 21 items and a 'NO' response for 5 items. The negative items are 9, 10, 15, 16 and 23. Item analysis of the scale using SPSS program resulted in Cronbach alpha coefficient of 0.817.

Procedure

The tests were administered to the subjects in groups of 6-10 subjects per group. Data collection was done in one session which lasted for about 15 minutes. Before administering the questionnaire, rapport was established with the subjects and they were asked to introduce themselves. The purpose of the study was made clear to them. They were given appropriate instructions and the questions were read out to them. They were asked to indicate their responses in the respective sheets given to them. Whenever they had doubt in understanding questions, the test administrator made those questions very clear to them in their local language. Whenever the meaning of certain words was not clear to the students, test administrator made them clear to them.

Scoring and Analysis

For the shyness questionnaire, items worded in the direction of shyness, responses were scored 2 for 'YES", 1 for 'DON'T KNOW", and 0 for 'NO". Scores were reversed for the items worded in the opposite direction. High scores indicate high level of shyness and low scores indicate low level of shyness. Two-way ANOVA was employed to test the significance of difference in the mean fear scores of students with three levels of shyness, grades and medium of instruction, where fear scores were taken as dependent variable, and shyness level and grades and shyness and medium of instruction as independent variables. The statistical analyses were performed through SPSS for Windows, Version 14 (Evaluation version).

Results

Table 10.1 shows mean shyness scores of the students belonging to urban and rural areas with gender and age groups. Table 10.2 shows results of 2-way ANOVA for mean shyness scores of the students belonging to urban and rural areas with gender and age groups

Area, Gender and Shyness Scores

Students studying in rural areas had significantly higher shyness scores than students studying in urban areas. ANOVA revealed a significant difference in the mean shyness scores of students studying in urban and rural areas. ($F_{(1,747)} = 26.441$; $P<.000$). The mean shyness scores for students studying rural and urban areas were 22.88 and 19.89 respectively. Further, gender-wise comparison revealed that female students (mean 22.91) were found to be significantly ($F_{(1,747)}$=9.885; P<.002) more shy than male students (mean 20.30). Even the interaction effect between area and gender was found to be significant ($F_{(1,747)}$ = 27.145; P<.000). From the mean values it is clear that female students from rural area had significantly higher shyness scores compared to rest of the groups.

Table 10.1. Mean Shyness Scores of the Students Belonging to Urban and Rural Areas with Gender and Age Groups

Para-meters		Area Urban			Overall Rural		
		Mean	S.D	Mean	S.D	Mean	S.D
Overall		19.89	7.55	22.88	7.72	21.55	7.79
Gender	Male	20.32	7.20	20.28	6.75	20.30	6.99
	Female	19.17	8.08	24.95	7.84	22.91	8.38
Age in	11-13	19.25	8.02	20.96	6.58	20.22	7.26
years	14-16	19.95	7.39	23.34	7.95	21.81	7.88
	17-19	23.80	11.03	22.80	6.63	23.13	7.95

Table 10.2. Results of Two-way ANOVA for Mean Shyness Scores of the Students Belonging to Urban and Rural Areas with Gender and Age Groups

Source of variation	Df's	F value	P value
Area (A)	1, 747	26.441	.000 (HS)
Gender (B)	1, 747	9.885	.002 (HS)
Interaction (A × B)	1, 747	27.145	.000 (HS)
Age (C)	2, 745	2.636	.072 (NS)
Interaction (A × C)	2, 745	1.127	.324 (NS)

Note: HS-Highly significant; NS-Non-significant

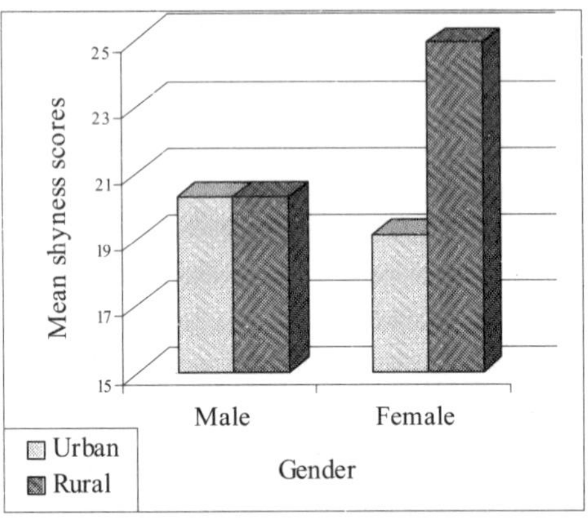

Fig. 10.1(*a*)

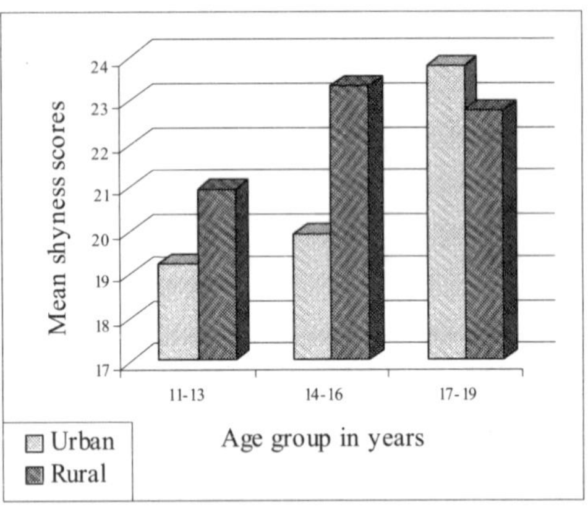

Fig. 10.1(*b*)

Fig. 10.1(*a*) and 10.1(*b*). Mean shyness scores of male and female students in different age groups studying in Urban and rural areas.

Area, Age Groups and Shyness Scores

Students with different age groups did not differ significantly in their shyness scores as the obtained F value of 2.636 was found to be non-significant. Further, the interaction effect between area and age groups are also found to be non-significant, indicating that pattern of shyness is same for students in different age groups irrespective of the area they belong to. Though not statistically significant, we can see a linear increase in the shyness scores from 11 to 19 years.

DISCUSSION

The main findings of the present study are;

1. Students studying in rural area had significantly higher shyness compared to students studying in urban areas.
2. Female students were found to be shyer than male students; shyest were rural female students.
3. Comparatively as the age increased, shyness also increased linearly.

Adolescents studying in rural areas had higher levels of shyness than urban area students. On of the important aspect to be highlighted that most of the students studying in rural areas are monolinguals and mostly they study in Kannada language, whereas in urban area students are coming from diverse areas and multilingual. Students in rural area studying in Kannada media they may have felt inferior to their counterparts in urban area, which may lead to increased shyness among rural students. Further, students in urban area are exposed to variety of situations – psychological, physiological and cognitive aspects than students studying in rural areas. Further, female students were shyer; shyest were rural females, where the customs and traditions are very strictly followed for females in rural area than urban area, which makes the rural females to be more withdrawn than urban females.

For the reasons not completely known yet, adolescents with higher age groups showed more shyness than their counterparts in lower age groups. The effect of physical transformation during pubescent are to adolescent ages which further continue till late adolescent age, where a series of physical and physical changes occur, which may lead to higher levels of shyness. Shyness is more common in teenagers, especially in early adolescence. Around the age of twenty, most adolescents have overcome or have substantially reduced this difficulty. There does not seem to be any correlation between Shyness in childhood and in adolescence. Mild Shyness in childhood could turn severe in adolescence. On the other hand, those with Social Anxiety Disorder/Social Phobia generally have a history of Shyness in childhood.

To conclude, therapists and mental health professionals should recognize the serious need for treatment of shy people, and should develop treatment approaches to liberate the millions of people who are trapped in their silent prisons of shyness. Also, the educationists/policy makers should plan English as a media of instruction from early schooling along with Kannada language even in rural areas.

REFERENCES

Anonymous (2000). Shy no more: New treatments for social phobia. *Health and Nutrition*, 12, (4), 92-95.

Crozier, W.R. (1995). Shyness and Self esteem. *British Journal of Educational Psychology*. 65, 85-95.

D'Souza, L. (2003). Influence of Shyness on Anxiety and Academic achievement in High school students *Pakistan Journal of Psychological Research*, 18, 3-4, 109-118.

D'Souza, L. (2005). Shyness/Social Phobia: Influence on self-concept and academic achievement in High school students.Suggested remedial measures. *Artha – a Journal of Social Sciences*. 4 (1), 23-29.

D'Souza, L., and Urs. G. .B. (2001). Effect of shyness on the adjustment of high school students. *Pakistan Journal of Psychological Research*, 16, 3-4, 85.

D'Souza, L., Singh, M. and Basavarajappa. (1999). Influence of shyness on Performance, personality and intelligence of students of physical education. *Psychological Studies*, 44, 92-94.

D'Souza, L., Urs, G.B., and James.M.S. (2000). Assessment of shyness: Its influence on the personality and academic achievement of High school students. *Indian Journal of Clinical Psychology*, 27, 286-289.

D'Souza, L., Urs. G. B., and Ramaswamy C. (2003). Relationship of self-esteem with shyness, personality and academic achievement in high-school students. *Artha-a Journal of social sciences*, 1, 228-234.

D'Souza, L., Gowda, H.M. R and Gowda, D.K.S. (2006). Relationship between shyness and fear among High school students. *Pakistan Journal of Psychological Research*, 21, 3-4, 53-60.

Henderson, L & Zimbardo, P (1996). *Encyclopedia of Mental Health*. San Diego: Academic Press.

Natesha, N. & D'Souza, L. (2007). Prevalence of shyness among children: A Developmental perspective of age and gender, *Asian Journal of Development Matters*, 1, 55-60.

Sreeshakumar, H Y., D'Souza, L & Nagalakshmi, K, 2007. Relationship between shyness and happiness among high school students. *Psychological Studies*, 52, 121-123.

CHAPTER

11

Reading Habits of Newspapers and Magazine among Students of Urban and Rural Areas : A Case Study of Dakshina Kannada District

—*Sudha S.T. and Harinarayana N.S.*

It seemed important to study the reading habits of students of rural and urban areas in the light of current political concerns about reading generally, that the issues raised in the appraisal about reading habits are discovered in greater detail. This study is conducted to explore students studying professional and non-professional colleges in their reading preferences. The data for this study are based on 1757 respondents from professional and non-professional college student respondents of rural (N=866) and urban (N=891) areas of Dakshina Kannada District. Results revealed that students from urban area were found to have higher preferences than students from rural areas in reading business magazines, Kannada newspapers, competitive magazines, subject journals and newspaper clippings. In general newspapers, students from urban areas had more frequency in 'most frequently', whereas; rural students had more frequency in 'frequently' categories. In crime news category, students from urban areas had more frequency in 'most frequently' reading categories, whereas, rural students had more frequency in 'frequently' category. In reading general magazines no difference was observed between students from rural and urban areas. Further, role of librarians and influence of electronic media reading habits are also discussed.

Introduction

There has been common belief in the society that the reading habit among youngsters is on decline. Among other factors, one of the important factors that are ascribed is the influence of internet, TV and other technologies. Another common belief is that internet has replaced the books in education institutions, these beliefs need to be studied and appropriate corrective measures need to be taken by the society in general and libraries in particular. The belief of influence of internet is perhaps, substantiated by the fact that there has been a quantum reduction in number of users visiting the libraries. This gives rise to a question. Whether the reading habit itself is on decline or readers have alternate sources such as internet for fulfilling their needs? This question is difficult to answer unless we collect substantiate data and come out with a result.

Demidov opines that "Reading activity shapes the abstracting power of the left hemisphere of the brain and besides develops the words relating to specific images. The last process is totally absent when viewing pictures on the television screen. As a result the reader develops more intellectual personality than the one who lives at the mercy of the visual perceptions without taking the trouble of couching them in words that is at the level of abstraction" (Ramaiah, 1996).

Reading is a basic tool of education. It provides us information, knowledge, recreation and education. It is one of the most important aspects of language, arts, and effective means of communication. Reading helps in all-round development of the human beings; it is an intellectual activity, which contributes to the growth of balanced personality. The present scientific and technological developments, attainments and achievements are the outcome of intellectual uniqueness of human beings. Reading is the gateway of knowledge and intellectual caliber. It helps us not only in improving our vocabulary better comprehension, but also the personality development of the individual. Once upon a time reading was looked as only means of receiving the messages now it has become a multi faceted mental process, which paves the way for human intellectual development.

In the present study an attempt is made to find out the differences in reading preferences among students studying in urban and rural areas of Dakshina Kannada district. It is hypothesized that urban sand rural students differ significantly in their reading preferences.

Sample

It seemed important to study the reading habits of students of rural and urban areas in the light of current political concerns about reading generally, that the issues raised in the appraisal about reading habits are discovered in greater detail. This study is conducted to explore young people their reading preferences in news papers and magazines. The data for this study are based on respondents from professional and non-professional college student respondents of rural and urban areas of Dakshina Kannada District. A total of 1757 students out of a total student population of 26083 respondents were included in the study of which 866 were from rural areas and 891 from urban areas. They were randomly selected from all the five taluks of Dakshina Kannada district.

Survey Tool

The first author prepared a tool for measuring the preferences of students from urban and rural areas in reading various types of newspapers and magazines. The tool is constructed on the basis of 4-point scale where options of 'not at all', 'some times', 'frequently' and most frequently' were given. The student had to read each option like reading general newspapers, business, Kannada newspapers, competitive magazines, crime news, general magazines, subject journals and newspaper clippings and indicated any one of the options he/she would prefer to choose. Along with the above items, the tool included the information on some of the demographic variables also.

Procedure

Each selected college in both urban and the first author personally visited rural areas and questionnaire was given individually to each student. Students were requested to go through the instructions carefully and answer honestly.

Once the data were collected, they were scored, coded and a master chart was prepared. Later, entire data on 1757 students were fed to the computer and subjected to contingency table analysis to see the association between categories of responses and area. SPSS for Windows (Version 15.0) was employed to do the statistical calculations.

Results

Table 11.1 presents the area-wise frequency and percent responses for reading various types of newspapers and magazines and results of contingency coefficient (CC) analysis.

(*a*) **Area and reading general newspapers:** A significant association was observed between area and type of responses where CC value of .091 was found to be significant at .002 level. From Table 11.1 it is clear that students from urban areas had more frequency in 'most frequently' and 'sometimes' reading categories, whereas, rural students had more frequency in 'frequently' and 'not at all' categories.

(*b*) **Area and reading Business magazines and newspapers:** Significantly, urban students were reading more of business newspapers and magazines compared to students from rural areas. Contingency coefficient value of .103 was found to be significant at .000 level.

(*c*) **Area and reading Kannada newspapers:** Significantly, in this category also urban students were reading more of Kannada newspapers compared to students from rural areas. Contingency coefficient value of .149 was found to be significant at .000 level.

(*d*) **Area and reading Competitive magazines:** Even in reading competitive magazines students from urban area excelled rural students and contingency coefficient of .077 was found to be significant at .014 level.

(*e*) **Area and reading Crime news:** A significant association was observed between area and type of responses where CC value of .077 was found to be significant at .015 level. From table 1 it is clear that students from urban areas had more frequency in 'most frequently' and 'not at all' reading categories, whereas, rural students had more frequency in 'frequently' and 'not at all' categories.

(*f*) **Area and reading general magazines:** A non-significant association was observed between categories of responses where the pattern of responses are similar in each category irrespective of the area they belong to.

(*g*) **Area and reading subject journals:** Significantly, in this category, urban students were reading more of subject journals compared to students from rural areas. Contingency coefficient value of .068 was found to be significant at .045 level.

(*h*) **Area and reading newspaper clippings:** Even in reading news paper clippings students from urban area excelled rural students and contingency coefficient of .088 was found to be significant at .003 level.

Discussion

Main findings of the present study are:

- Students from urban area were found to have higher preferences than students from rural areas in reading

Business magazines, Kannada newspapers, competitive magazines, subject journals and newspaper clippings.

- In general newspapers, students from urban areas had more frequency in 'most frequently', whereas, rural students had more frequency in 'frequently' categories.
- In crime news category, students from urban areas had more frequency in 'most frequently' reading categories, whereas, rural students had more frequency in 'frequently' category.
- In reading general magazines no difference was observed between students from rural and urban areas.

On the whole, it is clear that students from urban area had higher preference for reading magazines and newspapers compared to students from rural areas. Several reasons could be attributed for these preferences. In rural areas, availability of newspapers and magazines are relatively lesser compared to urban areas. Even though, in rural areas some newspapers and magazines available, in urban areas there is a wide variety of spectrum of news papers and magazines available for reading. Many a times in rural areas students are not only involved in studying, they may be involved in some other work like helping their parents, doing some additional work in agriculture fields or farms, which makes them to read lesser due to physical stress and lack of time.

In urban areas there are circulating libraries, where for a meager amount one can read newspapers and magazines of his/her choice. Even mobile libraries which go to place to place once in a week or fortnight, makes the students to read variety of magazines and newspapers. The concept of circulating and mobile libraries is not very popular among rural areas. Though regular libraries are functioning in rural areas, they may not be fully equipped with all the news papers and magazines satisfying reader's needs.

Considering the above facts, there is a serious need to improve the reading habits of the students especially in rural areas, since more than 80 per cent of the Indian population dwelling in rural and backward areas. Though, Dakshina Kannada district is considered as one of the highly literate district, educationists, administrators and planning experts should make their sincere efforts in improving reading habits of the student community by providing adequate facilities and improving/upgrading the existing facilities not only in colleges and schools, but in public libraries too.

Role of Library in Improving the Reading Habits of the Students

It needs to be identified as the libraries and the librarian play an important role in developing reading habits of the students. It is necessary to see that whether the teachers are cultivating standards in reading cultivating abilities of the students and for the conceptual growth of student themselves. As the library is the heart and brain centre of knowledge it is needed to see whether library functions well with the leading force, to see whether the teaching faculty motivate the students in enhancing their inquisitiveness, curiosity, and also building up irresistible learning pressures. It needs to be seen that how many students depend on library for their cognitive needs. In return this paves the way for assimilating and arriving at their inclinations. To identify whether the librarians are dynamic in promoting the reading habit of the students it needs to be identified whether students rely on lectures, or notes, internet, books guides, departmental libraries, and the factors that is helping them to use the library or the dependency of students for preparing assignments, projects, participating in curricular and co-curricular activities like quizzes, debates, intercollegiate competitions, colloquiums etc. these factors art to be identified to know the dependency of students for their informational requirements.

Shift from Print to Electronic Media

While going through the present trend of improving the reading habits of rural and urban students of Dakshina Kannada District, it is true that the electronic media has taken

Table 11.1. Area-wise Frequency and Percent Responses for Reading Various Types of Newspapers and Magazines and Test Statistics

Extent of reading		Newspapers/Magazines							
		GNP		Business		Kannada		Competitive	
		Rural	Urban	Rural	Urban	Rural	Urban	Rural	Urban
1	2	3	4	5	6	7	8	9	10
Not at all	F	20	8	247	180	206	112	112	76
	%	2.3%	.9%	28.5%	20.2%	23.8%	12.6%	12.9%	8.5%
Some times	F	172	219	390	419	178	219	333	356
	%	19.9%	24.6%	45.0%	47.0%	20.6%	24.6%	38.5%	40.0%
Frequently	F	382	340	174	225	244	310	308	318
	%	44.1%	38.2%	20.1%	25.3%	28.2%	34.8%	35.6%	35.7%
Most Frequently	F	292	324	55	67	238	250	113	141
	%	33.7%	36.4%	6.4%	7.5%	27.5%	28.1%	13.0%	15.8%
CC		0.091		0.103		0.149		0.077	
P Value		.002 (S)		.000 (HS)		.000 (HS)		.014 (S)	

Extent of reading		Newspapers/Magazines							
		Crime news		GM		Subject Journals		NPC	
		Rural	Urban	Rural	Urban	Rural	Urban	Rural	Urban
1	2	11	12	13	14	15	16	17	18
Not at all	F	79	96	34	26	112	87	93	63
	%	9.1%	10.8%	3.9%	2.9%	12.9%	9.8%	10.7%	7.1%
Some times	F	356	370	273	289	350	343	337	313
	%	41.1%	41.5%	31.5%	32.4%	40.4%	38.5%	38.9%	35.1%
Frequently	F	306	261	393	385	282	304	296	335
	%	35.3%	29.3%	45.4%	43.2%	32.6%	34.1%	34.2%	37.6%
Most Frequently	F	125	164	166	191	122	157	140	180
	%	14.4%	18.4%	19.2%	21.4%	14.1%	17.6%	16.2%	20.2%
CC		0.077		0.041		0.068		0.088	
P Value		.015 (S)		.392 (NS)		.045 (S)		.003 (HS)	

Note: CC - Contingency co-efficient; HS - Highly significant; NS - Non significant; S - Significant.
GNP - General News Paper; GM - General magazines; NPC - newspaper clippings

its own place in emerging as a global media of communication to impart education, as it has the capacity and capability to store, search and generate information and help in wider reach than the published and printed media. Learners by their skills are able to get access to information within the short span of time. But as far as the infrastructure and the media sections of the colleges are concerned we are still lagging behind as the paucity of funds and other technical problems faced by the college management. The students are still in the budding stage in learning through information technology that is web based education. It is true that special libraries have the Networking of institutions by electronic media that has resulted in consortium of institutes. It is very important to think whether our students are depending on web based education? Considering these fact the professional college students have progressed to that extent of using electronic media and to pursue their studies. Internet is a substantial communication tool for getting the information it helps in getting the information through Net. The web does the function of news paper, magazine, periodical, journal article, recreation, chatting it gives all kinds of information needed by the user. The advent of e-books and e-journals has enabled the professional students to browse and read through electronic media. Digital versions of books and journals are available and could be obtainable in online bookshop as the book will be downloaded to PC by payment. But the non professional colleges are still in the budding stage some colleges do not have separate library building also. It is unfortunate that the non professional colleges of rural and urban do not have adequate facilities. In course of time the government should give impetus to implement e resources but still print media has its own value it will never fade.

Conclusion

By considering all these factors it is necessary to help the youth by providing challenging opportunities that stimulate them to translate this ideas into reality. They need to be helped to shoulder responsibility and make decisions. The educational system must undoubtedly be overhauled if such programmers are to be started because the college is the right plan for the right plan of development in the company of the peers and under the guidance and leadership of enlightened teacher, a conducive atmosphere can be fostered. Today reading has become universal phenomena, and an essential Reading habit of the educated world, spreading through all their private and public lives of people.

This whole network of activities related to promotion of reading habits in school Libraries is a great task. It requires the cooperation of all concerned; but with all eyes focused on the same goal and imbued with the high spirit of service, success will not be that far. The journey may be long and difficult but the first step has to be made. This is a challenge we are committed to accept

REFERENCE

Ramaiah, L.S. (1996). The Reading habit and the role of libraries, University *news*, pp. 5-7.

CHAPTER

12

Study of Social Science Achievement by D.Ed Trainees: Influence of Type of Institute and Gender

—*Prabhuswamy B.S. and Parvathamma G.H.*

ABSTRACT

The present study reports the social science achievement of second year D.Ed trainees. Achievement test developed by the investigator on concepts like fill up the blanks, multiple choice, match the following, classification, true/false was employed to measure the influence of students studying government and private D.Ed colleges as well as male and female students. Two-way ANOVA was employed to find out the significance of difference between trainees studying in government and private D.Ed colleges as well as male and female students Results revealed that D.Ed trainees from government institutions scored significantly higher than D.Ed trainees from private institutions in classification and true/false subtests. D.Ed trainees from private institutions scored significantly higher than D.Ed trainees from government institutions in remaining subtests like fill up the blanks, multiple choices and match the following Gender-wise male and female D.Ed trainees had similar scores on social science achievement test

Key words: social science achievement, government and private institutions,

Introduction

The prime objective of education and society is all round development of the individuals to achieve the objective primary school. Teachers should aim at providing suitable learning experience in social science because the aim of providing, good citizens is rested on social science teachers. To achieve this, the objective of D.Ed., training institutions would be disseminating additional knowledge in social science to the trainees to the teacher trainees. The present study has been designed in this regard. There are limited studies at dissertation level at Ph.d., level. Content enrichment refers a process of programme, which enhances the master level of the knowledge from 1st to 7th Std., before entrance has teaching.

The present study is descriptive, comparative and correlative in nature. The objective of the study is to find out the influence of selected variables like gender, and type of institute on achievement in social science at the end of the training on social science.

The present study is conceptualized broadly under three levels:

1. To list concepts of the content enrichment in social science.
2. The construction achievement test in content enrichment of social science
3. Administration of the achievement test on the selected sample and to arrive at specific conclusions on the influence of selected secondary variables

METHOD

Subjects

A total of 1000 D.Ed trainees were selected from the jurisdiction of Mysore South Division. Of the 1000 trainees selected, 500 of them belonged to urban area and 500 belonged to rural area. Out of which 323 of them from government run institutions and remaining 677 from private institutes. They were randomly selected from 25 D.Ed training colleges coming under Mysore South Division in five districts of Mysore, Mandya, Hassan, Coorg and Chamarajanagar.

TOOLS

Social Science Achievement Test (Prabhuswamy, 2006)

The social science achievement test consisted of 285 items, which were classified into five groups. They were filling up the blanks (20 items), multiple-choice options (39 items), match the following items (97 items), classifications items (80 items) and true/false statements (49 items). All these items were prepared on the basis of content enrichment programme in D.Ed curriculum. Initially, a try out was done on a sample of 100 trainees, and later some of the items were modified/ deleted as per the opinion of the respondents. The final version was administered after discussion with subject experts and establishing psychometric properties to a satisfactory level.

Procedure

The tests were administered to the subjects in groups of 6-10 subjects per group. Data collection was done in 1 session and each session lasted for about 150 minutes. The investigator established rapport with the trainees and they were asked to introduce themselves. The purpose of the study was made clear to them. Then they were administered social science achievement test. They were given appropriate instructions and the questions were read out to them. They were asked to indicate their responses in the respective sheets given to them. Whenever they had doubt in understanding questions, the test administrator made those questions very clear to them in their local language.

Scoring and Analysis

For each correct answer one score was assigned, and calculated separately for different subtests fill up the blanks (20 items), multiple choice options (39 items), match the following items (97 items), classifications items (80 items) and true/false statements (49 items) and finally total scores were added.

Two-way ANOVA was employed to test the significance of difference in the mean social science achievement scores of

D.Ed trainees, where the scores in subtests and total scores were taken as dependent variable, and institution type and gender as independent variables. The statistical analyses were performed through SPSS for Windows, Version 14 (Evaluation version).

Results

Table 12.1 presents mean scores obtained on social science achievement scores by male and female D.Ed trainees in government and private institutions along with the results of 2-way ANOVA. Following are the major findings.

Main Effects

(*a*) Institution type and social science achievement scores: In all the subtests significant differences were observed between D.Ed trainees studying in government and private institutions. All the F values obtained for the subtests for the differences in mean scores between D.Ed trainees in government and private institutions. From table 1 it is evident that D.Ed trainees from government institutions scored significantly higher than D.Ed trainees from private institutions in classification and true/false subtests. However, D.Ed trainees from private institutions scored significantly higher than D.Ed trainees from government institutions in remaining subtests like fill up the blanks, multiple choices and match the following. On the whole, when total social science achievement scores are considered, no significant difference was observed between D.Ed trainees of government and private institutions.

(*b*) Gender and social science achievement scores : Gender-wise, no significant differences were observed in different subtests as well as in total social science achievement scores, as all the obtained F values for gender differences were failed to reach the significance level criterion. In other words, male and female D.Ed trainees had statistically equal scores in all the subtests of social science achievement test as well as in the total scores.

Table 12.1. Mean scores on various subtests of social science achievement test by male and female D.Ed trainees studying in government and private institutions

Sectors	Sex	Fill up the blanks		Multiple Choice		Match the following		Classification		True/false		Total Achievement	
		Mean	SD	Mean	SD	Mean	SD	Mean	SD	Mean	SD	Mean	SD
Govt	M	15.99	1.70	28.29	4.21	66.65	4.37	64.09	4.95	37.16	3.07	212.18	11.90
	F	15.92	1.65	28.39	3.96	67.58	6.11	63.82	4.96	36.84	3.56	212.54	13.33
	T	15.96	1.67	28.33	4.10	67.07	5.24	63.97	4.95	37.01	3.30	212.34	12.55
Private	M	15.40	1.77	31.18	4.07	67.85	4.52	61.32	6.03	35.96	3.40	211.70	12.85
	F	15.36	1.66	30.52	4.56	67.74	4.11	61.47	5.04	36.22	3.30	211.32	11.58
	T	15.38	1.71	30.83	4.34	67.79	4.31	61.39	5.53	36.10	3.35	211.50	12.20
Total	M	15.61	1.77	30.15	4.34	67.43	4.50	62.30	5.82	36.39	3.34	211.87	12.51
	F	15.53	1.67	29.90	4.50	67.70	4.78	62.15	5.13	36.40	3.38	211.67	12.12
	T	15.57	1.72	30.03	4.42	67.56	4.64	62.23	5.48	36.39	3.36	211.77	12.31
Sector		**F=24.647; P< .000**		**F=75.423; P< .000**		**F=4.709; P< .030**		**F=49.703; P< .000**		**F=16.028; P< .000**		F=1.030; P< .310	
Gender		F=0.198; P< .656		F= .910; P< .340		F=1.722; P< .190		F=0.030; P< .863		F= .021; P< .886		F= .000; P< .990	
Sector*Gender Interaction		F=0.029; P< .866		F=1.711; P< .191		F=2.749; P< .098		F=0.343; P< .558		F=1.645; P< .200		F= .202; P< .653	

INTERACTION EFFECTS

All the interactions effects between the type of institute and gender were found to be non-significant, indicating that the pattern of scoring by male and female D.Ed trainees was same irrespective of the type of institute they study in. All the F values obtained for interaction effects were non-significant.

Discussion

Main findings of the present study are:

1. D.Ed trainees from government institutions scored significantly higher than D.Ed trainees from private institutions in classification and true/false subtests.
2. D.Ed trainees from private institutions scored significantly higher than D.Ed trainees from government institutions in remaining subtests like fill up the blanks, multiple choices and match the following
3. Gender-wise male and female D.Ed trainees had similar scores on social science achievement test.

In the present study no consistent trend was observed in the social science achievement of the D.Ed trainees as trainees from government institutions were better in classification and true/false statements, where as private college trainees excelled in like fill up the blanks, multiple choices and match the following. Chelini (1989) and in their investigations indicated that achievement level to be better in private institutions than in government institutions, where as, Paravathamma (1996) and Bhattacharya (1989) reported quite opposite findings.

Surprisingly, in the present study, no significant differences were observed between male and female trainees which is in agreement with few other studies (Parvathamma, 1996; Narasimaiah, 2000). Studies by Nadabi (1986) and Prasanna Kumar (1975) and Lalithamma (1978) indicated that male subjects had higher achievement compared to female subjects. On the other hand Barrick and Stanley Wayne (1980), Chelini (1989) and Mani (1980) indicated in their study female students were better than male students.

On the whole the total sample had a mean achievement score of 211.77, out of 285, which accounted for 74.30 per cent for D.Ed trainees. Though, the trends seem to be good, teacher educators and education planners should plan seriously to improve the social science knowledge of the future teachers, who are going to deal with 21st century generation children.

REFERENCES

Barrick and Stanley, Wayne (1980), Ed.D. University Of The Pacific, Achievement in and Towards High School Mathematics With Respect to Sex and Socio Economic Status, *Dis. Abs.* Nov 1980, Vol. 41, No. 5, P 1989-A

Bhattacharya (1989), *Vividha Shaleglalina Vidyarthigal shala sadhne hagu Abiprerane mathu shikshakarugala samrthya,* Unpublished thesis, Culcutta University, Kolkatta.

Chelini (1989), *Hiriya prathmika Shal Vidyarthigal Mula bootha grhikegal mathu koushalgal sadhne,* unpublished thesis, Mysore University, Mysore.

Lalithamma, K.N. (1978), Some Factors Affecting Achievements of Secondary School Pupils in Mathematics, in Secondary Survey of Research in Education, Ed. By M.B. Buch, M.S. University of Boroda, p. 349

Mani, Mohan, R. (1980), *A Study Of Pupils Achievement With Reference To Basic Understandings In Biology At Pre-university Level,* M.Ed. Dissertation, Un published, University, Mysore

Narasimaiah., (2000), *Vishkapatnam Jileya hathane thraragathi Vidyarthigal kshishanika sadhne malae sambandhitha mano samajika amshagala prbhava ondhu hadhyayana,* Unpublished thesis, Mysore University, Mysore.

Ndabi (1986), Daniel Manwawishwima, Ed. D., The Relationship Between Selected Student Background, School Characteristics and Academic Achievements in Standard Seven Primary School Students In Tanzania, *Dis. Abs.* June 1986, Vol. 46, No. 12, P 3698-A

Paravathamma (1996) *Kiriya prathmika Shal Vidyarthigal Mula bootha grhikegal mathu koushalgal sadhne,* Unpublished thesis, Mysore University, Mysore.

Prabhuswamy, B S (2006). *The social science achievement test for D.Ed trainees.* Mysore: University of Mysore.

Prasannakumar, S. L. (1975), *A study of high school Pupils, Understanding of geometric Concepts,* M.Ed. Disstrtation, Un published, University, Mysore.

CHAPTER

13

Influence of Shyness on Academic Achievement of Children and Adolescents : A Developmental Perspective of Age and Gender

—*Lancy D'Souza, Jayaraju R, Venugopal P N & Natesha N*

ABSTRACT

The present study reports influence of shyness on academic achievement of children and adolescents. A total of 1220 students studying in classes I to X were employed in the present study of which 425 (171 boys + 254 girls) were children and remaining 795 (410 boys+ 385 girls) were adolescents. They were administered Shyness questionnaire (Crozier, 1995) and their academic achievement scores were collected from respective school records. Results revealed that for the overall sample shyness correlated significantly and negatively. Shyness had significant influence over academic achievement. Shyness affected the achievement negatively more for adolescents than children. Only physiological domain of shyness did not influence academic achievement of the sample selected. Treatment aspects of shyness also delineated.

Key words: Shyness, academic achievement, children, and adolescents

Introduction

Shyness is a form of excessive self-focus, a preoccupation with one's thoughts, feelings and physical reactions. Shyness may vary from mild social awkwardness to totally inhibiting social phobia. It may be chronic and dispositional, serving as a personality trait that is central in one's self-definition. Situational shyness involves experiencing the symptoms of shyness in specific social performance situations but not incorporating it into one's self-concept.

The reactions for shyness can occur at any or all of the following levels: cognitive, affective, physiological and behavioral, and may be triggered by a wide variety of arousal cues (Henderson and Zimbardo, 1996).

Shyness in and itself is not a psychological disorder, and therefore doesn't warrant medication. But, if bashfulness prevents a person from functioning, or depression or anxiety accompanies it, then medication can be helpful. A common observation in most of the shyness research is that the consequences of shyness are deeply troubling. Shyness leads to higher levels of anxiety (D'Souza, 2003), decreased levels of happiness (Sreeshakumar, *et al.*, 2007), neurotic tendency and lower academic performance (D'Souza, *et al.*, (2000), lowered performance in physical education students (D'Souza, *et al.*, 1999), lowered self-esteem and decreased self concept (D'Souza, 2005; D'Souza, *et al.*, 2003), increased fear reactions (D'Souza, 2007, D'Souza, *et al.*, 2006) and social and emotional maladjustment (D'Souza & Urs, 2001). Some other studies revealed that (Bell *et al.*, 1994) young adults with high shyness may be at risk for Parkinson disease later in life.

Childhood shyness is strongly related to the complex subtype of social phobia in the general population (Coyne, 1994).

A degree of shyness is normal whenever social expectations are new or ambiguous. Shyness begins to emerge as a problem if it becomes not merely situational but dispositional, so that the child is labeled as shy. The studies related to shyness and academic achievement in India is not very well documented specially on children and adolescents. In the present study an attempt is made to assess the influence of shyness on academic achievement and to see any influence of gender and age on shyness.

METHOD

Samples

Primary and high school children studying in classes I to X were selected for the present study. Of the total 1220 students included in the study 581 were boys and remaining 639 were girls. They were studying in six primary schools and 10 high schools in and around Mysore city. Of the total sample of 1220, they were further classified into children (425) and adolescents (795). Out of 425 children, 171 were boys and 254 girls and in 795 adolescents, 410 were boys and remaining 385 were girls. Stratified random sampling technique was used to select the sample. The sample involved students studying in both Kannada and English medium. Their age varied from 5 to 18 years.

Tool used: Shyness Questionnaire

This questionnaire was developed by Crozier (1995) of University' College of Cardiff. It consists of 26 items and requires the subject to indicate his/her response by ticking "YES/ 'NO" OR 'DON'T KNOW". The items of the questionnaire are based on situations or interactions like performing in front of the class, being made fun of, being told off, having one's photograph taken, and novel situations involving teachers, school-friends interaction and so on. The items pertain to three domains Physical, Psychological and Social. Of the 26 items, shyness is indicated by a 'YES' response for 21 items and a "NO" response for 5 items. Item analysis of the scale using SPSS program resulted in Cronbach's alpha coefficient of 0.817. Further, in the present investigation the questions were further classified into three domains-social, psychological and physiological.

Procedure

The tests were administered to the subjects in groups of 6-10 subjects per group. Data collection was done in single session the session lasted for about 25-30 minutes. First, the researcher, established rapport with the subjects and they were asked to introduce themselves. The purpose of the study was made clear to them. Then they were administered the Shyness questionnaire. They were given appropriate instructions and the questions were read out to them. They were asked to indicate their responses in the respective sheets given to them. Whenever they had doubt in understanding questions, the test administrator made those questions very clear to them in their local language.

Scoring and analysis

For the shyness questionnaire, items worded in the direction of shyness, responses were scored 2 for 'YES', 1 for 'DON'T KNOW' and 0 for 'NO' Scores were reversed for the items worded in the opposite direction. High scores indicate high level of shyness and low scores indicate low level of shyness. To find out the relationship between shyness and academic achievement, product moment correlation technique

Results

Table 13.1 presents results of correlation coefficients between different domains of shyness and academic achievement of the total sample selected. From the table it is clear that shyness correlated negatively and significantly with all the domains and total shyness scores among male sample. However, in females shyness did not correlate with physiological domain of the shyness and correlated significantly and negatively with social domain, psychological domain, and for total shyness scores. When the total sample is considered, except for scores on physiological domain, all the scores on remaining domains and total shyness were correlated significantly and negatively with academic achievement scores.

Table 13.1. Gender-wise and total correlation coefficients of academic achievement with different domains of shyness for the entire sample

Domains of Shyness	Gender		Total
	Male	Female	
Social	–.191**	–.135**	–.159**
Psychological	–.195**	–.089*	–.134**
Physiological	–.095*	.028 NS	–.029 NS
Total shyness	–.233**	–.127**	–.172**
N	581	639	1220
df	579	637	1218

Note: * Sig at .05 level; ** Sig at .01 level; NS - Non-significant.

Table 13.2 presents results of correlation coefficients between different domains of shyness and academic achievement of the children alone. From the table it is clear that shyness correlated negatively and significantly only with physiological domain scores of shyness. All the remaining correlation coefficients obtained for different domains and total shyness scores with academic achievement scores were found to be non-significant.

Table 13.2. Gender-wise and total correlation coefficients of academic achievement with different domains of shyness for children

Domains of Shyness	Gender		Total
	Male	Female	
Social	–.028 NS	–.092 NS	–.077 NS
Psychological	–.145 NS	–.015 NS	–.038 NS
Physiological	.196**	.082 NS	–.002 NS
Total shyness	–.125	–.045 NS	.121 NS
N	171	254	425
df	169	252	423

Note: ** Sig at .01 level; NS - Non-significant

Table 13.3 presents results of correlation coefficients between different domains of shyness and academic achievement of the adolescents alone. From the table it is clear that shyness correlated negatively and significantly with all the domains and total shyness scores among male, female and total sample except for physiological domain.

Table 13.3. Gender-wise and total correlation coefficients of academic achievement with different domains of shyness for adolescents

Domains of Shyness	Gender		Total
	Male	Female	
Social	–.216**	–.234**	–.225**
Psychological	–.202**	–.263**	–.232**
Physiological	–.053 NS	–.057 NS	–.057 NS
Total shyness	–.248**	–.271**	–.258**
N	410	385	795
df	408	383	793

Note: ** Sig at .01 level; NS - Non-significant

Discussion

Main findings of the present study are:

1. For the overall sample shyness correlated significantly and negatively.
2. Shyness had significant influence over academic achievement
3. Shyness affected the achievement negatively more for adolescents than children
4. Only physiological domain of shyness did not influence academic achievement of the sample selected.

Higher levels of shyness resulted in lower academic achievement. The results of the present study with reference to shyness and academic achievement are in partially in agreement with studies done earlier. Lower academic performance (D'Souza *et al.*, 2000) was related to higher levels of shyness in one study; however in another study Shyness did not influence academic achievement. Shyness can also be acquired later on, instigated at times of developmental transition when children face new challenges in their relationships with their peers. For instance, entering the academic and social whirl of elementary school may leave them feeling awkward or inept with their peers. Teachers label them as shy and it sticks; they begin to see themselves that way and act it.

Adolescence is another hurdle that can kick off shyness. Not only are adolescents' bodies changing but their social and emotional playing fields are redefining them. Their challenge is to integrate sexuality and intimacy into a world of relationships that used to be defined only by friendship and relatives (Psychology Today, 1995)

The treatment for shyness is multi-fold. In support of the benefits of the "tend-and-befriend" response, parents and teachers should encourage shy individuals to become more involved in social clubs and activities as a means of establishing a social support network. Service learning programs through the school and other community volunteer activities have been proposed as offering shy individuals non-threatening opportunities for practicing and developing their social skills in a semi-structured social environment while minimizing feelings of social anxiety and self-consciousness (Carducci, 2000). In addition, to help shy individuals in their efforts to make conversation with others, teachers should consider including in the general curriculum information on such topics as the basic elements and protocol for approaching and engaging others in social conversation. Shy individuals tend to use alcohol and drugs to deal with their shyness, parents, teachers, and mental health professionals should also be sensitive to the possibility of substance abuse issues.

REFERENCES

Bell, I. R., Schwartz, G.E., Amend, D., Peterson J.M., Kaszniak, A.W., and Miller, C.S. (1994). Psychological characteristics and subjective intolerance for xenobiotic agents for normal young adults with trait shyness and defensiveness, a Parkinsonian like personality type?. *Journal of Nervous and mental diseases*, 182, 367-374.

Carducci, B. J. (2000). Shyness: The new solution. *Psychology Today*, 33, 38-40.

Crozier, W.R. (1995). Shyness and Self esteem. *British Journal of Educational Psychology*. 65, 85-95.

D'Souza, L. (2003). Influence of Shyness on Anxiety and Academic achievement in High school students *Pakistan Journal of Psychological Research*, 18, 3-4, 109-118.

D'Souza, L. (2005). Shyness/Social Phobia: Influence on self-concept and academic achievement in High school students. Suggested remedial measures. *Artha – a Journal of social sciences*. 4 (1), 23-29.

D' Souza, L (2007). Relationship between shyness and fear among college students. *Journal of Psycho-social Research*, 2, 85-91.

D'Souza, L., & Urs. G. .B. (2001). Effect of shyness on the adjustment of high school students. *Pakistan Journal of Psychological Research*, 16, 3-4, 85-94.

D'Souza, L., Singh, M. & Basavarajappa. (1999). Influence of shyness on performance, personality and intelligence of students of physical education. *Psychological Studies*, 44, 92-94.

D'Souza, L., Urs, G.B., & James.M.S. (2000). Assessment of shyness: Its influence on the personality and academic achievement of High school students. *Indian Journal of Clinical Psychology*, 27, 286-289.

D'Souza, L., Urs. G. .B., & Ramaswamy C. (2003). Relationship of self-esteem with shyness, personality and academic achievement in high-school students. *Artha- a Journal of social sciences*, 1, 228-234.

D'Souza, L., Gowda, H.M. R & Gowda, D.K.S. (2006). Relationship between shyness and fear among High school students. *Pakistan Journal of Psychological Research*, 21, 3-4, 53-60.

Henderson, L & Zimbardo, P.(1996). *Encyclopedia of mental Health*. San Diego: Academic Press.

Psychology Today (1995). *Are you shy*? Sussex: Sussex publishers.

Sreeshakumar, H Y., D'Souza, L & Nagalakshmi, K, 2007. Relationship between shyness and happiness among high school students. *Psychological Studies*, 52, 120-122.

CHAPTER

14

Prevalence of Shyness among Adolescents in Iran : Influence of Gender and Age

—*Kazem Sheriatnia, Lancy D' Zouza*

ABSTRACT

The present study reports the prevalence of shyness among adolescents in Iran, their age ranging from 12 to 18 years. A total of 469 male (n = 234) and female adolescents (n = 235) studying in classes from 6 to 12 from Iran were randomly selected for the study. They were further classified on the basis of age as early and late adolescents. They were administered. The Shyness Assessment Test (SAT) developed by D'Souza (2006) in one setting. Data on shyness was collected on three domains-cognitive/affective, action-oriented and physiological, including total shyness scores. Of the total sample studies, 16% of them were found to have high levels of shyness, followed by 48.8% low and remaining 35.2 per cent of them had medium level of shyness. Iranian adolescents had higher shyness in cognitive/affective and physiological domains compared to action-oriented domain Female subjects expressed more shyness than male adolescents in total shyness. Early adolescents were shyer than late adolescents. Further, the treatment aspects of shyness are also discussed.[2]

Key Words: Shyness, adolescents, Iran

Introduction

Shyness is a form of excessive self-focus, a preoccupation with one's thoughts, feelings and physical reactions. Shyness may vary from mild social awkwardness to totally inhibiting social phobia. Some inhibited children move from shy teenagers to adults and are often extremely self-conscious, so much so that they may painfully and ruthlessly analyze their behavior after a social interaction, as unhappy incidents that lead them to avoid interactions with others in the future. The reactions for shyness can occur at any of the following levels: cognitive, affective, physiological and behavioral, and may be triggered by a wide variety of arousal cues. (Henderson and Zimbardo, 1996). Situational shyness involves experiencing the symptoms of shyness in specific social performance situations but not incorporating it into one's self-concept.

The percentage of adults in the United States reporting that they are chronically shy, so much so that it presents a problem in their lives, had been reported at 40%±3%, since the early 1970's. The research indicates that the percentage of self-reported shyness has escalated gradually in the last decade to nearly 50% (48.7% ± 2%). The National Co-morbidity Survey in 1994 revealed a lifetime prevalence of social phobia of 13.3%, making it the third most prevalent psychiatric disorder. Most referrals to shyness clinics meet criteria for generalized social phobia, and many meet criteria for avoidant personality disorder. Although it has been suggested that there is a greater heterogeneity of presentation among shy people than among those diagnosable with generalized social phobia, both shy and those with generalized social phobias demonstrate similar difficulties with meeting people, initiating and maintaining conversations, deepening intimacy, interacting in small groups in authoritative situations, and with self-assertion. Chronically shy individuals frequently have obsessive and /or paranoid tendencies. Shy individuals would prefer to be with others but are over restrained by the experience of shyness (Brophy, 1996).

Research in the United States typically indicates that shyness is highest among Asian Americans and lowest among Jewish Americans. This difference prompted efforts to assess shyness across diverse cultures. Using culturally sensitive adaptations of the Stanford Shyness Inventory, colleagues in 8 countries administered the inventory to groups of 18 to 21 year olds, usually in college or work settings. The overall pattern of results indicates a universality of shyness since a large proportion of participants in all cultures reported experiencing shyness to a considerable degree- from a low of 31 per cent in Israel to a high of 57 per cent in Japan and 55 per cent in Taiwan. In Mexico, Germany and New Found land, shyness was more similar to the 40 per cent U.S. statistics. Other data from this cross-cultural research shows that the majority in each country perceive many more negative than positive consequences of being shy, and 60 per cent or more consider that shyness is a problem (except for Israel where the figure is 42 per cent). There is no gender difference in reported shyness, but men have typically learned tactics for concealing their shyness because it is considered a feminine trait in most countries. In Mexico, males are less likely than females to report shyness (Henderson and Zimbardo, 1996). A recent study by Natasha and D'Souza (2007) indicated that in India, 26.2 per cent of the children showed high levels of shyness, followed by 36.6 per cent moderate and remaining 37.3 per cent of the children showed low levels of shyness.

A common observation in most of the shyness research is that the consequences of shyness are deeply troubling. Shyness leads to higher levels of anxiety (D'Souza, 2003), decreased levels of happiness (Sreeshakumar *et al.*, 2007), neurotic tendency and lower academic performance (D'Souza *et al.*, 2000), lowered performance in physical education students (D'Souza, *et al.*, 1999), lowered self-esteem and decreased self concept (D'Souza, 2005; D'Souza, *et al.*, 2003), increased fear reactions (D'Souza, *et al.*,) and social and emotional maladjustment (D'Souza and Urs, 2001). Some other studies revealed that (Bell *et al*, 1994) young adults with high shyness may be at risk for Parkinson disease later in life.

The studies related to prevalence of shyness in Iran are not very well documented, especially among adolescents. A thorough search of literature did not yield fruitful results on the prevalence of shyness in Iran. In the present study an attempt is made to assess the prevalence of shyness in various domains like cognitive/affective, physiological and action oriented and to see any influence of gender and age on shyness among adolescents in Iran.

Method

Sample: High school and pre university adolescents studying in classes 6 to 12 in Iran were selected for the present study. Of the total 469 students included in the study 234 of them were male students and remaining 235 were females. They were further classified into early and late adolescents (respective numbers 319 and 150). The sample was selected from Gonbad-e-kavoos city of Iran. Stratified Random sampling technique was used to select the sample.

Measures: Shyness Assessment Test (D'Souza, 2006)

The shyness assessment test was developed by D'Souza (2006) of Maharaja's College, University of Mysore. It consists of 54 items and requires the subject to indicate his/her response by marking Yes, or No. The items in the test pertain to three domains of shyness - Cognitive/Affective, Physiological and Action oriented. Item analysis of the scale using SPSS program resulted in Cronbach's alpha coefficient of 0.7119 for the Iranian population. Further, the scale had sufficiently high validity.

Procedure

The tests were administered to the subjects in groups of 6-10 subjects per group. Data collection was done in a single session the session lasted for about 25-30 minutes. First, the researcher, established rapport with the subjects and they were asked to introduce themselves. The purpose of the study was made clear to them. Then they were administered the Shyness questionnaire. They were given appropriate instructions and the questions were read out to them. They were asked to indicate their responses in the respective sheets given to them. They were instructed to answer 'yes' or 'no' for each question. Whenever they had doubts in understanding questions, the test administrator made those questions clear to them in their local language.

Scoring and Analysis

For the shyness questionnaire, items worded in the direction of shyness, responses were scored 3 for 'high', 2 for 'moderate', 1 for 'low' and 0 for 'NO". High scores indicate high level of shyness and low scores indicate low level of shyness. Lastly, the scores were cumulated under 3 domains-cognitive/affective, action oriented and physiological domain.

Once the scores were graded into low, medium and high levels, the frequencies under each level were subjected to chi-square test for various domains separately and to see the association between gender and age with shyness levels, contingency coefficient test was applied. All the statistical calculations were done through SPSS for windows (version 15, Evaluation version).

Results

Table 14.1 presents analysis and test statistics of shyness levels for various domains by demographic variables of gender and age.

Shyness Levels

(*a*) Total shyness : Of the 469 students studied in the present sample 16.0 per cent of them were found to have high levels of shyness, 35.2 per cent of them had medium levels of shyness and remaining 48.8 per cent of the sample had low levels of shyness. Chi-square test revealed a significant difference (χ^2=76.57; P<. 000) between frequencies of low, medium and high levels of shyness.

(*b*) Cognitive/affective Dimension : In this dimension, 47.3% of the sample had low levels of shyness, 35.2% of them medium and remaining 17.5% of them had high levels of shyness and chi-square test revealed a significant (χ^2=63.41; P<. 000) difference between these frequencies.

(*c*) Physiological dimension : As far as the physiological dimension is considered, a majority of the sample had low levels of shyness (55.4%), 24.5% of them had medium levels of shyness and remaining 16.2% of them had high levels of shyness and when chi-square test was applied to various frequencies a significant difference was observed (χ^2=108.49; P<.000).

(*d*) Action-oriented dimension : In this dimension, 59.3% of the sample had low levels of shyness, 35.2 5 of them medium and remaining 17.5% of them had high levels of shyness and chi-square test revealed a significant (χ^2=63.41; P<.000) difference between these frequencies.

Gender and Shyness Levels

A significant association was observed between gender and levels of shyness as the obtained contingency coefficient value of 0.159 was found to be statistically significant (P<.008). From the frequencies and percentages it is clear that female adolescents had significantly higher levels of shyness (30.2%) as against male adolescents (1.7%).

Age Groups and Shyness Levels

As far as the age groups and shyness levels are considered, a significant association was observed between age groups and shyness levels as the obtained contingency coefficient value of 0.311 was found to be significant at .000 level. From Table 14.1 it is clear that in high shyness levels, early adolescents showed higher levels of shyness (19.1%) than late adolescents (9.3%).

Discussion

- The main findings of the present study are:
- On the whole 16.0% of them were found to have high levels of shyness, 35.2% of them had medium levels of shyness and remaining 48.8% of the sample had low levels of shyness.

- Comparatively Iranian adolescents had higher shyness in cognitive/affective and physiological domains compared to action-oriented domains.
- Female adolescents had higher levels of shyness compared to male adolescents.
- Early adolescents had higher levels of shyness than late adolescents.

Rubin, *et al.*, (1990) theorized that certain children, from infancy, are predisposed towards behavioral inhibition. Such wariness and inhibition results in a failure to establish normative peer relations, which leads to consequent failure to develop appropriate social skills. This lack of social skills then leads to further anxiety, insecurity, and withdrawal that is likely to result in the child receiving a negative reputation among his or her peers, eventually culminating in peer rejection. Many pre-school, school going children and adolescents, show initial wariness on meeting a stranger, have doubts about one's ability to contribute effectively to social encounters and the belief that others will negatively evaluate one's action/behavior may contribute to the withdrawal behavior and social anxieties that characterize shyness or social phobia (Crozier, 1995). As explained by Bruch *et al.*, (1995), inhibition and withdrawal is often perceived as deviant by the peer group and responded to by rejection, isolation, or bullying.

In the present study almost 51% of the adolescents showed either high or medium levels of shyness. This is more or less in agreement with the prevalence of shyness rates in Asian countries like Taiwan, Japan and India. However, the prevalence of shyness in Iran is high when compared to countries like U.S., U.K. and the western countries. The reason could be, Iran is being a conventional society compared to other countries like U.S., U.K. and others. It should be mentioned here that the culture of Gonbad-e-Kavoos city is different from Tehran as it is the biggest city in the Middle

Table 14.1. Frequency and percent analysis and test statistics on various domains of shyness by demographic variables of gender and age

Variables/ Domains		Levels of shyness			Statistical	
		Medium	High	Low	Total	Inference
Total skyness	Frequency	229	165	75	469	χ^2=76.57; P<. 000
	Per cent	48.8	35.2	16.0	100.0	(HS)
Cognitive/affective	Frequency	222	165	82	469	χ^2=63.41; P<. 000
	Per cent	47.3	35.2	17.5	100.0	(HS)
Physiological	Frequency	260	125	84	469	χ^2=108.49; P<. 000
	Per cent	55.4	26.7	17.9	100.0	(HS)
Action-oriented	Frequency	278	115	76	469	χ^2=146.90; P<. 000
	Per cent	59.3	24.5	16.2	100.0	(HS)
Gender	Male Frequency	138	92	4	234	CC=0.159; P<. 008
	Per cent	59.0	39.3	1.7	100.0	
	Female Frequency	91	73	71	235	(HS)
	Per cent	38.7	31.1	30.2	100.0	
Adolescence	Frequency Early	164	94	61	319	CC=0.311; P<. 000
	Per cent	51.4	29.5	19.1	100.0%	
	Late	65	71	14	150	(HS)
	Per cent	43.3	47.3	9.3	100.0%	

Note: χ^2=Chi-square; HS-Highly significant; CC-Contingency coefficient

East. Whatever the situation may be, the culture of the Asian continent has different effects on human behavior including shyness when compared to other continents, which follow exclusively western culture.

Further, as age increased, shyness decreased linearly. In early adolescence age, immediately after puberty, the individual would undergo a rapid physical and psychological transformation, which is not very pleasant for the pre-pubescent, and may increase the level of shyness in that particular age group. As expected, female adolescents showed more shyness than male adolescents, since they are more restricted. The changes, which they undergo both physically and psychologically, are more prominent than male adolescents, and could be the reasons for higher levels of shyness. Several studies are in agreement with these findings (D'Souza & Urs, 2007).

The treatment for shyness is multi-fold ranging from medication to simple behavioural therapies. Psychotherapies apply to any difficulty in the mental or psychological arena, but some therapists dedicate themselves more to some of them, as is the case of shyness and the anxiety disorders. Cognitive behavior therapies aimed at treating shyness were found to be very effective than traditional therapies (Shariatnia and D'Souza, 2007). Equally effective was the cognitive behaviour group therapy (Shariatnia and D'Souza, 2007). There are dozens of approaches, but few of them are based on theoretical models and/or consistent experiments. In addition, to help shy individuals in their efforts to make conversation with others, teachers should consider including in the general curriculum information on such topics as the basic elements and protocol for approaching and engaging others in social conversation. Shy individuals tend to use alcohol and drugs to deal with their shyness. Parents, teachers, and mental health professionals should also be sensitive to the possibility of substance abuse issues.

REFERENCES

Bell, I. R., Schwartz, G.E., Amend, D., Peterson J.M., Kaszniak, A.w., & Miller, C.S. (1994). Psychological characteristics and subjective intolerance for xenobiotic agents for normal young adults with trait shyness and defensiveness, a Parkinsonian like personality type?. Journal of Nervous and mental diseases, 182, 367-374.

Brophy, J. (1996). *Teaching problem students.* New York: Guilford.

Bruch, M.A., Hamer, R.J., & Heimberg, R.G. (1995). Shyness and public self-consciousness: Additive or interactive relation with social interaction. *Journal of Personality, 63, 1,* 47-63.

Crozier, W.R. (1995). Shyness and Self esteem. *British Journal of Educational Psychology.* 65, 85-95.

D'Souza, L. (2003). Influence of Shyness on Anxiety and Academic achievement in High school students *Pakistan Journal of Psychological Research,* 18, 3-4, 109-118.

D'Souza, L. (2005). Shyness/Social Phobia: Influence on self-concept and academic achievement in High school students. Suggested remedial measures. *Artha – a Journal of social sciences.* 4 (1), 23-29.

D'Souza, L. (2006*). Shyness Assessment Test.* Mysore: University of Mysore.

D'Souza, L. & Urs. G. .B. (2001). Effect of shyness on the adjustment of high school students. *Pakistan Journal of Psychological Research,* 16, 3-4, 85-94.

D'Souza, L. & Urs, G.B. (2007). Assessment of shyness among adolescent students studying in rural and urban areas. *Asia Pacific Review of Rural and Tribal Issues,* 1, 10-14.

D'Souza, L., Singh, M. & Basavarajappa. (1999). Influence of shyness on performance, personality and intelligence of students of physical education. *Psychological Studies,* 44, 92-94.

D'Souza, L. Urs, G.B., & James.M.S. (2000). Assessment of shyness: Its influence on the personality and academic achievement of High school students. *Indian Journal of Clinical Psychology, 27,* 286-289.

D'Souza, L. Urs. G. .B., & Ramaswamy C. (2003). Relationship of self-esteem with shyness, personality and academic achievement in high-school students. *Artha- a Journal of social sciences,* 1, 228-234.

D'Souza, L., Gowda, H.M. R & Gowda, D.K.S. (2006). Relationship between shyness and fear among High school students. *Pakistan Journal of Psychological Research,* 21, 3-4, 53-60.

Henderson, L & Zimbardo, P.(1996). *Encyclopedia of mental Health.* San Diego: Academic Press.

Natesha, N. & D'Souza, L. (2007). Prevalence of shyness among children: a developemental perspective of age and gender, *Asian Journal of Development Matters,* 1, 55-60.

Rubin, K.H., LeMare, L.J., Lollis, S. (1990) "Social withdrawal in childhood: Developmental pathways to peer rejection" In: Asher, S.R., Coie, J.D. eds., Peer rejection in childhood. Cambridge studies in social and emotional development, Cambridge University Press, NY, pp. 217-249.

Shariatnia, K.& D'Souza, L. (2007). Effectiveness of Cognitive Behaviour Group therapy on shyness among Adolescent in Iran. *Psychological Studies*, 52, 372-376.

Sreeshakumar, H Y., D'Souza, L & Nagalakshmi, K, 2007. Relationship between shyness and happiness among high school students. *Psychological Studies*, 52, 121-123.

CHAPTER

15

Nutritional Status and Cognitive Performance of School Children form Mysore Taluk, Karnataka

—*Shekhara Naik R & Jamuna Prakash*

ABSTRACT

Malnutrition in Indian children is more or less 50 per cent, about a half of the children are underweight and 40 per cent are stunted but there is no gender bias with respect to nutritional status of females (NNMB Report-2000). Malnutrition has significantly correlations on cognitive development in childhood that reduces the work capacity (Wachs, 1995). Children from urban and rural do have little difference with socioeconomic status but nutritional both area children have one or other kind of malnutrition on deficient of nutrients in their diet. Therefore to assess the nutritional status and cognitive performance of schoolchildren from Mysore taluk was designed. The study recruited 1093 children, 575 male and 518 female for the cognitive performance (RCPM) test and measured the nutritional status according to the weight for height (waterlow). Study revels that, cognitive test scores among children of normal nutritional status scored 8.6, 11.44, 15.46, 20.55 and 7.93, 10.72, 14.08, 21.27 whereas malnourished status children scored 10, 10.75, 13.19, 15.77 and 7.64, 9.826, 12.34, 13.42 male and female respectively in the following age groups 4-6, 6-8, 8-10, 10 and above. Normal nutritional status of both sex children showed higher cognitive score than the malnourished children in all the age group, as both normal and malnourished status children of male gender had upper hand than the female. As the children age proceeds the cognitive scoring increased among both sex, male children were shown higher cognitive scoring than the female, the better nutritional status children shown superior cognitive scores than malnourished.

Introduction

School age is the most active stage of growth and lots more activities performed during this age. Malnutrition in Indian children is more or less 50 percent, about a half of the children are underweight and 40 per cent are stunted. There is no gender bias with respect to nutritional status of females (NNMB Report-2000). Recent studies indicated the relations between indexes of malnutrition and development is inconsistent. The significant correlations between Anthropometric measures thought to be indexes of chronic mild malnutrition and measures of cognitive development in childhood. Modest associations were also demonstrated between measures of Anthropometry (particularly weight) and activity (work capacity) (Wachs, 1995). Urban packets of children population are look like better in health but still they need attention towards better nutrition; improve their nutritional status that intern perform better in the cognitive and scholastic developmental activities, the rural packet of the population is socioeconomic and health is worst than urban areas. Therefore to assess the nutritional status and cognitive performance of schoolchildren from urban and rural areas Mysore is designed.

Methodology

Thousand school children were recruited in the study; 500 each from urban and rural area and there are between 4 to 10+ years age groups studying in 1st standard to 4th standard. The selection of schools and subjects was done in accordance with random sampling technique from both areas. Selected children Anthropometry observation was recorded with the help of standard measuring tools; nutritional classification done according to water lows qualitative cut off for the nutritional status. Each children cognitive performances of was recorded with the help of Raven's color progressive matrices (RCPM).

Raven's Colour Progressive Matrices

Raven's Colored Progressive Matrices have been used extensively as a "culture-fair" test of intelligence. They measure the ability to reason and solve problems. The battery of test book consisting of 3 sets i.e. A, Ab and B. each test set consisting of 12 visual problem in the form figures and the subject is shown a visual pattern with a missing section and is required to select 1 of 6 alternative sections to complete the overall pattern (each problem having six answer figure, among six one of figure solves the problem) as the test proceeds, the problems become progressively more difficult. The test is not timed, and the subject continues until satisfied with the choice made. The score is the number of correct items selected. Each correct answer were considered scored with one; finally total score of each child from three set was considered for Raven's classification; it was done based on percentile of score acquired within the age group. The percentile was calculated by taking the score of the within each age group; maximum score of the within the group was considered as cent percentile and calculated rest of the score for interpretation and reporting (Ravens CPM -1998). The data was statistically analyzed for the signification by SPSS10 version package.

Results

According to the Waterlow's classification the children were classified as normal and malnourished (stunted, wasted and both form of malnutrition were combined), the average cognitive (rcpm) score among nutritionally normal children of Mysore taluk were 8.37, 11.08, 14.85, 20.82 and 12.40 among 4-6, 6-8, 8-10, 10 & above and overall age groups respectively (Table 14.1).

Table 16.1. Nutritional status and cognitive performance (RCPM score) of school children according to Waterlow's classification from Mysore taluk

Age group		Water Low Classification					
		Normal		Mal nourished		Over all	
	Sex	Mean	SD	Mean	SD	Mean	SD
4-6	Male	8.6765	4.8513	10.0000	5.0166	8.8889	4.8708
	Female	7.9348	4.9008	7.6471	3.5697	7.8571	4.5538
	Total	8.3772	4.8634	8.6667	4.3417	8.4375	4.7463
6-8	Male	11.4444	5.3258	10.7500	5.4432	11.3320	5.3400
	Female	10.7233	4.7664	9.8261	4.3783	10.5595	4.7023
	Total	11.0847	5.0613	10.2558	4.8946	10.9419	5.0379
8-10	Male	15.4655	8.0753	13.1957	8.2748	14.9909	8.1510
	Female	14.0809	7.3907	12.3409	6.8095	13.6556	7.2731
	Total	14.8581	7.8005	12.7778	7.5636	14.3900	7.7871
10+	Male	20.5556	9.7873	15.7778	9.1348	18.9630	9.6734
	Female	21.2727	7.1287	13.4167	7.3911	17.1739	8.1556
	Total	20.8276	8.7426	14.4286	8.0534	18.1400	8.9625
Overall	Male	12.8908	7.2036	12.1204	7.1783	12.7461	7.1989
	Female	11.8371	6.3879	10.8067	5.8661	11.6004	6.2813
	Total	12.4053	6.8561	11.4317	6.5418	12.2031	6.8006

The mean cognitive (RCPM) score by the malnourished children were found with 8.66, 10.25, 12.77, 13.4 and 11.43 among 4-6, 6-8, 8-10, 10 and above and over all year's age groups respectively; it indicated that the malnourished children cognitive (rcpm) score was less than the normal children in all the age group except 4-6 year age group. In accordance with the gender; male children cognitive score was 8.6, 11.44, 15.46, 20.55 and 12.89 but female children score was 7.93, 10.72, 14.08, 21.27 and 11.83 among 4-6, 6-8, 8-10, 10 and above and over all age group were shown in normal cases, whereas malnourished male children score was 10, 10.75, 13.19, 15.77 and 12.12 whereas female children score was 7.64, 9.826, 12.34,13.42 and 10.43 among 4-6, 6-8, 8-10, 10 and above and over all age groups in the study area; the finding shown that, normal nutritional status of both sex children shown higher cognitive score than the malnourished children in all the age group, as both normal and malnourished nutritional status children of male gender had upper hand than the female gender except in 4-6 years age group. All together nutritional status children's mean cognitive (rcpm) score of male was 8.88, 11.33, 14.99, 18.96 and 12.74 whereas female were with 7.85, 10.55, 13.65, 17.17 and 11.60 among 4-6, 6-8, 8-10, 10 and above and over all years age groups; in all the age group male children cognitive score was greater than the female children. On combine both gender cognitive (rcpm) score was 8.43, 10.94, 14.39, 18.14 and 12.20 among 4-6, 6-8, 8-10, 10 and above and overall. The finding clearly indicated that, as children age proceeds the cognitive (rcpm) scoring increased among both sex with significant difference, male children were shown higher cognitive (rcpm) scoring than the female, the children of better nutritional status associated with superior cognitive scores than malnourished.

Discussion

School children of the urban and rural Mysore were assessed for their nutritional status and cognitive performance. The cognitive performance and normal nutritional status of the school children from Mysore taluk, were assessed with cognitive performance test, the mean score of the test to be 8.6, 11.44, 15.46, 20.55 and 12.89 score among male and 7.93, 10.72, 14.08, 21.27 and 11.83 among female children of 4-6, 6-8, 8-10, 10 and above and over all years age group. The malnourished status of male children cognitive scores are 10, 10.75, 13.19, 15.77 and 12.12 and female children score 7.64, 9.826, 12.34, 13.42 and 10.43 among 4-6, 6-8, 8-10, 10 & above and over all years age groups in the study area; the finding shown that, normal nutritional status of both sex children shown higher cognitive score than the malnourished children in all the age group, as both normal and malnourished nutritional status children of male gender had upper hand than the female gender except in 4-6 years age group. All together nutritional status children's mean cognitive score of male was 8.88, 11.33, 14.99, 18.96 and 12.74 whereas female were with 7.85, 10.55, 13.65, 17.17 and 11.60 among 4-6, 6-8, 8-10, 10 and above and over all years age groups; in all the age group male children cognitive score was greater than the female children. On combine both gender cognitive score 8.43, 10.94, 14.39, 18.14 and 12.20 among 4-6, 6-8, 8-10, 10 and above and overall years age group. The finding clearly indicated that, as children age proceeds the cognitive (rcpm) scoring increased among both sex with significant difference, male children were shown higher cognitive (rcpm) scoring than the female, the children of better nutritional status associated with superior cognitive scores than malnourished. The cognitive performance of children is associated with nutritional status of children shown significant, the relations between indexes of malnutrition and development is inconsistent; significant correlations between Anthropometric measures thought to be indexes of chronic mild malnutrition and measures of cognitive development in childhood, modest associations were also demonstrated between measures of Anthropometry and activity (Wachs. 1995).

Niehaus *et al.*, (2002) the early child hood diarrhea is correlated with reduced cognitive function among children, Pollit *et al.*, (1998), poor nutrition among schoolchildren has adverse effects on attention and memory processes effects that may be mediated by metabolic changes in plasma glucose regulation in the brain.

Conclusion

School children of the growing stage, the physical activities are more and pressure on mental activity too follows. Cognitive performance of the children is the active development of brain that promotes the brain cells to cognize the events observed and retain in the memory to recall depending on the circumstances. The cognitive performance associated with nutritional status of the children, as children age proceeds the cognitive performance increase among both sex with significant difference, male children were shown higher cognitive scoring than the female, the children of better nutritional status associated with superior cognitive scores than malnourished. Therefore, the cognitive performance of the children is associated with the nutritional status of children.

REFERENCES

Niehaus, Mark D., Sean R. Moore, Peter D. Patrick, Lori L. Derr, Breyette Lorntz, Aldo A. Lima, and Richard L. Guerrant, (2002) Early Childhood Diarrhea Is Associated With Diminished Cognitive Function 4 To 7 Years Later In Children In A Northeast Brazilian Shantytown. *Am. J. Trop. Med.* Hyg., 66(5), 590–593.

NNMB Survey report, NIN, ICMR 2000.

Pollitt Ernesto, Santiago Cueto, and Enrique R Jacoby (1998), Fasting and cognition in well- and undernourished schoolchildren: a review of three experimental studies. *Am J Clin Nutr* 67(suppl): 779S–84S.

Raven, J., Raven, J. C. and J .H Court (1998). Raven Manual: Section 2, *Coloured progressive matrices*, CPM49-51, Oxford Psychologists Press, Oxford.

Wachs T.D. (1995) Relation of mild-to-moderate malnutrition to human development: correlational studies. *J. Nutr.* 125: 2245S-2254S.

CHAPTER

16

Influence of Academic Performance, Gender and Area on Emotional Intelligence of Young Adults

—Madhu Ramdurg & K. Rajasekhara Reddy

ABSTRACT

The present study reports the influence of academic performance, gender and area on emotional intelligence of young adults. A total of 320 (189 male + 131 female) young adults studying in urban and rural areas were randomly selected for the study. They were administered with Emotional Intelligence Scale developed by Hyde, Pathe and Dhar (2001). Statistical techniques like 't' test and One-Way ANOVA. Results revealed that male and female young adults had statistically similar emotional intelligence scores. Area-wise comparison revealed that young adults from rural areas were more emotionally intelligent than urban young adults. However, academic performance of the young adults did not influence emotional intelligence of the young adults.

Key words: Emotional Intelligence, Academic performance, and young adults.

Introduction

Emotional intelligence refers to the capacity for recognizing our own feelings and those of others, for motivating ourselves and for motivating emotions well in us and in our relationships. It is the ability to perceive accurately, appraise and express emotions, generate feelings that facilitate thoughts and an ability to regulate emotions to promote growth. It is also defined as an array of non-cognitive capabilities competencies and skills that influence one's ability to succeed in coping with environmental demands and pressure. According to Goleman (1995), emotional intelligence has five elements: self-awareness, self-regulation, motivation, empathy, and social skills. With the dawn of 21st century, the human mind added a new dimension, which is now being held responsible more for success than intelligence. This is termed as emotional intelligence and is measured as EQ (emotional quotient). Over the past several years the term emotional intelligence has received much attention as a factor that is useful in understanding and predicting individual's performance at work, at home, at school etc. The concept of emotional intelligence was first introduced by Salovey and Mayer in the early 1990's and made popular by Daniel Goleman with publication of his book: *"Why it can matter more than IQ"* in 1995. Emotional intelligence is the capacity to create positive outcomes in relationships with others and with oneself. According to Mayer and Salovey (1993), emotional intelligence is the ability to monitor one's own and others' feelings and emotions, to discriminate among them, and to use this information to guide one's thinking and actions. Thus, emotional intelligence is an umbrella term that captures a broad collection of interpersonal and intrapersonal skills. Interpersonal skills consist of the ability to understand the feelings of others, empathise, maintain and develop interpersonal relationships and above all our sense of social responsibility. On the other hand, intrapersonal skills comprise of the ability to understand one's own motivation. Emotional intelligence plays a key role in determining life success. It becomes more and more important as people progress up the career ladder of their life. Emotions are our feelings, hence, emotional intelligence is our life. Emotional intelligence does not only measure emotions or intelligence. What it does is to open up a new way of looking at how our thinking and behavior could be seen intelligent.

Review Literature

Review of literature on emotional indicated following aspects. Harrod and Scheer (2005) found that emotional intelligence levels were positively related to females, parents' education and household income. Amirtha and Kadhiravan (2006) found that gender, age and qualification influenced the emotional intelligence of schoolteachers. The main aim of education is the all round holistic development of the students. Devi and Uma (2005) found that the parental education, occupation had significant and positive relationship with dimensions of emotional intelligence like social regard, social responsibility, impulse control and optimism. McDowelle and Bell (1997) found that lack of emotional intelligence skills lowered team effectiveness and created dysfunctional team interactions and most effective performers lost the best networking skills.

Tapia and Marsh (2001) found an overall significant main effect of gender and two-way interaction of gender - GPA on emotional intelligence. Annaraja and Jose (2005) found that rural and urban B.Ed., trainees did not differ in their self-awareness, self-control, social skills and emotional intelligence. Though studies are done in northern region of India, we do not find many studies in the south, especially on young adults. The present study aims at studying the influence of academic performance, gender and locality on emotional intelligence of young adults in urban and rural areas of young adults.

Sample

A total of 320 students were included in the present study. In the total sample there were 189 male participants and 131 were female participants. Of the 320 sample selected from the study, 130 were from rural area, and remaining 190 were from urban area. The age of young adults ranged from 19 to 23 years.

Tool Employed

The Emotional Intelligence Scale (EIS) developed by Hyde, Pathe and Dhar (2001) was used to measure EI. This instrument is made of 34 items and provides an indicator of the levels of perceived EI. The sub factors of the scale included self-awareness, empathy, self-motivation, emotional stability, managing relations, self-development, value orientation, commitment, and altruistic behavior. Respondents are asked to rate their degree of agreement of the items on a 5-point Likert-type scale ranging from 1 (strongly disagree) to 5 (strongly agree). The reliability of the scale was determined by calculating reliability coefficient on a sample of 200 subjects by split-half method and was found to be .88. The validity of the scale assessed through content validity, which was sufficiently high.

Procedure

The tests were administered in a group of 3-5 subjects in a single session for about 25-30 minutes. Initially, rapport was established with the subjects and they were asked to introduce themselves. The purpose of the study was made clear to them. Then they were administered the emotional intelligence scale. They were given appropriate instructions and the questions were read out to them. They were asked to indicate their responses in the respective sheets given to them. Whenever the meaning of certain words was not clear to the students, they were made clear to them by one of the test administrators. Later the questionnaires were scored according to the manual and a master chart was prepared for statistical analysis.

Once the scores were arranged, they were subjected to statistical analysis like Independent samples 't' test and One-way ANOVA using SPSS for Windows (version 11.5) software. To see the gender and area difference 't' tests were employed and to see difference between academic performance levels one-way ANOVA was employed.

Results

Table 16.1. Mean total emotional intelligence scores of male and female young adults hailing from urban and rural areas with different levels of academic performance and test statistics

	Variables	Mean	S.D	Statistical Inference	Significance
Gender	Male	136.74	13.61	't'=0.933	P=.352 (NS)
	Female	135.35	12.21		
Area	Urban	132.69	12.49	't'=14.827	P=. 000 (HS)
	Rural	140.75	12.42		
Academic performance	Distinction	139.48	10.67	F=1.573	P=. 181 (NS)
	I Class	135.04	13.85		
	II Class	136.04	12.21		
	III class	140.40	11.44		
	Fail	134.15	10.67		

Gender and Emotional Intelligence

Gender comparisons revealed that male and female young adults had statistically equal emotional intelligence scores (136.74 and 135.35 respectively). Further, t test revealed a non-significant (t=.933; P=.352) difference between mean scores of male and female young adults.

Area and Emotional Intelligence

Surprisingly, rural young adults (mean 140.75) had higher emotional intelligence scores compared to urban young adults (mean 132.69) and 't' test revealed a significant difference (t=14.827; P=.000) between mean scores of rural and urban young adults.

Academic Performance and Emotional Intelligence

Academic performance of young adults did not have significant influence over emotional intelligence of the young adults as the obtained F value of 1.573 was found to be non-significant (P=.181). In other words, young adults having different levels of academic performance from distinction to fail had similar emotional intelligence scores.

Discussion

The main findings of the present study are:

1. Male and female young adults had similar emotional intelligence scores.
2. Rural young adults were more emotionally intelligent than urban young adults.
3. Academic performance of the young adults did not influence the emotional intelligence scores.

The results of the study are in quite contrary with the other studies. The findings of studies reported by Bhosle (1999), King (1999), Sutarso (1999), Wing and Love (2001) and Singh (2002) found females to have higher emotional intelligence than that of males. However, study by Chu (2002) revealed that males have higher level of emotional intelligence than that of females. The present study did not reveal differences between male and female young adolescents.

As far the relationship between academic achievement and emotional intelligence is conodered, the opinions are diverse. Pool, the senior editor of Educational Leadership, stated in an article she wrote in 1997 that emotional well being is a predictor of success in academic achievement and job success among others. Finnegan (1998) argues that schools should help students learn the abilities underlying emotional intelligence. Possessing those abilities, or even some of them, "can lead to achievement from the formal education years of the child and adolescent to the adult's competency in being effective in the workplace and in society". In January 2000, Coover & Murphy conducted a study that examined the relationship between self-identity and academic persistence and achievement in a counter-stereotypical domain. The study revealed that the higher the self-concept and self-schema, the more positive the self-descriptions, the better the academic achievement at 18. The study also showed that self-identity improves through social interaction and communication with others, which would enhance achievement.

One important aspect of the present study was that rural young adults had higher Emotional intelligence compared to urban young adults. The probable reasons would be that the rural young adults can understand, empathize and ability to deal effectively than urban young adults.

This study is only a starting point in the area of emotional intelligence. Emotional intelligence requires much more in depth research work, especially in India. An understanding of all these aspects will provide a better insight into the success equation required in life. This research study will prove beneficial for psychologists, educators, parents, counselors etc. for providing better knowledge about this vital component of success and its important predictors.

REFERENCES

Amirtha, M. and Kadheravan, S. (2006) : Influence of personality on the emotional intelligence of teachers. *Edu Tracks* 5, 12, 25-29.

Annaraja, P. and Jose, S. (2005) : Emotional intelligence of B. Ed. trainees. *Research and Reflections in Education* 2, 8-16.

Bhosle, S. (1999) : Gender differences in EQ.

Chu, J. (2002): Boys development. *Reader's Digest* 94-95.

Coover, G. E., & Murphy, S. T. (2000) : The communicated self. *Human communication research,* 26(1), 125-148.

Culver, D. (1998) : A Review of Emotional Intelligence by Daniel Goleman: Implications for Technical Education.

Devi, U.L. and Uma, M. (2005) : Relationship between the dimensions of emotional intelligence of adolescents and certain personal social variables. *Indian Psychological Review,* 64, 01, 11-20.

Dhull, I. and Mangal, S. (2005) : Emotional intelligence its significance for school teachers. *Edu Tracks,* 4, 11, 14-16.

Finegan, J. E. (1998) : Measuring emotional intelligence: where we are today. (Clearinghouse No. TM029315)_Montgomery, AL: Auburn University at Montgomery, School of Education. (ERIC Document Reproduction Service No. ED426087).

Harrod and Scheer (2005) : An exploration of adolescent emotional intelliegence in relation to demographic characteristics. *Adolescence*, 40, 503-512.

Goleman, D. (1995) : *Emotional intelligence: why it can matter more than IQ*. New York: Bantam Books.

King,M. Measurement of differences in emotional intelligence of preservice educational leadership students and practicing administrators as measured by the multifactor emotional intelligence scale. Dissertation Abstracts International, 60(3): 606.

Mayer, J. D., & Salovey, P. (1993) : The intelligence of emotional intelligence. *Intelligence*, 17(4), 433-442.

McDowelle, J. O. & Bell, E.D.(1997) : Emotional intelligence and educational leadership at East Carolina University. Paper presented at the Annual meeting of the National Council for professors of Educational Administration. Retrieved from Internet on 27th June 2005 via ERIC Document reproduction service. Clearinghouse identifier: He030690

Pool, C. R. (1997) : Up with emotional health. *Educational Leadership*, 54(8), 12-14.

Sutarso, P. (1999) : Gender differences on the emotional intelligence inventory (EQI). Dissertation Abstracts International.

Tapia, M. and Marsh, G. (2001) Emotional Intelligence: The Effect of Gender, GPA and Ethnicity. Paper Presented at the Annual Meeting of the Mid-South Educational Research, Association Mexico. (ED 464086).

Wing, E. and Love, G.D. (2001): *Elective Affinities and Uninvited Agonies: Mapping Emotions With Significant Others Onto Health. Emotion, Social Relationships and Health Series in Affective Science*. Oxford University Press, New York.

CHAPTER

17 Impact of Study Method on Educational Aspiration of Mountain, Valley, Hill and Plain Sectors High School Students

—*Ram Chandra Aryal & G. Venkatesh Kumar*

ABSTRACT

Purpose of the study was to find the effectiveness of study method intervention for increasing the adjustment score of high school students. Students were divided into two groups e.g. experimental and control. The PQRST study method intervention was used for experimental groups after taking pretest. The sample was selected by using average basis (exam score of previous year) from mountain, valley, hill and plain sectors' schools of Nepal. The sample contains 240 boys and girls of grade nine. Educational aspiration scale (EAS), developed by Sharma & Gupta (1980) was used to measure educational aspiration scores of the students. General linear Model Repeated Measure of ANOVA was applied to measure the effect of study method intervention on educational aspiration increase. A significant "F" observed indicating differential increased in experimental groups. However, the interaction between sectors and groups within subjects' effects found non-significant.

Introduction

Nepal a land locked country between two big countries India and China has 1904 private and 3135 government high schools. About 2,68,390 girls and 31,886 boys are studying at high schools (Ministry of Education, 2005). Area of the country: 147,181 esq, total population of the country was 2,31,51,423 (male 11,56,39,21 and female 1,15,87,502), birth rate 30 : 62 per 1000 population and life expectancy at birth 62 : 8. The enrolment of high school students is growing every year. They are in need to know effective study method to continue their academic life. Level of educational aspiration is as psychological construct, which reflects a cognitive type of motivation of the individual (Sharma and Gupta, 1980).

The term level of aspiration involves the estimation of ones ability (whether over, under or realistic) for his/her future performance on the stern birth of his/her past experience (goal discrepancy) his/her ability and capacity, the efforts that one can make toward attaining the goal thus set by him.

All aspirations are strivings for something beyond the person's present status. Aspirations can be divided into three major categories: (*i*) positive and negative, (*ii*) immediate and remote, and (*iii*) realistic and unrealistic. Realistic aspirations lead to success, satisfaction and self-esteem. Unrealistic aspirations lead to failure accompanied by feelings of guilt, embarrass-ment, shame and unworthiness. The person who is unrealistic about what he wants to be and what he does usually finds it "burdensome". The more unrealistic the person is in his thinking, the greater will be the gap between his aspirations and achievement. This is where unreal ism has its most damaging effect on personality.

Educational aspiration is a strong desire to achieve higher education. Educational aspirations mainly depend upon academic performance. The prevailing trend among the students is that: when they know a better method to study and to achieve good score in the exams they are more inspired in their studies. Thus, aspiration is altered by performance.

Whatever tasks a student does are performed by a definite method. The same method does not apply to all tasks. Even the same task requires alternative methods as the time and situation changes. The same lesson applies to the students in their studies. They have to use different study techniques according to the nature of the subject matter for better performance, which will in turn yield more educational aspirations, Staton (1982). The effects of achievement have greater impact on the person's personality because the person expects more from himself then from others. Educational aspiration shapes the personality of a person. According to the educational aspirations the students evaluate themselves and their self-concept (Gibson and Mtchell, 2005).

A person's aspirations are determined by a feeling of inferiority in some physical or social relationship. In well adjusted people, the driving force behind the need for achievement or the "will to power", is adjusted to reality. In poorly adjusted people it is unrealistic and unrelated to social drives, thus leading to failure and maladjusted behavior. While the well adjusted person generally tries to compensate for failure or weakness by excelling in activities in which his ability is greatest, the poorly adjusted overcompensates or tries to excel where he is the weakest in an attempt to deny his weakness, (Adler, 1925).

Students who are bright have more realistic aspiration at all ages than those of average or below average intelligence. They are better able to recognize their own weakness and environmental limitations. But the less bright students overestimate their abilities and they set unrealistic goals. Boys and men usually set a greater aspiration in school work, athletics and vocational advancement than girls and women. As a result they set aspirations above their capacities in these areas. In adulthood, sex differences in aspirations are even more marked than in childhood and adolescence. Men's aspirations concentrate on achievement whereas women's concentrate on personal attractiveness and social acceptance

(Turner, 1964). If the schools' system and government authorities are dictators, people are discouraged from developing higher aspirations. In democratic system people are encouraged to aspire high and are lauded for having higher aspirations. From the child hood they are told that everyone can be successful and they get equal opportunity for the success.

This is sad that often in democratic societies people are encouraged to have unrealistic aspirations. Most people discover that competition with those who are superior rarely leads to success. As a result they lower their aspirations. By adulthood, the pattern of aspiring to what others aspire to has become a well-established habit. Thus aspirations are more often influenced by competition with others than by individual's interests, abilities and needs.

The adolescence period is as follows: early adolescence 10-12 initial adolescence 13-16 late adolescence 17-21. According to *Encyclopedia of Educational Psychology* the period of adolescence of girls is generally 13-21 years and in the boys from 15 to 21 years.

Future success of an adolescent depends upon the norm of group. Cooperation education aspiration forms the group they belong. Adolescent learn the value of education from the teachers and the family members. They are too conscious about their own personality. This is thinking, logical power and decision-making age. The heart of adolescence is full of aspiration. They want to achieve some thing great. They want to follow the model of their heroes of great ideal person. If they are properly guided to give an outlet their energy for better education, they will utilize their abilities at optimum level (Kochhar 1989).

An investigation conducted by researchers Holland *et al.* (1990), found that classified vocational aspirations—singly or in combination—of Navy recruits (467 men and 250 women) were superior to the Vocational Preference Inventory. Predictions for persons with coherent vocational aspirations

(aspirations all in the same occupational category) were very predictive over a short time interval.

To ensure academic success, the careful planning of class schedule is important. Study schedule should be realistic including other responsibilities. One of the worst habits students can develop are waste their time and money. The ability to retain and recall large amounts of information is essential for becoming an effective student; a good memory alone is not enough. In other words, being a good student requires more than the simple regurgitation of facts in an exam. One must also be able to take factual information and use it as a critical thinking to address key questions and solve problems (Brophy and Good, 1986).

Schraw *et al.* (2007) conducted a grounded theory study of academic procrastination to explore adaptive and maladaptive aspects of procrastination and to help guide future empirical research. The authors describe in detail informants' perceptions of procrastination, which were used to construct a 5-component paradigm model that includes adaptive (i.e. cognitive efficiency, peak experience) and maladaptive (i.e. fear of failure, postponement) dimensions of procrastination. These dimensions, in turn, are related to conditions that affect the amount and type of procrastination, as well as cognitive (i.e. prioritizing, optimization) and affective (i.e., reframing, self handicapping) coping mechanisms.

Different authors like Grouzet *et al.,* (2005), investigated the structure of goal contents in a group of 1854 undergraduates from 15 cultures around the world. Results suggested that the 11 types of goals the authors assessed were consistently organized in a circumplex fashion across the 15 cultures. The circumplex was well described by positing two primary dimensions underlying the goals: intrinsic (e.g. self-acceptance, affiliation) versus extrinsic (e.g. financial success, image) and self-transcendent (e.g. spirituality) versus physical (e.g. hedonism). The circumplex model of goal contents was also quite similar in both wealthier and poorer nations, although there were some slight cross-cultural variations.

A study by O'Brien *et al.* (2000), tested a proposed model investigating the relations among attachment to and separation from parents, career self-efficacy, and career aspiration over a 5-year period with a sample of 207 young women. Results suggested that being attached to parents may lead to the development of confidence in pursuing career-related tasks, which in turn influences career aspiration. Separation from parents did not have direct effects on career self-efficacy.

O'Malley *et al.* (1979), did an investigation where the self-esteem of 3183 male and female seniors in a nationwide sample of the high school class of 1977. Comparisons were drawn with 1715 males from the class of 1969. thus the study showed that educational accomplishments underwent a reduction in centrality—became less important-for self-esteem during the late teens and early twenties.

Korman (1971) reports five studies which support the general proposition that high expectancies of competence by others are positively related to performance. Rosenfeld; Zander (1961) conducted an investigation and the data were obtained from a questionnaire given to 400 boys in the 10th grade. Students tend to accept the teacher's suggestions for aspirations when they are rewarded, but tend to ignore or oppose what teachers desire when indiscriminate coercion is perceived. These tendencies affect the degree to which students set their aspired grades congruent with their perceived capacities. Disapproval of inadequate performance appears to have no effect on aspiration, but disapproval of a good performance seems to have a negative effect. Tendencies to accept teacher influence are lowered under indiscriminate reward but increased by reward for adequate performance

Method

A pre- and post-test design with an intervention programme for experimental group is used. The independent variables were same in experimental and control groups. The dependent variable is the educational aspiration score of the students. There are two groups of participants: (*a*), experimental group for which study method intervention is given and (*b*), control groups for which no study method intervention is given.

Sample

The sample is selected by using average basis (performance score of previous exam), from mountain, valley, hill and plain sectors' schools of Nepal. The sample consists 240 boys and girls who were average performer in their classes. The age ranges from 13-18, mean age is 15.5 years. Then randomly assigned them in to two groups equally as experimental and control groups.

Measures

1. Personal information sheet used to know the following information: (*i*), Gender, (*ii*), age, (*iii*), grade, (*iv*), name of school, (*vi*), district and (*vii*) date.
2. Educational Aspiration Scale (EAS) for high school students, developed by Sharma and Gupta (1980) was used to obtain the educational aspiration score of participating students. The EAS, consists 45 items alternative response either 'a' or 'b'. The participants have to response only one alternative for all 45 items.

The total educational aspiration score was obtained by adding the scores according to the following manner:

(*i*) Alternate "A" for question no: 2, 3, 5, 6, 10, 22, 23, 24, 25, 28, 29, 33, 35, 37 and 41 will count score 1.

(*ii*) Alternate 'B' for question no 1, 4, 7, 8, 9, 11, 12, 13, 14, 15, 16, 17, 18, 19, 20, 21, 26, 27, 30, 31, 32, 34, 36, 38, 39, 40, 42, 43, 44 and 45 will count score 1. The total score determines the standing on the scale of the individual.

Procedure

The selected 240 boys and girls participants were equally divided into two experimental groups and control groups randomly. The experimental groups were given PQRST study method intervention programme developed by Staton (1982). No intervention was given to control groups.

The intervention programme continued for eight months and end of the every month one session (20 minutes motivating lecture and 80 minutes PQRST study method is taught to practice) by the investigator. After the intervention, the experimental and control groups were measured again on the dependent variable and obtained post test scores.

Result and Discussion

To assure the randomization data of the sample is tested using independent sample 't' test in the pre-test. The experimental and control groups mean score and S.D. are 28.62-4.54 and 29.60-3.73 respectively. The 't' values for the EAS is -1.833 and "P" is .068 Indicating a non-significant difference between experimental and control groups. General linear Model Repeated Measure of ANAOV is applied to know the effect of intervention programme on adjustment.

Between pre-test to post-test scores there is no significant difference. But in compare to pre and post with group a significant difference was observed (F= 12.902; P< .000). Mean score of experimental group increased by 1.76 (pre - 28.62 - Post 30.38) where control group has reduction by -.0.93(Pre 29.60 - post 28.67). However, between subjects effect between experimental vis control and sector was found non significant. Subject's effects were found significant (F=1351.998; P < .000). Thus, experimental group has better educational aspiration. From the mean aspiration s score it is evident that schools of plain sector improved mean aspiration by 3.8 (pre 26.85- post 30.65) through the PQRST study method intervention.

The PQRST study method intervention increased educational aspiration of the students of experimental groups. This study method is useful to promote academic performance. The study also has significance for school teachers, parents, counsellors and government policy-maker. Finding can be use by these specialists to design intervention program, for better educational aspiration of high school students.

Table 17.1. Mean and S.D of pre-test and post-test score on educational aspiration of mountain, valley, hill and plain sectors' schools of both experimental and control groups on educational aspiration

Group	Sectors	Pre-test		Post test		Change
		Mean	S.D	Mean	S.D	
Experimental	Mountain	29.70	5.32	30.75	4325	1.05
	Valley	29.25	3.83	30.65	5.10	1.04
	Hill	28.33	4.96	29.78	5.21	1.45
	Plain	26.85	3.82	30.65	4.25	3.8
	Total	**28.62**	**4.54**	**30.38**	**4.84**	**1.76**
Control	Mountain	30.65	3.13	29.95	4.47	0.7
	Valley	29.55	3.62	28.83	4.63	0.72
	Hill	29.60	3.38	27.75	5.52	1.85
	Plain	28.65	5.00	28.90	5.78	0.22
	Total	**29.60**	**3.73**	**28.67**	**5.11**	**0.93**
Total	Mountain	30.17	4.22	30.35	4.36	0.18
	Valley	29.4	3.72	29.74	4.38	0.34
	Hill	28.96	4.17	28.76	5.36	0.2
	Plain	27.75	4.41	29.77	5.01	2.22
	Total	**29.07**	**4.13**	**29.65**	**4.89**	**0.58**

Table 17.2. Result of Repeated Measure ANOV A - Within and between subjects' effects for mean pre- and post-test scores of mountain, valley, hill and plain in experimental and control group on educational aspiration.

Source of Variances	Sum of Squares	df	Mean Square	F	P
Within-Subjects Effects					
Pre-post test	36.426	1	36.426	2.451	.119 **
Exp-con	191.709	1	191.709	12.902	.000 *
Sectors	68.362	3	22.787	1.534	.207 **
Exp-Con	15.029	3	5.010	.337	.798 **
Between- Subjects Effects					
Exp-Cont	7.176	1	7.176	.264	.608 **
Sectors	139.304	3	46.435	1.705	.167 **
Exp-Cont	13.238	3	4.413	.162	.922 **

* = Significant, ** = No significant

REFERENCES

Adler, A. (1925). *Individual Psychology.* New York: Harcourt Brace.

Brophy, J, E., and Good, T. (1986). *Teacher behaviour and student achievement: Handbook of research on teaching.* In M. Wittrock (Ed.), New York: Macmillan, 328-375.

Gibson, Robert L., & Mtchell, Marianne H. (2005). *Introduction to Counselling and Guidance* (6th Ed.). Delhi: Pearson Education.

Grouzet, Frederick M. E., Kasser, Tim., Ahuvia, Aaron., Dols, Jose Miguel Fernandez., Kim, Youngmee., Lau, Sing., Ryan, Richard M., Saunders, Shaun., Schmuck, Peter., Sheldon, Kennon M (2005). *Journal of Personality and Social Psychology,* 89(5), 800-816.

Holland, John L., Gottfredson, Gary D., Baker, Herbert G. (1990). Validity of vocational aspirations and interest inventories: Extended, replicated, and reinterpreted. *Journal (if Counseling Psychology,* 37(3), July, 337-342.

Kochhar, S.K. (1989). *Guidance & Counseling.* New Delhi: Sterling Pub. Pvt. Ltd. L-10 Green Park.

Ministry of Education, Nepal in Figure-2005. *Central Bureau of Statistics.* Retrieved Jan 4.

O' Brien, Karen M., Friendman, Suzanne Miller., Tipton, Linda c., Linn, Sonja Geschmay (2000). Attachment, separation, and women's vocational development: a longitudinal analysis. *Journal of Counseling Psychology*, 47 (3), 301-31

O' Malley, Patrick M., Bachman, Jerald G (1979). Self-esteem and education: Sex and cohort comparisons among high school seniors. *Journal of Personality and Social Psychology*, 37(7), 1153-1159.

Rosenfeld, Howard & Zander, Alvin (1961). The Influence of teachers on aspirations of students. *Journal of Educational Psychology*, 52(1), 1-11.

Schraw, Gregory; Wadkins, Theresa; Olafson, Lori,(2007). *Journal of Educational Psychology*. Vol 99(1) 12-25.

Sharma, V.P. Gupta, Anuradha (1980). *Manual for Educational Aspiration Scale (EAS)* Agra: National Psychological Corporation.

Staton, Thomas F. (1982). *How to Study?* Nashville TA: Distributor: Post Box; 40273, 37204.

Turner, R.H. (1964). Some Aspects of Women's Ambition. *Amer. J. Social.* 70, 271-285.

CHAPTER

18

Transformational and Transactional Leadership: An Assessment of Secondary School Managers' Leadership Style in Iran

—Alireza Rezaei Abgoli

The purpose of this study was to determine if the leadership style of secondary school managers in Iran is transformational and/or transactional. Also is there any relation between managers' leadership style and their demographic variables? Managers were defined as individuals who manage secondary schools. In this research, secondary school teachers judged about their managers' leadership style as they perceive it. Findings of this study imply that managers of secondary schools in Shiraz City have a more transformational leadership with the mean of 55.73 in comparison with transactional leadership style with the mean of 27.25. In transformational subscales Inspirational Motivation had the highest scores with the mean of 12.72 and Individual Consideration received the lowest scores with the mean of 10.20. Additionally, managers' leadership style had not any significant relationship with their demographic variables such as age, gender, educational qualification, subject and experience.

Introduction and Theoretical Framework

Effective leaders will need to include their subordinates and employees, their peers, and perhaps even their superiors. In order to use the thinking skills of other people, leaders will have to engage them in the process of thinking innovatively and creatively, rather than telling them what to do. When leaders concentrate on the process of finding and solving important problems, they concentrate on the process.

Effective leadership requires leading others to think innovatively and promoting the continual discovery of new solutions. Getting people to work toward a common goal is not easy. The leader must know when and how to synchronize the thinking of others. People tend to lack skills in problem-solving and divergent thinking, as well as the ability to create innovative solutions to complex problems. Research shows involving people in using their creativity is itself motivating. By encouraging people to think for themselves, the leader creates intrinsic motivation in their followers. Good leadership fosters change that is both transformative and sustainable. It can be concerned with moral or organizational matters. It can define the college's [schools'] role in the world beyond its walls, or it can determine their internal dynamics of the institution. Most importantly, it requires a worthy goal-vision, if you will—but it also requires persistence (Eckman, 2003).

The dean's [managers'] role may be multifaceted from college to college or university to university [or school to school], yet there is one role that all deans must face: dealing with "change." While undergoing change, researchers have found that followers have to be empowered so that they are willing to work for new change. Research suggests that leaders need to have qualities that facilitate followers to transform from one situation to another that is transformational leadership (Shamir *et al.*, 1993; Yukl, 1999). Transformational leadership may motivate people to go beyond their own self-interest and to pursue goals and values of the collective group. Effective leadership is central to change and, in particular, to the ability to produce "constructive or adaptive change" as leaders "risk disorder and instability as they seek out opportunities for change" (Bedeian & Hunt, 2005). Leadership requires the development of a vision, communication of that vision, and the ability to set purpose or direction (Bedeian & Hunt, 2005).

How secondary school managers lead their schools and teachers through the change and their style of leadership could ensure the success of their education institutions. The leadership of secondary schools will be a determining factor of whether the secondary schools will be able to successfully and effectively manage the change. The managers of secondary schools in Shiraz have been designated as the individuals responsible for guiding their schools during this time of change.

It is obvious that managers can not solve problems alone. In today's complex world problems call for the combined expertise of multiple resources and assistants. For these reasons, strong emphasis is placed on promoting teamwork and strong leadership. Due to the complex challenges created which exist in secondary schools these days, it is imperative for secondary school managers to solve problems efficiently and make the most of available resources. Managers must recognize the creativeness of all the schools' members across multiple disciplines. Suggestions and ideas need to be implemented quickly and efficiently. Managers must promote collaboration and teamwork. In order to facilitate change, managers must respect teachers' expertise and find ways to identify and solve complex problems and challenges.

Transformational leadership involves the ability to inspire and motivate followers. It is important to provide followers opportunities to participate by having the chance to present their thoughts and opinions. These thoughts and opinions can then be considered and incorporated into management decisions. Followers are more willing to accept change when they have input in the change process. Transformational leadership has five components including Idealized Influence (behavior), Idealized Influence (attributed); Inspirational Motivation; Intellectual Stimulation and Individualized Consideration. Each of the four components describes characteristics that are valuable to the "transformation" process. When managers are strong role models, encouragers, innovators, and coaches, they are utilizing the "four I's" to help "transform" their associates into better, more productive and successful individuals. Northouse (2001) states that in 39 studies of transformational literature, individuals who exhibited transformational leadership were more effective leaders with better work outcomes. This was true for both high and low-level leaders in the public and private sectors (Northouse, 2001). Therefore, it can be very advantageous for managers to apply the transformational approach in the workplace.

Because transformational leadership covers a wide range of aspects within leadership, there are no specific steps for a manager to follow. Becoming an effective transformational leader is a process. This means that conscious effort must be made to adopt a transformational style. Understanding the basics of transformational leadership and the four I's can help a manager apply this approach. According to Northouse (2001), a transformational leader has the following qualities:

- Empower followers to do what is best for the organization;
- Is a strong role model with high values;
- Listens to all viewpoints to develop a spirit of cooperation;
- Creates a vision, using people in the organization;
- Acts as a change agent within the organization by setting an example of how to initiate and implement change;
- Helps the organization by helping others contribute to the organization.

Sample

The population for this study was secondary school managers in Shiraz City in Iran. Each participant was contacted because he or she held the title of secondary school's manager. Researcher collected manager' demographic variables such as gender, age, educational qualification, subject and experience by giving them a separate questionnaire. Then the Rater Form of leadership style questionnaire was distributed between 200 teachers in the same 30 secondary schools to judge about their managers' leadership styles. So, collected data are about secondary school managers from their teachers' perspective.

Instrumentation

In order to accomplish the research objectives a packet containing the research instrument was given to each teacher. Leadership styles of the study's participants were determined by scoring each participant's response to the Multifactor Leadership Questionnaire. The Multifactor Leadership Questionnaire (MLQ) is based on the Full Range Leadership Model developed by Bass and Avolio (2000). The survey is a short and comprehensive assessment with 45 items that measure a full range of leadership behaviors. The MLQ has been repeatedly validated by leadership experts. The MLQ is strongly predictive of leader performance (Bass, 1997). The MLQ measures transformational and transactional leadership styles. The reliability of the MLQ, as reported by Bass and Avolio for each leadership factor, ranges from .74 to .91.

The MLQ measures individual leadership styles as being transformational and transactional as well as scales of leadership. The MLQ was utilized to measure elements or scales of transformational and transactional leadership of the secondary school managers. The MLQ scale scores are measures of characteristics, or behaviors of leaders. These characteristics include: Idealized Influence (behaviour), Idealized Influence (attributed); Inspirational Motivation, Intellectual Stimulation and Individualized Consideration associated with Transformational Leadership; Contingent Reward, Management by Exception (active), Management-by-Exception (passive) and laissez-faire associated with Transactional Leadership.

Transformational leadership encourages followers to accomplish more than what would normally be expected of them. They become motivated to transcend their own self-interests for the good of the group or organization (Northouse 2001, Bass & Avolio, 1990).

The leader in which followers react to the leader and his/ her behavior is defined by the leaders idealized influence score. Idealized influence leaders have high moral and ethical values and are able to provide their followers with a sense of vision and mission. Followers deeply respect the idealized influence leader. Inspirational motivation is shown in leaders when they inspire and motivate followers to demonstrate commitment to the shared vision of the group or team. The inspirational motivational leader engages in clearly communicating high expectations to followers and increases team spirit and enthusiasm. Intellectual stimulation is demonstrated by the transformational leader when they support followers to be creative and innovative, to try new approaches, and challenge their own beliefs and values. This type of leader promotes problem solving to find creative solutions to the task at hand. Individualized consideration is shown by the transformational leader by creating a supportive climate, listening to followers, and acts as a coach and mentor. The leader pays attention to individual differences and treats individual employees in a caring way. Leaders also help individuals achieve goals and grow personally. This type of leader also uses delegation to get followers to grow through personal challenges (Northouse, 2001).

Contingent Reward is how the leader and followers exchange specific rewards for outcomes or results. Goals and objectives are agreed upon by both the leader and followers and the achievement is rewarded or punished. The MLQ measures a leader's degree of possessing Contingent Reward leadership attributes which are demonstrated by leaders that engage in a constructive path to goal transaction and exchange rewards for performance. These leaders clarify expectations, exchange promises and resources, arrange mutually satisfactory agreements, negotiate for resources, exchange assistance for effort, and provide commendations for successful follower performance.

Table 18.1. Leadership scale scores measured by the MLQ represent transformational and/or transactional leadership

1. Idealized (Behaviour)	Influence		
2. Idealized (Attributed)	Influence	Transformational Style	leadership
3. Inspirational Motivation			
4. Intellectual Stimulation			
5. Individualized Consideration			
6. Contingent Reward			
7. Management-by-Exception (Active)	Transactional style	leadership	
8. Management-by-Exception (Passive			
9. *Laissez-faire*			

Management-by-Exception (active) is when a leader makes corrective criticisms or uses negative reinforcement. This leadership behavior monitors followers closely so they can point out mistakes and errors. Leaders with Management-by-Exception with "active" behaviors have characteristics of monitoring followers' performances and taking corrective action if deviations from the set standards occur. These leaders enforce rules to avoid mistakes.

Management-by-Exception (passive) is only intervening when goals have not been met or a problem arises. The Management-by-Exception leader with a "passive" behavior would not intervene until problems become serious. The Management-by-Exception leader (passive) waits to take action until mistakes are brought to his or her attention. *Laissez-faire* behaviors are ones that delay decisions and give up responsibility. Laissez-faire leaders offer no feedback or support to the follower. *Laissez-faire* leadership is a "hands-off" approach to leadership (Northouse, 2001). *Laissez-faire* leadership is also termed a non-leadership style. The *laissez-*

faire leader avoids accepting responsibilities, is absent when needed, fails to follow up on requests for assistance, and resists expressing his or her views on important issues. The *laissez-faire* leader gives the majority of control in the decision-making process to the followers. *Laissez-faire* leadership assumes that followers are intrinsically motivated and should be left alone to accomplish tasks and goals. The *laissez-faire* leader does not provide direction or guidance.

Procedure

Each of the nine leadership scales measured by the MLQ as well as the transformational and/or transactional leadership style scores are presented in Table 18.1. Transformational and/or transactional leadership style scores are presented in Table 18.2. Leadership scale scores have a range possibility of 0 to 4. A score of 0 meant the style was not used at all while a 4 was a style used frequently, if not always. A score of 0-1 represents a style used minimally or never. A score of 1-2 demonstrate behaviours used once in a while to sometimes. A MLQ score between 2 and 3 demonstrates behaviors or traits used fairly often. Leadership styles used frequently, if not, always scored between 3 and 4. Of the nine scale scores, Inspirational Motivation received the highest mean score (M=12.72, SD=1.62), and Contingent Reward scale scores received the lowest mean score (M=5.38, SD=1.73).

The range of style scores for the respondents for transformational leadership style scores ranged from 10.20 to 12.72 and transactional leadership was 5.38 to 9.99. Transformational leadership scores reported by the participants were the highest of the leadership style scores (M=55.73, SD=6.77 out of total score of 80). Participants reported a score for transactional leadership style of (M=27.25, SD=4.00 out of total score of 64).

Coded data were analyzed with the help of SPSS software. ANOVA-one way was used to compare the managers' leadership style and also to find the relationship between managers' leadership style and their gender, age, educational qualification, subject and experience. Table 18.2 presents the scores for the two leadership style scores; transformational and transactional leadership.

Results

Table 18.2. Mean scores of leadership subscales of managers belonging to different schools

Leadership Scales	Mean	S. D
Idealized Influence (Behavior)	11.99	1.40
Idealized Influence (Attributed)	11.36	1.55
Inspirational Motivation	12.72	1.62
Intellectual Stimulation	10.45	1.59
Individual Consideration	10.20	1.59
Contingent Reward	5.38	1.73
Management-By-Exception (Active)	4.84	1.60
Management-By-Exception (Passive)	7.04	1.63
Laissez Faire	9.99	1.97

Table 18.3. Mean scores and standard deviations of leadership styles of managers belonging to different schools

Leadership Style	M	S.D
Transformational Leadership Style	55.73	6.77
Transactional Leadership Style	27.25	4.00

By scrutinizing mean scores of transformational and transactional leadership styles no significant relationship was observed between managers' leadership style and their gender, age, educational qualification subject and experience. (Wolverton *et al.*, 2001; Moore, 2003; Stedman, 2004) proved that no significant relationships could be found between managers' leadership style and their gender, age, educational qualification, subject and experience. In this research, researcher found the same results.

Table 18.4. t value of transformational and transactional leadership styles and managers' gender, age, educational qualification, subject and experience

Managers' personal factors		t	Sig.
Gender	Transformational	0.170	0.866
	Transactional	-1.628	0.115
Age	Transformational	1.131	0.268
	Transactional	-1.230	0.129
Educational	Transformational	0.113	0.911
Qualification	Transactional	1.077	0.291
Subject	Transformational	0.527	0.602
	Transactional	-0.310	0.759
Experience	Transformational	0.182	0.857
	Transactional	-1.172	0.251

Discussion

The purpose of this study was to determine if the leadership style of secondary school managers was transformational and/or transactional. Current managers appear to have a more transformational leadership style, as demonstrated by a mean score in transformational leadership (M=55.73), while exhibiting some characteristics of transactional leadership (M=27.25).

The findings of the research show managers use transformational leadership style (mean=55.73) more often than transactional style (mean 27.25) in all subscales. The findings of this study imply secondary school managers, both male and female, are using transformational leadership styles more often than transactional leadership style. This is a positive reflection of the current secondary school managers because the literature states transformational leadership behaviors are more successful for attaining and fulfilling goals (Tichny & Devanna, 1990).

The findings of the current study found secondary managers in Shiraz tend to use transformational leadership more often than transactional leadership. This is an important finding for the education community in Iran. Eagly *et al.* (2003) reported effective-successful leaders use transformational leadership style more often than transactional leadership. Bass (1990) stated that transformational leadership is the prototype of leadership that people have in mind when they describe their ideal leader. Bass also stated transformational leaders are more effective and successful. If school managers are using transformational leadership more often than transactional leadership, the chances for success and the continued viability for educational institutions is promising.

Since demographic variables did not significantly influence the leadership style of the school managers in regards to their being transformational or transactional becomes evident that educational institutions should continue to recruit diverse leaders with diverse backgrounds. Further research needs to be conducted to determine if managers' personal factors relate to the development of their leadership style.

REFERENCES

Bass, B. M. (1990). *Bass & Stogdill's handbook of leadership. Theory, research and managerial applications.* (3rd ed.), New York: The Free Press.

Bass, B. M., & Avolio, B. J. (2000). *MLQ: Multifactor questionnaire:* Third edition manual and sampler set. Redwood City, CA: Mind Garden.

Bedeian, A. G., & Hunt, J. G. (2005). Academic amnesia and vestigial assumptions of our forefathers. Unpublished Manuscript, Area of Management, The Texas University Press.

Eagly, A. H., Johannesen-Schmidt, M. C., & Van Engen, M. (2003). Transformational, transactional, and laissez-faire leadership styles: A meta-analysis comparing women and men, *Psychological Bulletin*, 129, 569–591.

Eckman, R. (2003). Standing up when it matters. *CIC Newsletter*, April 2, 2003.

Moore, L. L. (2003). Leadership in the cooperative extension system: An examination of leadership styles and skills of state directors and administrators. Unpublished doctoral dissertation, University of Florida, Gainesville.

Northouse, P (2001). *Leadership Theory and Practice,* second edition. Thousand Oaks, CA: Sage Publications, Inc.

Shamir, R. J. House, & Arthur, M. B. (1993). The motivational effects of charismatic leadership: A self-concept based theory. *Organization Science,* 4, 577–594.

Stedman, N. P. (2004). Leadership, volunteer administration and 4-H: Leadership styles and volunteer administration competence of 4-H state volunteer specialists and county faculty. Unpublished doctoral dissertation, University of Florida, Gainesville.

Tichny, N. M., & Devanna, M. A. (1990). *The transformational leader.* New York: John Wiley & Sons.

Wolverton, M., Gmelch, W., Montez, J., & Nies, C. (2001). The changing nature of the academic deanship, 28, (21). San Francisco, CA; Jossey Bass (ASHEERIC Higher Education Report No. ED 457 708).

Yukl, G. (1999). An evaluation of conceptual weaknesses in transformational and charismatic leadership theories. *The Leadership Quarterly,* 10(2), 285–305.

CHAPTER

19 A Study of Feelings of Security/Insecurity and Academic Achievement among Girl Students of Mysore City

—*Nahid Zeini Hassanv and CG Venkatesha Murthy*

The present study was undertaken with the twin objectives of studying the feelings of Security and Insecurity girl students in Mysore city in Karnataka, as well as of studying the differences between girl students of 14 years and 16 years on their feelings of Security and Insecurity in relation to the academic achievement. The sample comprised 1035 students drawn randomly from the North, South, West, and East of Mysore city. They were only girl students and their age group was in 14 and 16 years old. The responses on the measure of the Security/Insecurity Scale revealed that there are significant differences between two age group on their feelings security/insecurity. Marks obtained by subjects in their annual examination were taken as measure of Academic achievement. Relation between feelings of security/insecurity and academic achievement among two groups revealed that there is significant differences between secured and in secured girl students on their academic achievement.

Introduction

The terms "security" and "insecurity" have been accepted recently by many behavioral scientists and related practitioners who use them extensively. They appear principally in the literature of social psychology and allied subjects; sociology, psychiatry, abnormal or clinical psychology, and social work. The security phenomenon describes one's relationship with himself /herself and his/her world. Lack of security creates insecurity caused by deprivation. Security not only as the essence and the goal we try to obtain through our daily living, but also as an ever-present thread of truth that weaves its way through our existence. The feelings of security are a very important condition in human beings in order to achieve anything in life.

There are an estimated 105 million adolescent girls in the age group of 10-19 in India (CEDPA, 2001). In many places around the world, women have little or no access to education. On a grand scale, research has illustrated that educating women and girls lead to an increased overall development and well being both in communities and countries. They are more aware of health and reproductive health issue, political affairs, and the importance of children's education (Bruchfield, and Rocha, 2002).

As human beings, who are civilized, we all need to feel secured in all lives. It is to ensure this feeling of security we have social norms, rules, laws, judiciary etc. Security in life depends more on how we manage our self than on any other person or thing. Security has been defined as "a sense of confidence, safety, and freedom from fear or anxiety, particularly with respect to fulfilling one's present (and future) needs." This is closely related with the feeling of being at home, safety, friendliness, calm, easy, relaxation, uncomplicated, emotional stability, self- acceptance, and well based self-feeling of security strength. (Murthy, 2002).

Objectives

The present study has focused on the following objectives:

- To study the feelings of Security and Insecurity in relation to academic achievement among girl students of Mysore city.
- To study the differences between girl students of 14 years and 16 years on their feelings of Security and Insecurity.

Hypotheses

1. There is no significant difference between secured and in-secured students on their academic achievement.
2. There is no significant difference between students of 14 years and 16 years on their feelings of security/ insecurity.

Methodology

The present study is a descriptive research which has used ex-post facto design. The population comprises high school girl students who are 14-year and 16-year old who are studying, in Mysore city of Karnataka in India. They are drawn using stratified random sampling method. On the whole 1035 girl students have served as sample for the present study.

The tools used included, Security/Insecurity Scale (SIS), (Beena Shah 1989) contains 75 items, distributed over eight areas of security-insecurity scale covering; Family Security (13 questions)- School Security (12 Q) - Security Peer group (12Q) - Study – Context Security (08 Q) - Prospective-Context Security (08Q)-Test-Context Security (04Q) - Self-Context Security (10Q)- and Existence - Context Security (08 Q). The other tool used was Personal Data Blank prepared by the researcher.

The tabulated scores have been treated with descriptive and inferential statistics hypothesis wise. Mean and SD have been used. Among the inferential statistics, one way ANOVA and t-test have been used.

Results and Discussion

Hypothesis 1: To test hypothesis 1 the scores of all the subjects on the security-insecurity and the academic achievement scores were pooled. Based on the levels of security-insecurity the subjects were categorized and their academic achievement scores were tabulated.

The mean of the entire groups have been found to be 102.82, on composite security score, and Std. Deviation has come out to be 20.04. There are three groups among studied samples.

The first group is 'Secured Group' of 192 students, about 19% of the sample, has the mean score of 360.71. The Second group is 'In-between Group' 625 students, which has covered around 60% of the sample has the mean score of 392.77. The last group is 'Insecured Group' comprising 218 students, which covers about 21% of the sample has the mean score of 429.37.

Table 19.1. The scores on Academic achievement of students who are on different levels of security

Groups	N	Mean	SD	F	P
Secured	192 (19%)	360.71	112.24	20.468	.000 (S)
In-between	625 (60%)	392.77	110.34		
In-secured	218 (21%)	429.37	101.01		
Total	1035 (100%)	394.53	111.01		

Table 19.1 clearly indicates that between categories students have differed significantly on their feelings of security-insecurity as the obtained F value of 20.468 is found to be significant at 0.01 level. It means, all the three groups (secured, in-between and in secured), have differed significantly on their academic achievement. To see how groups have differed significantly, post-hoc comparison of the three groups scores are subjected to Duncan's multiple range test (DMRT), and it yield in the following:

The Mean differences on Post-Hoc Comparisons using Duncan's Multiple Range Test among three levels of the feelings of Security/Insecurity on their Academic Achievement clearly indicates that there are significant mean differences between Secured, In-between and In secured groups on their Academic Achievement. The In secured group with mean score (429.37), have the best position in academic achievement, In-between group with the mean score (392.77) is in the second rank in academic achievement, and the last rank is belong to Secured group with mean score of (360.71). It implies as the Security increases, academic achievement decreases but as the Insecurity increases, academic achievement increases. Which means, the security and achievement are inversely related. This contradicts many studies such as Caprova, *et al.* (2000).

This finding matches with Murthy's (2002) study. In her study she studied significance of difference among different levels of security on their English language achievement and found that the three groups have differed significantly. Further, when different group means were compared, the highest mean score was seen among those students who were insecured. This factor of link between Insecurity and English language achievement were consistently seen throughout. The findings of both studies show that those students who feel insecured have performed far better, may be because they might be thinking they have no option but to plan well and perform. Those who feel secured may not be as serious as those who insecured.

Hypothesis 2: To test hypothesis 2, the academic achievement scores of students who are 14 years and 16 years were segregated and then they were subjected to t test. The following emerged.

Table 19.2. The mean scores of 14 and 16 years old groups on their Feelings of security /insecurity and their significance level

Age Group	N	Mean	SD	F	P
14 years	553	100.15	20.99	-4.649	.000 (S)
16 Years	482	105.89	18.43		
Total	1035 (100%)	394.53	111.01		

The above table clearly indicates that there are significant mean differences between 14 and 16 years old groups on their Feelings of security /insecurity at 0.01 level. The mean of the 14 years old group has been found to be 100.15, and standard deviation has come out to be 20.99. The mean of the 16 years old group has been found to be 105.89 on security score, and standard deviation has come out to be 18.43. The above table clearly indicates that the 14-year and 16-year old students have differenced significantly on their feelings of security-insecurity as the obtained t-test value of -4.649 is significant at 0.01 level. It means, two groups have differed significantly on their feelings of security /insecurity in favor of 16-year old students as their mean score is higher than the 14-year old students. Since higher score on this test indicates insecurity, the 16-year old have been found to be higher in their insecurity as compared to the 14-year old girls.

The inference one can make from the above result is that as the age increases the feelings of insecurity increases among girls.

Conclusions

The following conclusions can be drawn from the above study.

- As the feelings of Security increases, academic achievement decreases but as the feelings of Insecurity increases, academic achievement increases. Which means, the security and achievement are inversely related.
- As the age increases the feelings of insecurity increases among girls.

REFERENCES

Caprova, G., Barbanelli, C., Pastorelli, C., Bandura, A., & Zimbardo, P. (2000). Prosocial foundations of children's academic achievement. *Psychological Science*, 11(4), 302-306.

Center for Development and Population Activities (CEDPA) (2001). Better Life Options Program.

Murthy, Shyla. (2002). English language achievement: Some Psychological Correlates. Rajat Publications. New Delhi (INDIA).

Chapter

20

The Effect of Motivation on Learning Foreign Language Skills

—*Shaban Barimani Varandi*

ABSTRACT

So far different factors have been explored to find the reason of learning differently in the same educational setting by learners. One of these prominent factors is motivation. In this study the effect of motivation on learning foreign language (FL) skills has been investigated. The obtained data have been analyzed through 't-test to determine the homogeneity of the participants and Carl Pearson Moment Correlation was applied to find the effect of motivation on learning foreign language skills. The participants have been given three different tests to find their level of proficiency, their type of motivation, and their reading comprehension ability respectively. The results have shown that the higher the learners were intrinsically motivated; the more successful they were in doing reading comprehension.

Key Words: motivation, orientation, intrinsic, extrinsic, reading comprehension.

Introduction

The reason why individuals in the same situation of learning and teaching and in the same educational setting, learn differently is a matter that has not received a definite answer so far. As it has so been proved, there are various factors to be considered in learning a language and its skills.

Apparently, the factors such as psychological, social, sociocultural, economic, biological, cognitive, and affective are directly involved in learning L2 skills. It seems that the last two items – cognitive and affective – play a prominent role in this regard. The cognitive characteristics include intelligence, memory, aptitude, age, and etc. The affective factors include emotion, motivation, anxiety, self – esteem, empathy, personality, and among all these characteristics, the affective factors, especially one of its particular dimensions i.e. "motivation" has been chosen and investigated in the present study.

Defining Motivation

How is motivation defined? Here are the following dictionary definition drawn from a number of different sources. Motivation is the extent to which you make choices about (a) goals to pursue and (b) the effort you will devote to that pursuit.

Brown (2001:73) believes that "this definition can be interpreted in varying ways; depending on the theory of human behavior you adopt". For the sake of simplicity, let us look at theories of motivation in terms of two opposing camps. In one of these camps there is a traditional view of motivation that accounts for human behaviour through a behavioristic paradigm that stresses the importance of rewards and reinforcement. In the other camp there are a number of cognitive psychological viewpoints that explain motivation through deeper, less observable phenomena. These two traditions are described below.

Behaviouristic Definition

A behavioristic psychologist like Skinner or Watson stresses the role of 'rewards' in motivating behaviour. In Skinner's operant conditioning model, for example, human beings like other living organisms, will pursue a goal because they perceive a reward for doing so. This reward serves to 'reinforce' behavior to cause it to persist.

A behaviourist would define motivation as *"the anticipation of reinforcement."* We do well to heed the credibility of such a definition. There is no question that a tremendous proportion of what we do is motivated by an anticipated reward.

Cognitive Definition

A number of cognitive psychological view-points offer a different perspective on motivation. While rewards are very much a part of the whole picture, the difference lies in the sources of motivating and in the power of self – reward.

Motivation

Motivation is probably the most frequently used catch – all term for planning the success or failure of virtually any complex task. It is easy to figure that success in a task is due simply to the fact that a learner will be successful with the proper motivation. Such claims are of course not erroneous, for countless studies and experiments in human learning have shown that motivation is a key to learning. Crooks and Schmitt (1991) state, "but these claims gloss over a detailed understanding of exactly what motivation is and what the subcomponents of motivation are". What does it mean to say that someone is motivated? How do you create, foster, and maintain motivation? Keller (1983:389) argues that "motivation is commonly thought of as an inner drive, impulse, emotion, or desire that moves one to a particular action. Or, in more technical terms, motivation refers to "the choices people make as to what experiences or goals they will approach or avoid, and the degree of effort they will exert in that respect."

Motivation is something that can, like self – esteem, be global, situational, or task-oriented. Learning a foreign language clearly requires some of all three levels of motivation. For example, a learner may possess high "global" motivation to perform well on, say the written mode of the language. Motivation is also typically examined in terms of the intrinsic and extrinsic orientation of the learner.

Brown (1984) says:

"Those who learn for their own self – perceived needs and goals are intrinsically oriented and those who pursue a goal only to receive an external reward from someone else are extrinsically motivated."

We will return to this extremely important concept below.

Intrinsic and Extrinsic Motivation

Perhaps one of the most powerful dimensions of the whole motivation construct in general is the degree to which learners are intrinsically or extrinsically motivated to succeed in a task. Decei (1975:23) defined intrinsic motivation as:

> Intrinsically motivated activities are ones for which there is no apparent reward except the activity itself. People seem to engage in the activities for their own sake and not because they lead to an extrinsic reward. Intrinsically motivated behaviors are aimed at bringing about certain internally rewarding consequences, namely feeling of competence and self-determination.

Extrinsically motivated behaviors on the other hand, are carried out in anticipation of a reward from outside and beyond the self. Brown (1984) says that typical extrinsic rewards are money, prizes, grades, and even certain types of positive feedback. Behaviours initiated solely to avoid punishment are also extrinsically motivated, even though numerous intrinsic benefits can ultimately accrue to those who, instead, view punishment avoidance as a challenge that can build their sense of competence and self-determination.

The intrinsic/extrinsic continuum is applicable to foreign language classrooms around the world. Regardless of the cultural beliefs and attitudes of learners and teachers, intrinsic and extrinsic factors can be quite easily identified – much more universally so than the integrative/instrumental continuum that relies exclusively on a social – psychological approach. Crooks and Schmitt (1991) argue that:

"One's attitude toward target language culture is but one of many aspects of complex phenomenon that we call motivation. But looking at motivation in terms of choice, engagement, but persistence, as determined by interest, relevance, expectancy, and outcomes, the concept of motivation will have a more satisfactory connection to language-learning process and language pedagogy."

Which form of motivation is more powerful? Most of the researchers strongly favor intrinsic one especially for long – term retention, Piaget (1972) and others:

> "point out that human beings universally view incongruity, university, and 'disequilibrium' as motivating."

Moslow (1970) claims that:

> "intrinsic motivation is clearly superior to extrinsic. According to his hierarchy of needs, we are ultimately motivated to achieve "self-actualization" once the basic physical, safety, and community needs are met. No matter what extrinsic rewards are present or absent, we will strive for self-esteem and fulfillment."

Statement of the Problem

In learning any skill or language apparently various factors are involved such as cognition, affection, situation, learners' purposes, and the like. Although these factors are more or less considered in pedagogical processes i.e. preparing materials and syllabus design, it seems that one of the most significant factors being directly involved in the process – motivation – is mostly ignored by the theorists and practitioners. Reading Comprehension skill is not an exception. One of the main factors to be considered is why the learner is going to attempt to learn a language e.g. English. Specifically speaking whether s/he has an intrinsic or an extrinsic motivation to learn it. That is, has he or she decided to learn a language by her or his own or some other external factors persuaded him or her to do so? Obviously, such factors should receive a special attention by the teachers and theorists because each of these factors leads to special strategies to be used and applied. The main problem that exists in the textbooks and language teaching programs is that they seldom pay attention to such issues. Apparently applying strategies and styles based on these elements, the learner can gain more attainments of his endeavor.

Research Question

What is the effect of Motivation on learning FL skills?

Null Hypothesis

Motivation has no effect on learning FL skills.

Significance of the Study

The importance of learning and teaching a foreign language especially English is quite obvious. These days, by improving technology such as computer and internet and other communication devices, this need grows larger and larger. Moreover people's attempt in this field is distinctly developing. Among the various dimensions and skills of foreign languages, ***Reading Comprehension Skill*** has a more significant role, because it is more widely used in comparison to other skills such as writing or listening. For example in any language courses and ESP, this skill has an active role. Internet that is being quite widely used is reading. But undoubtedly, there are some blocks and barriers in the flows of teaching and learning this skill. Up to now an ocean of studies have been made to withdraw such blocks or at least to weaken them. In this study the researcher's attempt is to consider a very common problem in the area of language learning skills – Motivation. Since the learners trying to learn an FL have different desires, it's necessary for the language teachers or syllabus designers to design syllabuses in accordance with such factors. Being intrinsically or extrinsically motivated is a factor which deserves to receive more attention. This is a problem that the language practitioners encounter in the process. At the end of the research, the researcher hopes to draw results so that they can help the text-book writers to provide materials in reading skill which promotes the rate of language learning.

What is Reading?

Before considering efficient approaches to the development of skill in reading, it is essential to distinguish two activities which go by this name but must not be confused with each other. A student who stands up in class and enunciates in the conventional way the sounds symbolized by the printed or written marks on the script may be considered to be "reading". Rivers (1993:161) argues:

> "The 'reading' may be comprehensible to a listener, without the reader drawing much in the way of meaning from what he or she is enunciating. Such an activity is one aspect of reading for which the student may usefully be trained, but it is a minor goal. The student must also be taught to derive meaning from the word combinations in the text and to do this in a consecutive fashion at a reasonable speed, without necessarily vocalizing what is being read. This is reading for comprehension."

According to Fries (1963:121) "the student is developing a considerable range of habitual responses to a specific set of patterns of graphic shapes". Reading is certainly an important activity for "expanding knowledge of a language", but only under certain conditions.

We may ask ourselves questions. First, have the difference between spoken and written language been taken into account in relation to the course objectives? Have the students been made aware of these differences, so that they are expanding their knowledge of both spoken and written language and not of some unrecognized conglomeration of the two?

Methodology

Subjects

Subjects consisted of 155 intermediate English learners (both males and females) from two institutes. Their ages ranged from 15 to 20. In order to determine the proficiency level of test takers, a Nelson English Language Tests (250 A and B) was administered to all the subjects, through which, 107 subjects were selected to answer the motivation questionnaire provided by Noel and expanded by the researcher. Of these, 30 intrinsic and 30 extrinsic subjects were selected to answer a reading comprehension test.

Instrumentation

Three paper- and-pencil tests were used for this study. First a standard proficiency test i.e. Nelson English Language

Test (250 A and B) was administered to act as an indicator of the subjects' proficiency levels. This test consisted of reading comprehension, vocabulary and grammar. The second was the motivation test, which had already been prepared and administered by Noel and et.al. in their study on Canadian students and expanded by the researcher, used in order to distinguish the two motivation oriented i.e. intrinsic and extrinsic ones. The questionnaire contained 20 items. It was also designed to show basic motivation preference on three dimensions: Intrinsic, Extrinsic, and Amotivation, but since the main focus of this study is on intrinsic/ extrinsic motivation, the researcher measured these aspects. Although the questionnaire has been originally developed for the Canadian students and was in English and French, the researcher translated it into his subjects' mother tongue i.e. Persian. The original questionnaire contained only ten items, but the researcher considering his own subjects, expanded it up to twenty items.

The third test was Reading Comprehension test. It included one cloze passage and two reading passages. The cloze passage and one of the reading passages followed by multiple choice questions, but the other reading passage followed by information questions.

Procedure

The first step was to administer a proficiency test to 155 subjects. The obtained scores were utilized to capture homogeneity. Those subjects who scored one standard deviation above and one below the mean were selected to take motivation questionnaire. It was a collection of 20 Yes/ No items in about 10 minutes. In order to obtain valid results, subjects were required to answer all the sheets. The papers were scored according to the scoring key. Based on the questionnaire score, 30 intrinsic and 30 extrinsic subjects were selected for this study. Then three reading passages with different types of questions were distributed. The subjects were asked to do the passages in about 45 minutes. The passages were selected from "Intermediate Reading Comprehension" published by Rahnama Publication.

Design

This research employs an ex post facto design. The researcher doesn't have any control over the manipulation of the independent variables. There is no cause - and - effect relationship between variables and the researcher was going to find a degree of the effect of variables through corelational analysis.

Results and Discussions

As it was mentioned in the earlier pages, this study was concerned with one research question. "What is the Effect of Motivation on learning FL skills". Along with the above research question, a null hypothesis was stated. In order to test the null hypothesis, Pierson Moment Correlation was carried out and the results are shown below.

In Table 20.1 a descriptive analysis of subjects' test scores before analyzing the data is presented.

Table 20.1. Descriptive Statistics of Subjects' Scores on TOEFL

	TOEFL
N	11
$\bar{X}$	52.4
SD	22.9
VAR	524.91

Table 20.2. Descriptive Statistics of Subjects Scores on Motivation

	Intrinsic	Extrinsic
N	66	41
$\bar{X}$	15.96	11.42
SD	2.68	3.15
VAR	7.19	9.95

As it was mentioned before, 107 subjects out of 155 subjects were given proficiency test were chosen to be given the motivation test to see whether they are intrinsically or extrinsically motivated in learning English. The states that those who were intrinsically motivated have a higher motivation than those who were extrinsically motivated.

Table 20.3. Descriptive Statistics of Subjects' Scores on Reading Test

	Reading
N	60
$\bar{X}$	14.5
SD	1.88
VAR	3.55

Analysis No. I

In the first step, to indicate the two groups' homogeneities, the means of intrinsic and extrinsic subjects on proficiency test were compared with each other through T-test. Table 20.4 shows the result of the T-test between the two groups.

Table 20.4. Comparison of the two means on Proficiency Test

	N	C	SD	T. Value
Intrinsic	30	64.5	5.69	
Extrinsic	30	63.5	6.05	0.52

d.f = 58 P<05 T. cri = 2.000

As it is shown in Table 20.4, the t-critical is higher than t-value and we can conclude that the difference between the two groups is not significant and they are at the same level of proficiency.

Analysis No. II

In order to find the answer to the research question of the study, a correlational analysis was employed between the subjects' scores on Motivation test and Reading Comprehension Test. The result of the statistical analysis is shown in table 20.5.

Table 20.5. Pearson Product Moment Correlation between Intrinsic and EFL Reading

	N	X	R
Intrinsic	30	18.46	
Reading	30	14.6	.64

d.f = 28 P< .05 R.cri = .3494

According to Table 20.5. correlation of .64 existed between two sets of scores. After checking the table of critical values of the Pierson Product Moment Correlation, the researcher concluded that Intrinsic motivation has a very positive effect on learning a foreign language skills. Therefore the null hypothesis was rejected.

Analysis No. III

In order to examine the probable effect of extrinsic motivation on EFL Reading, the researcher again concluded a Pierson Product Moment Correlation. The result is shown in table 20.6.

Table 20.6. Pearson Product Moment Correlation between Extrinsic and EFL Reading

	N	X	R
Extrinsic	30	16.6	
Reading	30	14.7	.36

d.f = 28 P < .05 R. cri = .3494

As Table 20.6 shows, the R-value is too near to the R.cri. Therefore the researcher could conclude that although the very slight rides in R-value can show a kind of effect, it is not significant at all. Especially in comparison with the R-value in the previous Table 20.5. which shows a very significant relation, it can be strongly claimed that its effect is insignificant on Reading Comprehension ability.

Discussion

This study investigated the effect of motivation (intrinsic/ extrinsic) and learning foreign language skills. As it's proved in the previous pages, the results showed that there was a significant effect ($p<0.5$) between intrinsic motivation and EFL Reading ($r = .64$). In terms of extrinsic motivation, the answer to the research question is "no". Because as it shows, there is an insignificant or no effect by extrinsic motivation on EFL Reading ($r = .36$). Therefore, intrinsic motivation as an affective factor can impact on test takers' performance on reading test. In conclusion, the hypothesis that believed in no significant effect of motivation on learning FL skills was rejected. The results of correlational analysis of this study supported the predicted effect of motivation on learning. The integrative orientation correlated most strongly with the intrinsic orientation. "Intrinsic motivation is the most self – determined form of motivation. A person who is motivated intrinsically learns an L2 because of the inherent pleasure in doing so. These feelings of enjoyment are hypothesized to stem from the fact that engagement is voluntary (i.e. not imposed on the learner by some outside sources) and because the activity challenges the learner's abilities, fostering a sense of L2 competence."

The outcome of this study is in line with the present belief possessed by most teachers that the learners who voluntarily take part in the process of learning gain more success than those who try to learn it by the force of some factors out of the learner's willingness.

Pedagogical Implications

The result of present research can be beneficial to test developers on the ground that considering such studies, they can make modifications on their approaches and methods to both language teaching and testing. That is, they can adapt their teaching and testing styles to students' motivation orientation.

On the other hand, the result of such studies warn language test developers not to ignore non-linguistic factors such as field independence, personality traits, etc. That is, instead of ignoring such factors, they must identify them to minimize their potential effects.

The findings of this study have also certain implications for teacher training programs and SL/FL teachers themselves. The researcher suggests that teacher training programs involve some practical courses, which have two aspects: teaching methods and psychology. Choosing appropriate method and approach, suitable techniques, and practical technems refer to the methodology domain. Helping the teachers to gain a deep understanding of the nature of the human learning, their motivation, personality traits, attitudes, etc. belong to another noticeable area called psychology.

REFERENCES

Brown, H.D. (1984). *Principles of Language Learning and Teaching*. Englewood Cliffs. Prentice Hall International.

Brown, H. Douglas. (2001). *Teaching by Principles: and Interactive Approach to Language Pedagogy/ 2nd ed.* Addison Welsley Longman, inc.

Crooks, Graham and Schmidt, Richard, W. (1991). *Motivation: Reopening the Research Agenda. Language learning* 41:469 - 512

Deci, Edward L. (1975): *Intrinsic Motivation*. New York. Plenum Press.

Fries C. (1963). *Linguistics and Reading*. New York, Holt Rinehart and Winston.

Keller, E., Taba – Warner, s. (1983). *Gambits 1*. Ottawa: Supply & Services Canada.

Moslow, Abraham, H. (1970). *Motivation and Personality*. Second Edition. New York: Harper & Row.

Piaget, Jean. (1972). *The Principles of Genetic Epistemology*. New york: Basic Books.

Rivers, Wilga. (1993). *Teaching Foreign language Skills:* Chicago. The University of Chicago Press.

Stern. H. H. (1993). *Fundamental Concepts in Language Teaching:* Oxford: Oxford University.

CHAPTER

21

Stressors and Mental Health in Adolescence

—*Seyed Younas Mohammadi Yousef Nejad and Dr. Raju S.*

ABSTRACT

The adolescent stage of life is a fascinating and crucial period characterized by change, transition, and challenge. During adolescence, children experience a number of stresses associated with the tremendous developmental changes in physical, cognitive, emotional and social spheres and the consequent adjustment difficulties. The school and peer group experience, development of sex roles and morality, and assumption of new roles within family structure all become very critical at this stage . Adjustment difficulties at this stage of life can substantially contribute to low self-esteem and self-efficacy, sense of inadequacy, unrelatedness, helplessness and powerlessness. These adjustment difficulties contribute significantly to mental health problems in adolescence and adulthood. Age and gender were important variables in mental health situations. More systematic descriptions of Stressors and Mental Health in Adolescence.

Key Words : Stressors, Mental health and Adolescence.

Introduction

Recent epidemiological data indicated that 15 per cent to 22 per cent of children and adolescents have mental health problems severe enough to warrant treatment. However, fewer than 20% of these youth with mental health problems currently receive appropriate services. Research also indicates that 25% to 50% of the general population of adolescents engage in multiple high-risk behaviors such as drug use, unprotected sexual intercourse, and violence. Therefore, adolescents today are at high risk for emotional, behavioral, and physical health difficulties due in part to their likelihood of engaging in dangerous activities.

Studies on risk and protective factors for children and adolescents have led mental health professionals to become interested in prevention programs. One well-studied prevention effort is life skills training. Life skills training is an effective prevention method for a range of problems with adolescents, as well as an effective intervention for adolescents experiencing a wide variety of emotional, behavioral, and physical problems.

Theoretical Model of Mental Health

Ecological-Developmental Perspective

An ecological approach to human development involves scientific study of a 'progressive, mutual accommodation' between an individual and the environment, in view of the social, cultural and historical contexts in which the immediate environment is embedded (Bronfenbrenner, 1979).

From an ecological perspective, an individual's interaction with the environment are not only influenced by the immediate environment but also by the individual's personal characteristics or history that were in part influenced by one's prior interaction with the same or similar environments (Nastasi & DeZolt, 1994). Development of personal-social competencies within the family involves a continuing process of mutual accommodation to the needs, demands and rules of the family. Behaviours that facilitate the stability of the system are thus reinforced among the family members. In a family, if gender-appropriate behavior is reinforced among the children and maintains the stability of the family, it is likely that the children will develop gender-specific behaviors.

So, in order to understand an individual's environment, it is necessary to examine the wider context, such as culture, or society, apart from the person's immediate environments like family, school or community. It should be noted that family, school or community rules, practices and values reflect the existing cultural or societal norms and values. For example, when the American parents expect their sons to be superior in science and mathematics compared to their daughters, the differential expectation explained by the widespread belief and expectation of male superiority in mathematics or science achievement over females in the American society.

Person-Centered and Environment-Centered Perspectives

Elias and Branden (1988) explained mental health of an individual from person- and environment-centred perspectives. The person-centered model postulated that behavioral and emotional difficulties in the individual are a function of stress that is experienced and physical vulnerability to stress, in relationship to the personal coping mechanisms, social resources and self-esteem of that individual. In an environment-centred model, the occurrences of behavioral-emotional disorders within a community or culture are influenced by the prevalent stressors and risk factors, in relationship to socialization practices, social resources and opportunities for relatedness (Elias and Branden, 1988; Nastasi and DeZolt, 1994). Nastasi has adapted the person- and environment-centered model of mental health suggested by Elias and Branden (1988), by incorporating some changes into that model. She has proposed that mental health is influenced by the interaction between critical person- and environment-centered factors. Mental health of the individual is determined by the personal vulnerabilities in relationship to socially or culturally valued competencies and personal mechanisms for coping with stress. The mental health within the community is influenced by the social-environmental stressors, in relationship to available social resources and culture-specific socialization practices (Jayasena & Nastasi, 1997).

Based on the person- and environment-centred model of mental health mentioned above, several general constructs related to mental health identifical :

(*a*) *culturally-valued competencies (e.g.,* academic competence, physical attractiveness) and *adjustment difficulties (e.g.,* behavioral problems);

(*b*) *personal vulnerabilities* due to personal and family history (e.g., school failure and family history of mental illness or domestic violence);

(*c*) *social stressors (e.g.,* violence, drug abuse);

(*d*) culture-specific *socialization practices* and socialization agents (e.g., family, school, community) responsible for influencing the development of the competencies;

(*e*) *personal resources (e.g.* problem-solving and decision-making skills) for coping with daily and other major life stresses;

(*f*) *social-cultural resources* available to youth (e.g., peers, family, teachers, religious organizations or professional services) to facilitate coping with the stressors.

Primary Prevention of Mental Illness through Promotion of Personal-Social Competence

The primary prevention model postulates the necessity to increase individual strengths and decrease individual limitations in order to prevent mental health problems and promote mental health of individuals. Among other models, integrating training programs to promote an individual's personal-social competence within the school curriculum was espoused by several researchers (Elias & Weissberg, 2000; Hall & Tones, 2002; Kapur, 1997; Nastasi & DeZolt, 1994). This model of primary prevention of mental health problems and promotion of personal-social competence is also consistent with World Health Organization's emphasis on providing life skill training to the children within school setting (Kapur, 1997).

Stressors and Mental Health

Adolescence has been described as a period of tremendous tumultuous development, a time of emotional upheaval and one marked by mental disorders and deviant behaviors more commonly than any other period of life (Erikson, 1968; Freud, 1958). Although some recent researchers have criticized these 'myths' of adolescence as simplistic overgeneralizations (Bandura & Walters, 1963; Offer & Schonert-Reichl, 1992), there is still concern regarding the extent of the stress experienced by adolescents as part of the normal development process, the degree to which present-day adolescents are exposed to stressors, and the extent to which they have developed and used coping strategies for dealing with the stresses and stressors they encounter (Deanda *et al.*, 1997). Increasing rates of adolescent suicide, depression, substance abuse and juvenile delinquency in almost every part of the world have been cited as indicators of increasing stressors and adolescents' inability to effectively cope with the resulting stress (Deanda *et al.*, 1997).

In addition to normal developmental stresses, other stressful life events also influence the adolescent's adjustment. Numerous studies have found significant relationships between the stressful life events in adolescents' lives and health, mental health and adjustment problems (Deanda *et al.*, 1997). Strong relationships have been found between stressful life events and the incidence of psychological and emotional disturbances among adolescents, particularly with regard to depression.

Some scholars have suggested that life stressors have an additive effect on the mental health of an individual (Biswas et al., 1995). Some studies have shown that there is a positive relationship between the numbers of recent stressful life events (SLEs) and adjustment difficulties, between SLEs and behavioral problems, and between adjustment difficulties and behavioral problems, indicating that with the presence of one factor, the chance of the presence of the other factor is significantly high (Cowen *et al.*, 1984; Sterling *et al.*, 1993). The major life stressors in adolescents are significantly related to mental health status, decreased self-esteem, disruptive and delinquent behavior and poor academic performance.

Several research studies have identified the sources of stress and stressors most frequently encountered by the adolescents. These major life stressors included economic hardship (Lempers, *et al.*, 1989; and illness and family discord (Fontana & Dovidio, 1984). Poverty was strongly associated with mental health problems. Unemployment, housing problems and other problems resulting from poverty were reported to be important risk factors that can trigger clinical depression. Children and adolescents are particularly vulnerable to problems associated with poverty. It is argued that familial poverty jeopardizes children's mental health and productivity. Lack of food, shelter, clothing, education and other materials may exert adverse effects on children's mental health. In addition, economic difficulty is related to ineffective parenting, parental psychopathology, and family hostilities, each of which can be additive sources of mental health problems. Furthermore, socioeconomic disadvantages often cause or aggravate marital dissatisfaction, conflict, aggression and violence within the family, thus increasing the risk of mental health problems among children (Beiser et al., 2002).

However, other researchers argued that cumulative daily stressors have the greatest impact on the lives of the adolescents (Armacost, 1989). Among these daily stressors were academic problems, schoolwork demands, academic pressures, and relationships with family and peers (Omizo *et al.*, 1988) including same-and opposite-sex peers.

Resources and Mental Health

Resources for coping with stressors have been investigated by many study, and both personal and social factors have been thought to affect coping in stressful situations. Researchers have indicated that perceived resources at a person's disposal to deal with a stressor influence the person's evaluation of the threat underlying the situation. Perceptions of abundant resources are associated with lower levels of perceived threat and the more efficacious coping. High self-esteem and self-efficacy, and good social network and personal support system have been reported to function as buffers in stressful environments and mediate healthy psychological adjustment. For example, personal-social competencies like self-esteem, self-efficacy and interpersonal relationship are the personal resources that are available and influential in helping an adolescent coping with major or daily life stressors. Parents, peers, siblings, teachers and mental health professionals in the schools and community are some of the social resources that may be available to the adolescents as part of their social network for coping with stressful situations. Researchers have also suggested that coping methods influence the social resources available to an individual (Deanda *et al.*, 1997). Coping in a prosocial manner, such as tending to others' needs and concerns for social aspects of behaviors, may bolsters an individual's support network, which in turn provides additional resources for successfully coping with stress in the future. On the other hand, coping in an antisocial manner, such as through aggression and self-focus, strains one's support network, thereby depleting the social resources needed for the future. Antisocial methods may address and answer personal needs, but alienate the supporters, thereby reducing and exhausting the availability of social resources. Prosocial methods, in addition to effectively meeting personal needs, may help build relationships, and thus enhance the individual's social network (Deanda *et al.*, 1997).

Mental Health, Culture and Gender

In defining mental health, cultures have ideal roles as well as normative expectations that may differently influence the sense of well-being in different individuals under very different conditions. Other things being controlled for, cultural norms determine whether the traits of submissiveness and nuance or assertiveness and competitiveness are related to a sense of well-being in women. Individualism may be valued in one setting, and despised in another. There may be very different threshold for mental well-being in agrarian versus industrial economies (Kleinman & Good, 1985). Furthermore, researchers have suggested that cultural context similarly plays a major role in the course of psychiatric disorders. So, investigating the role of culture as a mediating factor in the course of psychiatric disorders has the potential to improve research and practice in the field of mental health (Stanhope, 2002).

Researchers have argued that gender, as a cultural variable, creates differences in roles, beliefs, practices, specific vulnerabilities to mental health problems, and the presentation of mental illness.

Figure 21.1 depicts the distribution of individuals with a superimposed normal curve. Mental health emergencies appear to decrease with age, but early adulthood and middle age especially troubling.

Gender and cultural differences in the psychological constructs related to the mental health have been documented extensively by the researchers. Researchers have shown that physiological, social, psychological, and environmental factors each predict gender differences in mental health constructs such as personal-social competencies (self-esteem, self-efficacy), perceptions of stressors and use of coping strategies. Sociocultural factors play a very important role in influencing mental health of individuals through the process of socialization. For instance, socialization practices within a particular culture impact the process of gender role socialization. Through its various agents of socialization (e.g., family, school, peers, media), culture fosters development of gender role attitudes, beliefs/stereotypes, and gender-specific behavior which contribute to the gender differences in mental health constructs.

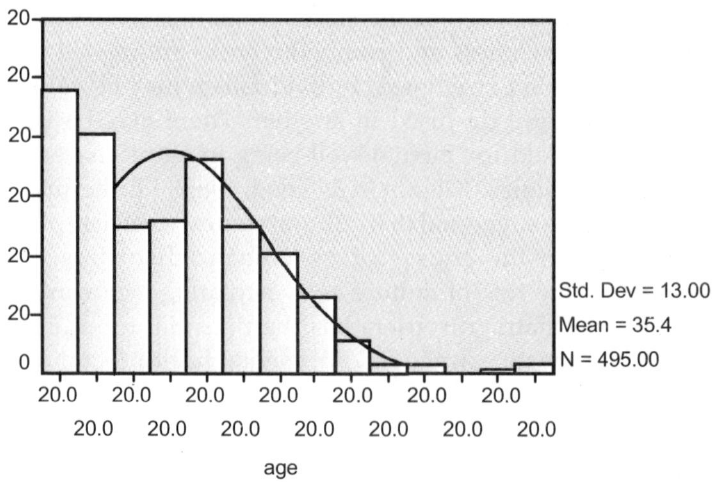

Fig. 21.1. Age Distribution

Conclusion

Females are particularly high utilizers of Severe Level crisis services are likely accounted for by the incidence of mental health disorders. Keep in mind that Depressive Disorders comprised 56% of our Severe Level contacts and the ratio of females to males for major depressive disorder is 2:1 (American Psychiatric Association, 1980).

Age appears to be inversely related to the incidence of mental health emergency. Young and middle age adults access mental health emergency services the most. This finding would be consistent with notions of adolescent and adult development theory wherein stressors are higher in early and middle adulthood. Also, many mental health disorders do not manifest until early adulthood (APA, 1994).

The coping process is particularly important during adolescence as it may be the first time that young people confront many different types of stressors and they may not yet have a wide range of coping strategies at their disposal. Moreover, the styles of coping with stress that develop during one's younger years influence how the individual handles new life events occurring in later adolescence and adulthood.

High self-esteem and self-efficacy, and good social network and personal support system have been reported to function as buffers in stressful environments and mediate healthy psychological adjustment (Bright et al., 1998).

REFERENCES

American Psychiatric Association (1980). Diagnostic and statistical manual of mental disorders(DSM-III), Third Edition, Washington D.C.: APA.

American Psychiatric Association (1994). Diagnostic and statistical manual of mental disorders (DSM-IV), Fourth Edition, Washington D.C.: APA.

Armacost, R. L. (1989). Perceptions of stressors by high school students. *Journal of Adolescent Research, 4,* 443-461.

Bandura, A. & Walter, R. (1963). *Social learning and personality development.* New York: Holt, Rinehart & Winston.

Beiser, M., Hou, F., Hyman, I., & Tousignant, M. (2002). Poverty, family process, and the mental health of immigrant children in Canada. *American Journal of Public Health, 92 (2).* 220-227.

Bronfenbrenner, U. (1979). *The Ecology of Human Development: Experiments by Nature and Design.* Cambridge, MA: Harvard University Press.

Cowen, E. L., Weissberg, R. A., and Guare, J. (1984). Differentiating attributes of children refered to school mental health program. *Journal of Metropolitan Child Psychology, 12,* 397-410.

Deanda, D., and Bradley, M., Collada, C., Dunn, L., Kubota, J., Hollister, V., Miltenberger, J., Pulley, J., Susskind, A., Thompson, L. A., and Wadsworth, T. (1997). A study of stress, stressors, and coping strategies among middle school adolescents. *Social Work in Education, 19 (2),* 87-98.

Elias, M. J. and Branden, L. R. (1988). Primary prevention of behavioral and emotional problems in school-aged population. *School Psychology Review, 17,* 581-592.

Elias, M. J. & Weissberg, R. P. (2000). Primary Prevention: Educational approaches to enhance social and emotional learning. *Journal of School Health, 70 (5), 186-190.*

Erikson, E. (1968). Identity, youth and crisis. New York: Norton.

Fontana, A., and Dovidio, J. F. (1984). The relationship between stressful life events and school-related performance of type A and type B Adolescents. *Journal of Human Stress, 10,* 50-54.

Freud, A. (1958). Adolescence. *Psychoanalytic Study of the Child, 13,* 255-278.

Hall, A. S., & Tones, I. (2002). Partnerships in preventing adolescent stress: Increasing sef-esteem, coping, and support thorough effective counseling. *Journal of Mental Health Counseling, 24 (2), 97-109.*

Jayasena, A., and Nastasi, B. K. (1997, August). *Education and mental health.* Paper presented at the 6th Sri Lanka Conference, Kandy, Sri Lanka.

Kapur, M. (1997). *Mental Health in Indian Schools.* New Delhi, India: Sage Publications.

Kleinman, A., and Good, B. (Eds.) (1985). *Culture and Depression.* Berkeley: University of California Press.

Lempers, J. D., Clark-Lempers, D., and Simons, R. L. (1989). Economic hardship, parenting, and distress in adolescence. *Child Development, 60,* 25-39.

Nastasi, B. K. & DeZolt, D. M. (1994). *School interventions for children of alcoholics.* New York, NY: Guilford.

Offer, D., and Schonert-Reichl, K. A. (1992). Debunking the myths of adolescence: Findings from recent research. *Journal ofAmerican Academy of Child and Adolescence Psychiatry, 31 (6),* 1003-1014.

Omizo, M. M., Omizo, S. A., and Suzuki, L. A. (1988). Children and Stress: An exploratory study of stressors and symptoms. *School Counselor,* 267-274.

Pies, T. Reducing Anxiety in the adult writer. Adult Learning, January/ February 1994, pp. 14-15.

Stanhope, V. (2002). Culture, control, and family involvement: A comparison of psychosocial rehabilitation in India and the United States. *Psychiatric Rehabilitation Journal, 25 (3),* 273-280.

Sterling, S., Cowen, E. L.,Tennen, H., & Affleck, G. (1993). The pil77les of self-esteem: A clinical perspective. In R. Baumeister, (Ed.). Self-esteem: Thepn77le of low self-regard. New York: Plenum.

CHAPTER

22

Relationship between Adjustment and Self-esteem among Adolescents

—Ningamma C. Betsur & Armin Mahmoudi

ABSTRACT

In the present study an attempt is made to see whether self-esteem is related to adjustment among adolescents studying in class 9 in Mysore city. A total of 100 adolescent students studying in Mysore city were randomly selected. They were administered Bell's Adjustment Inventory (BAI) (1968) (which measured adjustment of an individual in 4 areas - home, health, social and emotional) and self-esteem inventory developed by Coopersmith (1987), which measured self esteem of an individual in 5 areas - general self, social self, home parents, lie scale and school academic. Further, the students were classified into low and high self esteem groups. Independent samples 't' test was applied to see the differences between students having high and low self esteem in their adjustment scores. Results indicated that home parents self-esteem had positive influence over emotional adjustment of the students, where the analysis revealed that higher the self esteem better the adjustment. School academic self-esteem had positive influence over health adjustment of the students, where the analysis revealed that higher the self-esteem better the adjustment. Lastly, in other areas of self-esteem, there was no significant of self-esteem over adjustment of the students in individual areas as well as in total adjustment scores.

Introduction

Adolescence is a transitional period of one's life between childhood and adulthood, during which some important biological, psychological and social changes take place. It is a period of storm and stress. Adolescents have to adjust with their own changes in personality on one side and the changing socio-economic environment on the other side. Some adolescents find it difficult to adjust normally with these changes and experience some problems, which are characteristic of this developing stage.

The adolescence boy or girl may be faced with serious problem of adjustment when there is a difference of opinions, ideas and attitudes with their parents. Conflicts may arise between the adolescent and the parents that are difficult to resolve if both of them want to willing compromise. It takes all the tact and understanding of parents to handle their adolescent. (Coleman, 1974). Families of delinquent or uncontrollable adolescents are characterized by poorer family relationships and less social connectedness and adjustment. In general, these families are lower on cohesion and independence and higher on conflict and control (Fox, 1998).

Necessity is the most remarkable element in making all people have various needs including biological adjustment and mental ones. The former comprises the needs such as sleep, subsidiaries which cause the survival and satisfy the basic human demands, and the latter contributes to making a healthy personality and growth and removing the mental illness or breakdown. The needs can be named as self – esteem, security and invention

Indicating the importance of a healthy environment. On the whole, satisfying the needs leads to every single individual adjustment. Man lives in a world full of challenges resulted in depression and conflict as hindrances in achieving the goals. In other words, when a man's needs are not satisfied, he she suffer mental breakdown and tension. Thus, removing disappointment, shortcomings and life challenges ends in adjustment.

Self-esteem is the judgement we make about our own worth and the feelings associated with those judgements. According to Rosenberg (1979) a person with high self-esteem is fundamentally satisfied with the type of person he is yet he, may acknowledge his faults while hoping to overcome them. High self-esteem implies a realistic evaluation of the self's characteristics and competencies, coupled with an attitude of self-acceptance and self-respect. The persons with high self-esteem which shoulder more responsibilities can be more resistant and steadfast against mental pressure and the rest of ups and downs. High self-esteem causes prosperity, flourishing the hidden talents, initiative and economic, social and cultural achievements.

Self and peripheral adjustments are the bare necessities for every creature. Lack of due attention to the adjustment reactions amongst the youth will be gradually disguised as mental disorders, then it is significant to pay considerable and equal attention to the youth affairs as it is done to the adults to prevent from further consequences. Stank (2001) in his study demonstrated that there is a positive relationship between self-esteem and a given person's assumptions or of his/her capabilities; in other words, if the ratio of self-esteem in a person is lowered, the person feels debility. Conversely, high self-esteem will resuscitate empowerment feeling in a person. If a person feels that his/her self-esteem is exposed to instability, he/she preserves and defends from his self- worth by various behaviors and strategies.

Therefore, the adolescence with the same age group who are present at school can feel the tangibility of Pedagogical changes. Since school is a social environment, it is fundamental that every single individual keeps in touch with his/her peer groups Besides, the adjustment conflict can be posited in terms of the manner of adjustment to the school atmosphere, principals, teachers and subject matters is incorrect behaviors and will be pessimist to the future.

Objectives

(1) To find whether there is a significant difference between the adjustments of Standard (IX) students having different levels of General self-esteem.

(2) To find whether there is a significant differences between the adjustments of Standard (IX) students having different levels of Social self-esteem.

(3) To find whether there is a significant differences between the adjustments of Standard (IX) students having different levels of Home, Parents self-esteem.

(4) To find whether there is a significant differences between the adjustment of Standard (IX) students having different levels of School Academic self-esteem.

Methodology

Population and Sample

Population: The population of the study consisted of all the Standard (IX) student in Mysore city. The present study was conducted on the random sample of 100 Standard (IX) students (N = 100), male (N_1 = 50) and female (N_2 =50) of secondary schools of Mysore city. The age of the subjects of class (IX) ranged between 14 and 15 years.

Tools

1. Adjustment inventory for adolescent students developed by Bell's Adjustment (BAI) (1968). The inventory comprises of 140 items in relation to five areas of adjustment (Home 35, Health 35, Social 35, and Emotional 35 items). The test is helpful in screening the poorly adjusted students who may need further psycho-diagnostic study and counseling for their adjustment problems. The reliability coefficients were determined by spilt half and test retest methods, where the reliability coefficients varied from .81 to .89 for various areas of adjustment through split half and reliability coefficients varied from .89 to .92 through test retest method for different areas of adjustment. Cross validation of the scale with K. Kumar's adjustment inventory resulted in Pearson's *r* of .72,

.79, .82 and .81 for home, health, social and emotional areas respectively.

2. Self-Esteem Inventory for adolescent Students developed by Coopersmith (1987). The inventory comprises of 58 items in relation to five areas of self-esteem. (General self 25, Social self 8, Home parents 8, Lie scale 8, School Academic 8). The alpha coefficient for the total self-esteem scale was .88 and .79 for the Anglo-Indian and Vietnamese-Australian samples respectively. The validity of the scale was ascertained by Convergent and discriminate validity using EPQ (Eyesenck Personality Questionnaire), where negative and significant correlations were obtained for neuroticism scale and positive and significant correlations were obtained for extroversion dimension.

Procedure

The inventories were administered on the sample of 100 adolescent subjects. The data collection was one in two sessions. Before administering the scale proper rapport was established with the students. In the first session data were collected on personal information and self-esteem scale was administered. In the second session after a gap of 2-3 days the sample was administered Bells Adjustment Inventory. The questionnaires were administered in a batch of 2-3 students. They were given instructions for answering as prescribed in the respective manuals. The items in the answer sheet were scored with the help of scoring keys for four different areas for self-esteem and adjustment.

The obtained scores were recorded on master sheet and later fed to the computer using SPSS for Windows software (version 16.0). Depending on the scores the subjects were classified into two levels of self-esteem-low and High. Using Independent samples 't'test, influence of self esteem was verified on four areas of adjustment and total adjustment scores, taking self esteem as independent variable (varied at 2 levels-low and high) and adjustment scores as dependent variables.

Analysis and Interpretation of Data

Tables 22.1 to 22.5 show influence of self esteem on adjustment scores and results of independent samples't' test.

(*a*) General self esteem and adjustment : From Table 22.1, it is evident that in all the areas of adjustment, self esteem did not have significant influence as all the obtained't' values found to be non-significant. In other words students with low and high levels of general self esteem had statistically equal scores on different areas of adjustment. Self esteem was independent of adjustment in various areas as well as total adjustment scores.

Table 22.1. Mean adjustment scores (on various areas) of the sample having low and high general self esteem with the results of Independent samples't' test

Areas of adjust-ment	Level of self-esteem	Mean	S.D	't' value	P value
Home	Low	12.81	4.49	1.205	.231
	High	11.70	3.58		
Health	Low	8.90	5.12	.637	.526
	High	8.20	4.84		
Social	Low	16.69	4.82	.593	.555
	High	16.03	5.54		
Emotional	Low	13.69	5.69	1.129	.262
	High	12.40	3.86		
Total	Low	51.83	14.57	1.136	.259
	High	48.60	8.25		

Social self peer self esteem and adjustment : As in the case of social adjustment, the students with low and high self-esteem did not differ significantly in their adjustment scores in various areas and total adjustment scores. Here also, self-esteem did not have significant influence over adjustment scores. In the areas of home, health, social and emotional, the students with low and high self-esteem did not differ significantly in their adjustment scores. Even with respect to total adjustment students with high and low self-esteem didn't differs significantly. That means, self-esteem didn't have significant influence over adjustment scores

Table 22.2 : Mean adjustment scores (on various areas) of the sample having low and high social self peer self esteem with the results of Independent samples 't' test

Areas of adjust-ment	Level of self-esteem	Mean	S.D	't' value	P value
Home	Low	12.69	4.53	.649	.518
	High	12.11	3.73		
Health	Low	8.45	4.91	.627	.532
	High	9.11	5.27		
Social	Low	17.11	4.79	1.657	.101
	High	15.39	5.30		
Emotional	Low	12.80	5.32	1.288	.201
	High	14.19	5.00		
Total	Low	51.08	14.00	.222	.825
	High	50.47	11.31		

Home Parents Self-esteem and Adjustment : In the case of parents self-esteem only in the case of emotional adjustment, those with low self esteem had higher emotional maladjustment (mean 14.36), and those with higher self-esteem (mean 12.24) had better adjustment and the obtained 't' value of 2.061 was found to be significant at .042 level. In other words self-esteem had positive influence over emotional adjustment and not on other areas and in total adjustment.

Table 22.3. Mean adjustment scores (on various areas) of the sample having low and high home parents self esteem with the results of Independent samples 't' test.

Areas of adjust-ment	Level of self-esteem	Mean	S.D	't' value	P value
Home	Low	13.16	4.76	1.613	.110
	High	11.80	3.59		
Health	Low	9.16	5.26	.935	.352
	High	8.22	4.78		
Social	Low	17.10	4.66	1.217	.227
	High	15.88	5.35		
Emotional	Low	14.36	5.66	2.061	.042
	High	12.24	4.57		
Total	Low	53.22	14.95	1.831	.070
	High	48.50	10.44		

Academic self-esteem and adjustment : In the case of school academic self-esteem only in the case of health adjustment, those with low self esteem had higher health maladjustment (mean 9.42), and those with higher self esteem (mean 7.34) had better adjustment and the obtained 't' value of 1.998 was found to be significant at .049 level. In other words self esteem had positive influence over health adjustment and not on other areas and in total adjustment.

Table 22.4. Mean adjustment scores (on various areas) of the sample having low and high school academic self esteem with the results of Independent samples 't' test

Areas of adjust-ment	Level of self-esteem	Mean	S.D	't' value	P value
Home	Low	13.03	4.42	1.786	.077
	High	11.46	3.75		
Health	Low	9.42	5.36	1.998	.049
	High	7.34	4.06		
Social	Low	16.69	5.16	.547	.586
	High	16.11	4.83		
Emotional	Low	13.32	5.47	.060	.952
	High	13.26	4.82		
Total	Low	52.43	14.45	1.655	.101
	High	48.17	17.46		

Total self-esteem and Adjustment : In all the areas of adjustment, self-esteem did not have significant influence as all the obtained 't' values found to be non-significant. In other words students with low and high levels of total self esteem had statistically equal scores on different areas of adjustment. Self esteem was independent of adjustment in various areas as well as total adjustment scores.

Main Findings of the Study

1. Home parents self-esteem had positive influence over emotional adjustment of the students, because students with higher self-esteem had better emotional adjustment.
2. School academic self esteem had positive influence over health adjustment of the students, because students with higher self-esteem had better health adjustment.

Table 22.5. Mean adjustment scores (on various areas) of the sample having low and high self esteem with the results of Independent samples't' test

Areas of adjust-ment	Level of self-esteem	Mean	S.D	't' value	P value
Home	Low	13.18	4.80	1.662	.100
	High	11.78	3.53		
Health	Low	8.42	4.97	.536	.593
	High	8.96	5.11		
Social	Low	17.08	4.57	1.176	.242
	High	15.90	5.43		
Emotional	Low	13.74	5.90	.841	.403
	High	12.86	4.48		
Total	Low	51.86	15.01	.765	.446
	High	49.86	10.79		

3. In other areas of self-esteem, there was no significant influence of it over adjustment of the students in individual areas as well as in total adjustment scores.

(Except, in the above mentioned two uses).

The results obtained in the present study are some what in agreement with the studies done aboard. In a study on advantaged and disabled groups, self-esteem correlated positively with general self-efficacy. Both variables correlated positively with adjustment (Saracoglu, *et al.*, 1989). David *et al.*, (1998) investigated (*a*) global self-esteem and (*b*) social-contextual incongruity in factors contributing to the development and maintenance of self-esteem as predictors of the emotional, behavioral, and academic adjustment and found that higher reported levels of global self-esteem were associated with more favorable scores on most measures of adjustment. Incremental predictive contributions also were found, however, for indices of social-contextual incongruity in factors contributing to the development and maintenance of self-esteem. Incongruity in the direction of domain-specific self-evaluations being relatively stronger for peer-oriented domains in comparison to the domains of school and family was linked consistently with less positive adjustment.

Study by Duncan (1949) adopts a multi-dimensional construct of self-esteem to examine the relationship between self-perception and psychological adjustment in order to identify specific dimensions that discriminate between disturbed and non-disturbed groups. Results indicate that dimensional self-concept scores are significantly lower for clinical subjects while there are no significant differences between groups on the mathematics, honesty, and physical ability dimensions. These findings provide a more fine grained understanding of the relationship between self-esteem and psychological adjustment and emphasize the need to examine self-esteem in terms of its particular dimensions.

Descriptive views of the self and standards for self-evaluation will be more favorable and lenient than parental views and standards in corresponding areas results in poorer adjustment. Results indicate the importance of social-contextual factors for understanding the role of self-esteem in adaptation during adolescence. Implications for esteem enhancement as a prevention and health promotion strategy with this age group should be focused.

REFERENCES

Coleman, J. (1974). *Personality psychology, theories and researches.* Translated by Javad Jafari, Parvin Kadivar (1993): Rasa Publicarion.

Cooper Smith. (1987). *Self-esteem inventory.*

Douglas, C. Kimmel Irving, B. Weiner (1968). *Adolescence develpmentl transition.*

David, L. DuBois, Catherine A. Bull, Michelle D. Sherman & Magie Roberts (1998). Self-Esteem and Adjustment in Early Adolescence: A Social-Contextual Perspective. *Journal of Youth and Adolescence*, 27, 557-583.

Duncan, M.H. (1949). *Home adjustment of stutterers versus non-stutterers*.journal of '*Speech and Hearing Disorders*, *14*, 225-259.

Fox, M. (1998). *Adjustment psychology*. Bonyad Press.

Ojha, R.K. (1968). *Bell's Adjustment inventory*.

Rosenberg, M. (1979). *Conceiving the self*. New York: Basic Books.

Saracoglu, Berenice, Harold Minden, Marc Wilchesky (1989). The Adjustment of Students with Learning Disabilities to University and Its Relationship to Self-Esteem and Self-Efficacy. *Journal of Learning Disabilities*, 22, 9, 590-592.

Stank, J.D. (2001): "Conformity, Ability and self-esteem", Representative New Search in Social Psychology, Vol. 30, No. 2.

CHAPTER

23

Monitoring of Academic Achievement of Students in Tribal Schools of Andhra Pradesh

—*Malli Gandhi*

ABSTRACT

So far as the tribal education programme is concerned, there is a shift in approaches and policies from the provision of equal opportunities and incentives to that of effective participation, participatory development and receiving good quality education on the part of the child. May be a tribal child or a non-tribal child, the present emphasis is on quality improvement in schools. A tribal child should in no way lag behind as regards quality. Thus, there is a need for effective monitoring of the academic achievement of children in tribal schools.

The Chapter provides a detailed account of the various issues connected with the monitoring of the academic achievement in tribal schools. What is academic monitoring, what is academic monitoring of students, who is responsible for this, what are the steps in monitoring, how to collect information and what type of assistance is to be provided are dealt with in detail. It is reported that the three important steps in monitoring are knowing, identifying and assisting. Some hints are also suggested to the administrators in the process of academic monitoring of students.

Why Education?

Modern educationists believe that every individual is endowed with certain innate abilities or potentialities and these are to be brought out to achieve a harmonious development. The purpose of education is to promote the development of abilities to enable the individual for exercising such responsibilities in the society as his powers allow. Education has to make the individual physically strong, intellectually sound, emotionally stable, culturally fit and socially efficient. According to National Policy on Education 1986, Education has to produce self-assured, more productive, more capable and more thinking type of citizens. It is not the imitator that is to be developed, but it is exploratory that is to be developed. Education has to promote productivity, achieve social and national integration, step up the process of modernization, and inculcate social, moral and spiritual values.[1] This is what is expected of education.

In order to achieve these objectives suitable curriculum has been formulated and introduced at different levels of the education system. At the primary stage children are exposed to three academic subjects and five activity subjects. The academic subjects comprise of Language, Mathematics and Environmental Studies (EVS I - Social Studies and EVS II - Science). The activity subjects consist of Health Education, Physical Education, Socially Useful Production Work, Creative Activities and Moral Education. From class III level, English is introduced and from Class VI Hindi is also introduced as Second Language. Secondary education begins to expose students to appreciate the roles of science, humanities and social sciences.[2]

Each subject in the curriculum has a specific objective. Language is a means of communication. Teaching of language should aim at developing the four skills of listening, speaking, reading and writing. Mathematics should be visualized as the vehicle to train a child, to think, reason, analyze and to articulate logically. Science education needs to develop in the child well-defined abilities and values such as the spirit of inquiry, creativity, objectivity, the courage to question and an aesthetic sensibility. It should enable the learner to acquire problem solving and decision-making skills. In our culturally plural society, education should foster universal and eternal values, oriented towards the unity and integration of our people. The value education should help eliminate obscurantism, religious fanaticism, violence, superstition and fatalism.

The teacher who is the main dynamic force in the system of education needs to transact this curriculum by adopting appropriate strategy. Today there is a shift from Epistemic approach to Reconstructionist approach, from teacher centered approach to that of child-centered approach. The present emphasis is on the adoption of child centered, activity-oriented and competency based teaching-learning process. Student is the center of the education system. "The child is the starting point, the center and the end. His growth and his development is the ideal of education" felt John Dewey.[3] His Excellency the President of India, Dr. A.P.J. Abdul Kalam, has stated

> "What is more important is that teachers should not transmit their frustration to their students, but should constantly try to upgrade their skills and encourage the children to think big".[4]

The child should be the focal point in the system of education. Here comes the role of academic monitoring.

What is Monitoring?

Monitoring is defined as a periodic review and surveillance by Management at every level of the implementation of an activity in order to ensure that the inputs, deliveries, work schedules, targeted outputs and other required actions are proceeding according to a plan. It is a process of recording, collecting, processing, and disseminating information to assist the project management and decision-making.[5] Monitoring is a managerial function that begins with the start of a project and ends with the completion of the project. It is a continuous process during the implementation of the project. It is an essential process for successful implementation of a project. During the process of monitoring the shortfalls, deviations, problems and causes for the same are identified so as to take appropriate remedial and corrective action.[6]

What is Academic ?

Today in a school system academics include both theoretical as well as non-theoretical aspects. It includes subjects not only for intellectual development but also other types of development. It includes curricular, co-curricular and extra-curricular activities.[7]

What is Academic Monitoring?

Academic Monitoring is a periodic review of curricular, co-curricular and extra-curricular activities carried on in the school as scheduled/planned. It is a continuous process of knowing to what extent the objectives are realized, whether the objectives/targets/execution need any change. It involves measuring, recording, collecting, processing and communicating information to assist the management relating to the teaching-learning process. To bring about certain desirable changes in the behaviour of the child either at the thought level, perception level or psychomotor level is the ultimate objective of the teaching learning process. To what extent these are achieved should be known and necessary steps should be taken either to change the strategy or the objectives to be realized. Whether there is any problem with regard to teaching or problems with regard to learning are to be known and suitable measures are to be taken.[8]

What is Academic Monitoring of Students?

Academic monitoring involves three important issues, viz.) knowing, Identifying, and Assisting. *Knowing* involves-knowing whether the student is progressing in learning the academic as well as non-academic activities organized in the school, whether the expected learning outcomes are achieved or not, whether the desired behavioural changes have taken place in the child as a result of instruction. *Identifying* involves-identifying the strengths and weaknesses of the student, the deficiencies, the interests and attitudes etc. *Assisting* involves-

suggesting steps to make good the deficiencies, implementing the programmes to make good the weaknesses, taking up remedial instructional programmes, taking up individual care and attention, arranging for special coaching etc.[9].

Who are Responsible for Academic Monitoring of Students?

Since monitoring is a managerial function, all those who are involved in the project implementation should do monitoring. It is important to appreciate that monitoring is not an individuals' function but it is a collective function. However to be more specific the responsibility needs to be taken by the following personnel:

(1) Teacher in the school situation.

(2) Prefect in the dormitory.

(3) Parent at home.

(4) Warden in the hostel and

(5) Supervisor/Administrator/Manager in the System.[10]

How to Collect Information in Academic Monitoring?

Through the following Programmes, information for providing academic monitoring of students may be collected. The observation of classroom teaching-learning process, student participation in the process, interviews/putting questions, observing and checking the written work, class work and home work, attendance registers, performance in Unit Tests and Terminal Tests, assignments, pupils products, progress cards, cumulative record cards, pupils diaries, library work, laboratory work, project work, through peers, teachers, parents, participation in debates, discussion, quiz programmes, celebrations, co-curricular activities, review meetings, analysis of answer scripts of unit tests and terminal tests etc.[11]

What are to be identified?

After collecting the data for Academic Monitoring, the next step is identification of strengths, and weaknesses. Some students may be academically sound in some subjects and some others may not. In which areas they are sound and in which areas they are weak is to be identified. It is also important to identify the outstanding performance of the children and identify the deficiencies-in academic subjects, in activity subjects and personality traits.[12]

The current practice of academic planning for school education is largely a 'top down' annual exercise. Its focus is on how teaching time should be allocated for teaching of subject content over the year, and stipulating other activities that will be conducted in schools. This is done by SCERTs or the Directorates/Departments of Education, and prescribed uniformly for all schools in the State. The importance of school level planning was emphasized by the Kothari Commission.

To be meaningful academic planning has to be done in a participative manner by heads and teachers. One component of planning will include augmentation and improvement of physical resources of the school. The second is to address the diverse needs of students and to identify the inputs and academic support that the school needs in order to respond to these needs. The planning exercise is an important process through which schools can enlist the involvement and support of the larger community in the education of the children. This includes the village education committees and other statutory bodies. Micro planning, which includes village level mapping of school participation (non-enrolled children, attendance patterns, children with special needs, etc.) as well as identification of human resources allows the school to plan on a more realistic basis for every child.

The potential role of Headmasters in providing academic leadership to their schools is yet to be adequately realized. At present they are seen largely as the administrative authority within the school, though they lack the necessary control to exercise this authority, or even to ensure regular school functioning. Often they are equipped with neither the capacity nor authority to exercise choice and judgement relating to school curriculum. Headmasters and teachers need to be able to identify specific supports they require for their schools, articulate their expectations regarding the content of trainings and school visits from the cluster and block personnel and participate in the process of monitoring and supervision. Currently they are not differentiated enough from teachers with regard to their academic roles. The role that the headmasters can play within a cluster of schools must be highlighted.

Schools are now the focus of an increasing number of programmes to enhance quality, spread awareness about societal concerns relating to the environment, health and so on. Headmasters are often besieged by the numerous programmes they are called upon to conduct and participate. Programmes often lack clarity regarding their objectives and methodology and their activities tend to overlap. It is important that as part of the process of school level planning, they should be able to participate in decisions about programmes they need and how they should be integrated into regular school activities. These programmes could then be coordinated at the cluster and block level.

Conventionally, monitoring of schools has been through the Inspectorate system. This system has served largely to exercise authority and control rather than provide academic support to teachers. The School Inspectors perform a number of functions, one of which one is to visit schools under their purview. Their visits are usually few and far between, during which the students and teachers tend to present positive picture of the school, regardless of ground realities, due to fear of punishment. This reduces monitoring to a 'policing' function. Monitoring for quality must be seen as a process that enables and provides constructive feedback in relation to the teaching and learning processes within specific classroom contexts. The monitoring system put in place must be carefully analysed in relation to its objectives, and the norms and practices that are to be institutionalized to achieve the objectives. It must provide for sustained interaction with individual schools in terms of teaching-learning processes within the classroom context.[13]

How to Provide Assistance?

After identifying the strengths and weaknesses the next step is to provide assistance. The following are the ways through which assistance can be provided.

1. Suggest more and higher type assignments to gifted or outstanding students to progress further.
2. Give multilevel assignments based on individual differences.
3. Arrange for special coaching in time.
4. Arrange for remedial teaching.
5. Meeting the school Officials/Parents/Wardens.
6. Discussions with School Education Committees.
7. Examination of progress cards.
8. Organization of activities like debates, discussions, quiz programmes.
9. Working out the questions given in unit tests and terminals.
10. Regular Laboratory and Library work.
11. Correction of scripts before students.
12. Regular habit of studying.
13. Frequent testing.
14. Arranging extension lectures.
15. Timely supply of text books, writing materials, clothing etc.
16. Timely release of scholarships.
17. Supply of Nutritious food.
18. Health checkups.
19. Frequent visits.
20. Organization of co-curricular activities more in number.
21. Updation of syllabus.
22. Conduct of pre-final examination and correction of answer scripts before the students.
23. Working out the question papers of the last three years public examination and questions from question banks.

24. Adoption of students by staff.
25. Working out the exercises given at the end of the lessons in the textbooks.
26. Extra Drill.
27. Map pointing in Social Studies.
28. Organization of supervised study programme.
29. Training in letter writing and comprehension exercises
30. Emphasizing on co-operative learning etc.[14]

What are the Hints for Administrators in Academic Monitoring of Students?

The following are the hints for Administrators:

1. Maintain a register with names of students, their personal details and school details
2. Record their academic progress during personal visits
3. Interviews, discussions with teachers
4. Suggest measures for making good the deficiencies noticed based on the visits, putting questions etc.
5. Follow up
6. Visit at least once in a month the school and hostel and observe the academic progress of the students
7. Have direct interaction with students
8. Go through the school inspection reports
9. Hold review meetings
10. Maintain contacts with parents
11. Attend the review meetings organized by Education Department on academic issues and
12. Attend the Headmasters conference organized in the District level etc.[15]

REFERENCES

1. Government of India, *National Policy on Education, 1986*, Ministry of Human Resource Development, Department of Education, New Delhi, August 1986.

2. Aggarawal, J.C., *Education Policy in India, Retrospect and Prospect,* Shipra Publications, New Delhi 1992.
3. Dewey's philosophical views on educational aims, curriculum and pedagogy exercised an influence on the educational imagination of pedagogues and several national systems of education from the late nineteenth century and into the early half of the twentieth century. In his pedagogic creed, the teacher assumes the functions of an enquirer in order to set a model for the child. De-Wey's yardstick for judging authentic or meaningful education is that it must provide experimental learning for each child by introducing real life problems in the classrooms. Dewey's educational ideal is the problem-solving, self-reliant, articulate individual. See Krishna Kumar and Padma M.Sarangapani.
4. "History of the Quality Debate, in *Contemporary Education Dialogue", Vol.2 : 1, Monsoon 2004,* p. 34. Also see, Dewey, J., *Democracy and Education: The Middle works of John Dewey,* Vol. 9, Carbondale : South Illinois University Press, 1996.
5. The teacher, the child's window to learning and knowledge, has to play the role model in generating creativity in the child. If parents and teachers show the required dedication to shape the lives of the young, India would get a new life. See. A.P.J. Abdul Kalam, *Ignited Minds, unleashing the power within India,* Viking Penguin Book, India, 2002, pp. 25-26.
6. Mazda Jenkin, Jeff Jones, Sue Lord, *Monitoring and Evaluation for School Improvement,* Heinemann Educational Publishers, Oxford, 2000, p. 5.
7. At the level of monitoring and supervision due emphasis is given in the tribal schools of Andhra Pradesh. Special efforts were made for effective monitoring and academic supervision of schools at the local level by decentralizing the centers. Cluster Resource Centres have been responsible for this function. The Education Officers are being created by the Government to discharge monitoring and supervisory responsibilities. At the Community level, Village Level Committees (VEC) are vested with power to look after the academic and monitoring of the tribal schools to improve the quality of teaching and regular presence of teachers. The concept of 'school complex' has come into existence as means to improve the quality of teaching and break the isolation of teachers. Supervision was improved at the institutional level by empowering the VECs and ensuring community participation and involvement in the educational development of the tribal areas. The VEC members

have been given training in monitoring, supervision and administration of schools.

8. See K. Sujatha, *Education among Tribals, Year 2000 Assessment, Education for All*, National Institute of Educational Planning and Administration, Ministry of Human Resource Development, Government of India, pp. 17-18.
9. See P. Venkata Rao, *"Monitoring of Community Participation activities and School Education Committees"*, theme paper presented at a training programme conducted at Regional Institute of Education, NCERT, Mysore, March 2004.
10. Sujatha K., "Education among scheduled Tribes" in R.Govinda, *A profile of India Education Report*, Oxford University Press, New Delhi 2002.
11. *DPEP Calling*, Strategies for Tribal Education, District Primary Education Programme, April 1996, pp. 256 to 276.
12. The National Policy on Education 1986 (Programme of Action 1992) stated that: the monitoring of education in scheduled caste and scheduled tribe areas will be entrusted to the local community/ Village Education Committee with adequate representation of SC/ ST members specially women. The local community will take the total responsibility of planning the educational facilities in SC/ST areas. See Government of India, *The National Policy on Education, 1986, Programme of Action, 1992*, Government of India, Ministry of Human Resource Development, Department of Education, p. 13.
13. Krishna Kumar wrote "The examination system is actually cheating the masses by concealing the deep divisions that exist within the education system, where a poor mill worker's child from a neglected government school is made to compete with children from well-to-do public schools. The system submerges these ugly realities under a veneer of total parity among candidates. But it hardly needs probing to find that a majority of failures belong to the disadvantaged". See Probe team, *Public Report on Basic Education in India*, Oxford University Press, New Delhi, 1999, p.81. Also see Krishna Kumar, "Schooling in Rural India", *The Hindu*, January 11, 2005, p. 8.
14. See, K. Sesidhara Rao, *"Academic Monitoring of Students in Tribal Areas"* Paper presented at a Training Programme conducted at Regional Institute of Education, NCERT, Mysore, March 2004.
15. See, *Draft National Curriculum Framework 2005*, National Council of Educational Research and Training, New Delhi, 2005, pp. 92-93.

CHAPTER

24

The Effect of Shyness through the Life Cycle—View

Daryoush Ghasemian

Introduction

Shyness is a form of excessive self-focus, a preoccupation with one's thoughts, feelings and physical reactions. It may vary from mild social awkwardness to totally inhibiting social phobia. Shyness may be chronic and dispositional, serving as a personality trait that is central in one's self definition. Situational shyness involves experiencing the symptoms of shyness in specific social performance situations but not incorporating it into one's self-concept. We experience a personality trait as important as shyness in different ways at various points throughout our lives. As babies, we cannot rightly be said to be shy, but we may have been burn with a brain that is highly reactive to novelty. As young children, we must learn to make friends and play with others in the sometimes chaotic school environment. As adolescents, we may feel stigmatized by our shyness and seek ways to hide it. As adults, we struggle for strategies to connect with others – friends, lovers, coworkers – and assuage our loneliness. But although different issues arise at each of these life stages, the same underlying principles apply; in dealing with shyness of the body, mind and self we grapple with our slow-to-warm-up tendencies, the approach/avoidance conflict and restrictive comfort zones.

Carducci and Kaiser (2002) described her baby grand daughter to them:

> If Kelly were at my house and you walked in – no matter how much fun we were having – she would just stop and crawl over to where her mom and dad were sitting. When she was a year old, if anyone would go to her or talk to her, she would break out in tears. On her first birthday, the whole family was at her house. She was playing and was just fine. Then we sat her down in her high chair to have cake. Everyone gathered around to sing "Happy Birthday," and she looked at us with an expression like, "What are you doing to me?" She went from a happy lit the girl to one in tears in seconds!

Even now, when we first come into her house, she doesn't run up to us and give us a kiss. It takes five or ten minutes before you can approach her, and then she's loving.

The research of Pilkonis (1977) has identified different types of shy people: shy and those who are privately shy. Publicly shy people express distress as a consequence of more overt manifestation of their shyness, such as a through being too quiet, behaving awkwardly, and failing to respond appropriately in social situation(e.g., not acknowledging a compliment) (Pilkonis,1977). Privately shy people express distress as a consequence of more covert manifestations of their shyness, such as a through intense psycho physiological arousal (e.g., pounding heart, muscle tension, and anxiety reactions) (Pilkonis, 1977). Socially anxious shy people express distress as a consequence of more cognitive manifestations of their shyness, such as being excessively self-concious (e.g., do my clothes fit right) and overly concerned about being evaluated socially by others (e.g., I wonder what she thinks of my comment).

There are five types of shyness: those who are publicly shy and those who are privately shy. One is more concerned about behaving badly, the other about feeling badly. The chronically shy people often lead a pained existence. They experience shyness more frequently than other shy people and report being shy in significantly more situations. They perceive themselves as being more shy than their peers. They experience shyness as a personal problem more frequently and believe that they are less capable of overcoming their shyness than other people. The other type is transitionally shy, these individual act and feel shy during certain periods of their lives, usually when they leave one phase and being an other, such as entering college, starting a new job, or beginning to date after divorce. This is a common and normal response to uncertain, insecure, and unpredictable situations. In these threatening circumstance, they display all of the characteristics of the publicly shy, but once they have habituated and are able to cope with their new challenges, they become less shy and more confident about themselves and their abilities.

Are we born shy?

Temperament does not act alone to create shyness. Your biological make up, along with your life experiences and how you interpret those experiences, help to create shyness. Arcus and Kagan (1995) states:

> Biology influences your body's reactivity. You have been born with the capacity to handle a certain level of threatening stimulation. But biology is just a starting point, an influence you can surrender to or control through determination and wisdom. Its power will manifest throughout your life but will be most obvious when you are young – before experience and intellect come into play.

If you were born with a highly reactive system, your inhibited temperament may have been instrumental during the first two years of life because you had neither the mental capacity nor the experience upon which to rely. Consequently, like Kelly, you might have clung to your parents, cried when you were separated and fussed when strangers came near.

But after the age of two, biology ceases to be the most important factor. Caspi *et al.* (1988) explains:

> "environmental experiences come to the fore during the second year of childhood and beyond. How your parents and teachers treat you, the friendships you form, your relationship with your siblings, the classroom environment – all of these factors and the memories they evoke may instigate or extinguish shy behavior."

During adolescence the mind becomes the most potent force, and it will hold sway into adulthood. But it need not ordain a life of shyness. The shy adolescent, attempting to interpret his experiences as a highly reactive child, can begin to make appropriate choices that will calm his nervous system. He can select friends who support those choices by sparing him from overwhelmingly stimulating situations. He can build a strong identity based on his strengths and decide how he will use those strengths in the business and social world. Using his higher brain, he will be able to take charge of his life.

Almost half of the adult population claims to be shy, yet only 20 percent of babies are born inhibited. So, many of these adults must have acquired their shyness – through mental and emotional experiences and using their higher minds.

Just as parental care and experience influence temperamentally inhibited children, so are temperamentally uninhibited children shaped by these factors. But their shy minds interpret these circumstances and create shyness, scoring it into the brain's wiring with repetition and reinforcement. Their shyness comes from without. The shy mind is critical to this course.

Some people are born with bodies that make them highly reactive, but this does not mean they will become shy. In the next chapter we will explore how these biological processes are important during childhood, before we acquire learned shyness or the experience and wisdom to combat it.

Shyness in Pre-schooler

"I remember feeling mortified if someone noticed me," explained Jenny, a film maker in New York. Triandis (1994) expresses:

> When I was very young, before kindergarten, I remember hanging on to the back of my mother's skirt and trying to keep her between me and anybody whom I didn't want to notice me wile we were shopping or out in the world.
>
> I couldn't meet other children. The only kids I knew were my next-door neighbors. My parents tell me I wouldn't associate with anybody but my immediate family and the kids next door. I was terrified of my grandparents: I didn't even like to go to their house. With other relatives or family friends, I'd just hide in my room and hope that they'd leave me alone. I thought people could see through me – that burning sensation I still get occasionally – and I wanted to disappear through a hole in the floor. I'd even hide behind the furniture.

In addition to temperament, experiences within the family have a profound impact on the development of your child's personality traits, including shyness. The family is his first social environment; it teaches him how to cope with relationships. What he learns there will be reproduced in adulthood.

Siblings

A Pennsylvania college student explained to me why she believed she was shy. "I have a brother who is three years older than me," she wrote, "and as long as I can remember, he dominated the conversations where I was present, whether it be with our parents, relatives or friends. Because he did all the talking, I never had to. I could just fade into the background. To this day it continues."

Siblings are our first peers. How we interact with them often affects how we deal with others later in life. It may be a cliché, but its still true that older siblings seem to be overly responsible and mature, middle children want to be noticed as individuals and youngest, the "babies of the family," can shirk responsibility because their parents are permissive with them.

Intense sibling rivalries often affect how people see themselves and the world. Asendopf (1993) wrote:

> I don't know if I am genetically predisposed to being shy, but I do know that, while growing up, I always felt like I was second best to my six-years-older sister. I was nothing, and my opinions didn't matter to anybody. Maybe that wasn't the case in reality, but I always felt like it.

The Father's Role

Most dads teach their youngsters about power and self-expression through their style of play. They toss their kids into the air, give piggyback rides, scare and chase them, wrestle with them, or hold them tightly until they cry "uncle."

Your child learns many life lessons from this rowdiness. First, he sees that you and adults in general are stronger and more powerful than he is. He also must tolerate a certain level of frustration in a world that is rough, tough and scary; He carefully watches your moods and nonverbal cues, your face and body language, to predict what will happen next. He also learns to clearly communicate his emotions by giggling, crying, struggling, asking you to stop, or wandering away from the uncomfortable situation. This forces him to listen to his emotions, which may signal that the roughhousing is getting out of hand.

In short, through play, you train your children to hold their own in the world by teaching them to tolerate frustration, solve problems and interpret and communicate emotions.

The Impact of Divorce

Divorce is hard on children in general and can be especially difficult for a shy child, who reacts more to change, is more sensitive, and has less social support than his outgoing siblings.

Even when the breakup is relatively painless for the spouses, it is a trauma that can bring about shyness in temperamentally uninhibited children or make an inhibited child withdraw even further.

According to Asendopf (1990):

> Indeed, withdrawal is merely one sign of adjustment to the new situation. To cope with their confusion about divorce, young children may also become depressed, blame themselves, develop intense fears, create reconciliation fantasies, and even become aggressive and hostile. If you divorce, keep in mind that your children will be profoundly affected by the loss. Be sure that both of you are communicating with them clearly, compassionately and honestly.
>
> You and your family members will have the first and most fundamental influence on your child's shyness. But this may wane as your youngster discovers other children in the neighborhood, at play centers, and at school. IN fact, children naturally turn to playmates at the age of six or seven and enter what is called the latency period, during which they become sociable.

The latency period is a dress rehearsal for the roles children play as adults. Youngsters care for their dolls to practice parenting, play catch to mimic professional athletes, prepare tea parties to feel like hosts, and play war games to experience powerfulness. In the process, they learn valuable lessons about cooperation, sharing, friendship, leadership and negotiation. Not only do they want to play with each other, but they must in order to grow.

The latency period can be the most critical in the development of shyness. Children need to learn social lessons during this time but cannot do so if they isolate themselves by watching television, playing computer games, or reading. They need to be with friends and to explore the world.

The Growing Impact of Shyness in Latency

During the first few years of elementary school, young children seem oblivious to the fact that some of their peers are more reticent, but their attitudes change as they get older. Gradually, almost inevitably, the more dominant children begin to shun, reject and bully their shyer classmates. Sadly, those who are naturally less vocal and assertive and who do not benefit from a network of supportive friends can suffer for it.

Although they may emerge from their cocoons when among new children who don't label them, children tend to become stuck in their shyness with those who are familiar. If classmates believe a child is shy, no matter how much he wants to make overtures, he may be unable to break out and create a new persona.

This bias against shy children soon takes its toll. As early as the fourth or fifth grade, they realize bashfulness and anxiety are problems for them. In fact, surveys of shy fifth-graders show they have lower self-esteem than their more gregarious classmates.

Shyness in Adolescence

The development task of adolescence is to decide who we are and where we fit in the community that extends beyond our families. Teenagers must make these important decisions based on their needs and talents, not what others want them to be. Whether it's choosing a major, how to behave at a party, or how to dress, these decisions should reflect their true selves.

This is particularly true for shy teens who don't want their lives to reflect their shyness. They may try to deny that they feel insecure, socially anxious, and fearful. Consequently, they may follow the paths of others [and conform] rebel, or withdraw. Unfortunately, all of these choices work against self-awareness.

Shy teens need to come to terms with themselves and their shyness. If they are successfully shy at a young age, they will be prepared for the tasks of adulthood: expressing themselves through intimate relationships and work. We all discover who we are by interacting with others at work or at home. But if adolescents are uncertain about or quell their emotions and opinions, they will feel shackled by shy myths that can impede their growth.

In order to become successfully shy adults, teenagers must understand themselves and how shyness influences the many important choices they make. In fact, shyness in adulthood can become not just a personality trait but a quality-of-life issue. Researchers have correlated it with loneliness, depression, substance abuse, limited career advancement, low self-esteem, self-doubt, poor coping skills, the inability to solve problems, lack of community involvement, and poor health. Shy people view challenges as threats to their sense of self rather than sources of personal growth. Consequently, they are apt to shrink from them and live in a state of social and emotional stagnation.

Shyness in Adulthood

Shyness can be an issue at all stages of your life. Indeed, research has shown that adults who have been shy may have more difficulties as they age. They tend to be lonelier; have smaller and more unpredictable social and caregiving networks; have more difficulty replacing friends lost to retirement, illness, or death; and are more likely to be institutionalized. In many cases, adults grow into shyness and lose their old comfort zones following a divorce or the death of a spouse. The shy response alters as expectations and life circumstances evolve.

Conclusion

The many tasks of adulthood include developing a sense of community, discovering your place in society, finding and keeping love, raising a family, and engaging in meaningful work. Sadly, many of these tasks are difficult to achieve if your shyness makes you feel like a second-class citizen. Researchers have shown that shy people know what to do to make their lives more enjoyable but doubt their ability to carry through. For example, you may recognize that you must take a risk to begin a relationship but still worry excessively about self-disclosure, becoming the focus of attention, or rejection. You may want to make eye contact when talking with someone but feel too cautious and believe that you can't rise to the challenge. You may refrain from asking others questions because you fear you may be prying even though you know it just means you are showing an interest. You may have unreasonable expectations – you want immediate intimacy and paradoxically still expect others to draw you out.

Scientists have found that some shy people are highly anxious and may have poor emotional coping skills. They allow their feelings to run amok because they don't open up to others to seek reality checks or advice. They even deny themselves the comfort that comes from knowing that others have had the same experience. They feel lonely in new or challenging situations. When you don't rely on friends, social anxiety and self-doubt can fester, decreasing your ability to handle problems constructively. When you're anxious, you may find yourself unable to break problems into manageable components. Overwhelmed by your troubles, you soon fall into a vicious cycle. You constantly evaluate yourself negatively but never give yourself a chance to succeed.

Indeed, a in times of challenge you may engage in catastrophic, negative thinking and social avoidance and may fail to recognize opportunities for growth. Rather than solving your problems creatively, you become passive and just dwell on them. You may believe that other people can't relate to you because, unlike you, they seem so confident and able to work through their difficulties.

The result is plummeting self-esteem. Shy people constantly fail in their own eyes. They know what's expected, don't try, don't succeed, and feel miserable that they cant accomplish what they know they're supposed to. It is easy to see how shyness, unhappiness and loneliness are rightly interwoven.

Social support is imperative for happiness. It affects the way you think about the world and your place in it. It gives you hope and the belief in your ability to change your circumstances. It enhances problem-solving skills and motivation. Allen (1994) is reputed to have said, "ninety-nine percent of life is just showing up."

REFERENCES

Allen, O. (1994). Gender Differences in Selected psychological . Characteristics of adolescent Smorkers and Nonsmokers. *Healh Values,* 18, 34-39.

Arcus, D., and Kegan, J. (1995). Temperament and craniofacial variation in the first two years. *Child Development*, 33, 250-259.

Asendopf, J. B. (1993). Abnormal Shyness in Children. *Journal of Child Psychology and Psychiatry*, 34, 1069-1081.

Asendopf, J.B. (1990). *Beyond Social Withdrawal: Shyness, Unsociability, and Peer Avoidance*. Human Development, 33, 250-259.

Carducci, Bernardo J. and Kaiser, Lisa (2002). *Shyness: A Bold New Approach*. Harper Collins Publishers : New York.

Caspi, A. Bem, D. J., and Elder, G.H. Jr. (1988). Moving away from the World: Life-course Pattern of Shy Children. *Developmental Psychology,* 24, 824-831

Pilkonis, P.A. (1977). Shyness, Public and Private, and its Relationship to other measures of Social Behaviour. *Journal of Pesonalty*, 45, 585-595.

Triandis, H.C. (1994). *Culture and Social Behaviour*. New York: McGraw-Hill.

CHAPTER

25

Social Science Achievements among D.Ed. Trainees : Influence of Institutions and Locality

Prabhu Swami B.S.

ABSTRACT

The present study reports the social science achievement of second year D.Ed. trainees. Achievement test developed by the investigator on concepts like fill up the blanks, multiple choice, match the following, classification, true/false was employed to measure the influence of students studying government and private D.Ed., colleges as well as urban and rural students. Two-way ANOVA was employed to find out the significance of difference between trainees studying in government and private D.Ed. colleges as well as urban and rural students results revealed that government D.Ed. college trainees have scored better marks in fill up the blanks type, classification type and true/false type. Also they have scored better in total performance. Rural area D.Ed. trainees scored better marks in multiple choice items, match the following type and overall performance. Urban area D.Ed. students have scored better marks in classification type and true/false type. Locality has influenced positively on the marks scored. Rural government D.Ed. College trainees have scored better marks in fill up the blanks types, match the following type, classification type and total performance. Urban area government D.Ed. College trainees have scored better marks in true/false type.

Introduction

The prime objective of education and society is all round development of the individuals to achieve the objective primary school Teachers should aim at providing suitable learning experience in social science because the aim of providing, good citizens is rested on social science teachers. To achieve this, the objective of D.Ed., training institutions would be disseminating additional knowledge in social science to the trainees to the teacher trainees. The present study has been designed in this regard. There are limited studies at dissertation level at Ph.D., level. Content enrichment refers a process of programme, which enhances the master level of the knowledge from 1st to 7th Std., before entrance has teaching.

The present study is descriptive, comparative and correlative in nature. The objective of the study is to find out the influence of selected variables like gender, and type of institute on achievement in social science at the end of the training on social science.

The present study is conceptualized broadly under three levels:

1. To list concepts of the content enrichment in social science.
2. The construction achievement test in content enrichment of social science.
3. Administration of the achievement test on the selected sample and to arrive at specific conclusions on the influence of selected secondary variables.

Method

Subjects

A total of 1000 D.Ed. trainees were selected from the jurisdiction of Mysore South Division. Of the 1000 trainees selected, 500 of them belonged to urban are and 500 belonged to rural area. Out of which 323 of them from government run institutions and remaining 677 from private institutes. They were randomly selected from 25 D.Ed. training colleges coming under Mysore South Division in 5 districts of Mysore, Mandya, Hassan, Coorg and Chamarajanagar.

Tools

Social Science Achievement Test (Prabhuswamy, 2006)

The social science achievement test consisted of 285 items, which were classified into five groups. They were fill up the blanks (20 items), multiple-choice options (39 items), match the following items (97 items), classifications items (80 items) and true/false statements (49 items). All these items were prepared on the basis of content enrichment program in D.Ed. cirruculum. Initially, a try out was done on a sample of 100 trainees, and later some of the items were modified/deleted as per the opinion of the respondents. The final version was administered after discussion with subject and establishing psychometric properties to a satisfactory level.

Procedure

The tests were administered to the subject's in-group of 6-10 subjects per group. Data collection was done in 1 session and each session lasted for about 150 minutes. The investigator established rapport with the trainees and they were asked to introduce themselves. The purpose of the study was made clear to them. Then they were administered social science achievement test. They were given appropriate instructions and the questions were read out to them. They were asked to indicate their responses in the respective sheet given to them. Whenever they had doubt in understanding questions, the test administrator made those questions very clear to them in their local language.

Scoring and Analysis

For each correct answer one score was assigned, and calculated separately for different subtests fill up the blanks (20 items), multiple choice options (39 items), match the following items (97 items), classifications items (80 items) and true/false statements (49 items) and finally total scores were added.

Two-way ANOVA was employed to test the significance of difference in the mean social science achievement scores of D.Ed., trainees, where the scores in subtests and total scores were taken as dependent variable, and institution type and gender as independent variables. The statistical analyses were performed through SPSS for windows, Version 14 (Evaluation version).

Results

Table 25.1 presents mean scores obtained on social science achievement scores by urban and rural D.Ed. trainees in government and private institutions along with the results of 2-way ANOVA. Following are the major findings.

Main Effects

Between Institutions Type : Table 25.1 shows the government D.Ed. college trainees have scored better marks than private D.Ed. college trainees in fill up the blanks (F=25.896: P=.000), classification type (34.962: P=.000), and true/false (3.955: P=.046) and total performance (F=12.276: P= .00). Government D.Ed. College trainees have a mean score of 15.95 and private D.Ed. college trainees have a mean score of 15.40. In fill up the blanks type. Where as classification type. Government D.Ed. college trainees have a mean score of 63.97 and private D.Ed. college trainees has a mean score of 61.39. In true/false type government D.Ed. has 37.01 mean score whereas private D.Ed. college as a mean score of 36.01. In total performance government D.Ed. college trainees has a mean score of 212.34 mean and the mean score of private D.Ed. college is 211.50. With respect to multiple choice, fill up the blank items. Government and Private D.Ed. College trainees have equal statistical scores.

Locality and Social Science Achievement Scores: Except in fill up the blanks item in all the achievement items of social concepts, Rural D.Ed. College Trainees have better scores than urban D.Ed. College trainees in multiple choice (906.121:

Table 25.1. Mean Achievement scores in social science by teacher trainees having urban and rural area studying in government and private institutions and results of 2- way ANOVA

Instns	Locality	Tests											
		Fill up		Multiple choice		Match		Classification		True/false		Total	
		Mean	SD	Mean	SD	Mean	SD	Mean	SD	Mean	SD	Mean	SD
Govt	Urban	15.79	1.62	26.55	2.65	66.15	5.29	63.89	5.13	37.27	3.07	209.65	11.68
	Rural	16.41	1.73	33.24	3.28	69.60	4.17	64.17	4.45	36.31	3.80	219.74	11.91
	Total	15.95	1.67	28.33	4.10	67.07	5.24	63.97	4.95	37.01	3.30	212.34	12.55
Pvt.	Urban	15.89	1.72	26.89	3.14	68.47	4.41	63.33	6.51	37.26	3.23	211.84	13.64
	Rural	15.06	1.62	33.34	2.89	67.37	4.19	60.16	4.39	35.36	3.21	211.29	11.19
	Total	15.40	1.71	30.83	4.34	67.79	4.31	61.39	5.53	36.10	3.35	211.50	12.20
Total	Urban	15.84	1.68	26.73	2.92	67.37	4.98	63.60	5.90	37.26	3.15	210.80	12.78
	Rural	15.29	1.72	33.33	2.96	67.75	4.27	60.85	4.65	35.52	3.34	212.74	11.75
	Total	15.57	1.72	30.33	4.42	67.56	4.64	62.23	5.48	36.39	3.36	211.77	12.31
F: Institution (A)		F=25.296;P=.000		F=0.978;P=.323		F=0.014;P=.907		F=34.962;P=.000		F=3.955;P=.046		F=12.276;P=.000	
F: Locality (B)		F=0.799;P=.372		F=906.121;P=.000		F=12.218;P=.000		F=13.979;P=.000		F=35.123;P=.000		F=28.387;P=.000	
F: Interaction AxB		F=34.472;P=.000		F=0.288;P=.592		F=45.783;P=.005		F=20.020;P=.000		F=3.875;P=.049		F=35.298;P=.000	

P=.000), Match the following (F=12.218: P=.000), and total performance scores (F=28.387: P=.000).

Similarly the urban D.Ed. college trainees have better scores than rural D.Ed. College Trainees in classification type (F=13.979: P=.000) and True/False (F=35.123: P=.000). With respect to fill up the blank type in urban and Rural D.Ed. College trainees have scored statistically same scores.

Interaction Effects

Five interacting effects have been found significantly between locality and institutions. Rural government D.Ed. college trainees have better scores among fill up the blanks type match the following type, classification type and overall performance. Urban Government D.Ed. college trainees have better scores in true/false items. With the remaining item that is multiple choice items in there is no significant difference between locality and institutions. That means the rural and urban D.Ed. College trainee's scores are not dependent on locality.

Discussion

The result of the presence studies of:

1. Government D.Ed. college trainees have better scores among fill up the blanks type, classification type, true/false type and overall performance.
2. Localities have positive effect on total scores. Rural D.Ed. College trainees have better scores among multiple choice, match the following type and overall performance. While urban D.Ed. college trainees have significantly scores among classification type and true/false type.
3. Rural D.Ed. college trainees have better scores among fill up the blanks type, Match the following type, classification type and overall performance. While urban D.Ed. college trainees have better scores in true/false type.

The present study reveals the positive influence of the locality on the Social science achievement scores. There are direct studies pertaining to the relationship between locality and achievements, for the positive influencing of the locality. The following few studies could be named. Rural area students achievement are better than urban area students-Bountry (1970), Lowlar James Edward (1980) and but Lalithamma (1975), Aruna (1981), Mishra M (1986), Chakravarthy, S (1988) and Chelini A.B (1989) have revealed opposite result. Similarly there is no significant difference in school achievement among rural and urban area students-Kumar Rajiv (1989). While Narasimhaiah, C.V (2000) has revealed there is significance difference between rural and urban area students in achievement.

In total we can see locality place and important role in students achievements. In this background it can be conformed that locality influences achievements in different dimensions. Therefore the DIET is required to give suitable training at different levels by different resource persons for rural and urban primary teachers separately. These two classes of teachers required content based training for better teaching.

REFERENCES

Aruna, N.S (1981) "A study of the Factors influencing the Achievement of Standard VII students belongings to Scheduled Castes and Scheduled Tribes whose medium of Instruction is Kannada" The survey of Research in Education, Edited by M.B. Buch, M.S. University of Baroda.

Bountry (1978): "Construction and standardization of achievement test in Physical Science for high school class in Uttar Pradesh" in Secondary survey of research in education edited by M.B. Buch, M.S, University of Baroda.

Chakraborthy, S (1988). "A critical study of the socio-economic background of the family education environment in the family and quality of schools an academic achievement of childrens of standard Vth. A case study of some schools in and around Poona" Ph.D. thesis, Poona University.

Chelini, A.B. (1989), Hiriya prathamika Shal Vidyarthigal Mulabootha grhikegal mathu koushalgal sadhne, Unpublished thesis, Mysore University, Mysore.

Edward, Lowlar James (1981). "An assignment of selected variables social study skills and variables in six Indian public high schools" dessertation abstracts, ball state University.

Kumar, Rajiv, (1989). "Children curiosity intelligence and scholastic achievement" Ph.D Education, Agra University.

Lalithamma (1975) " A study of the relationship between atitudes towards academic work and achievement of the high school stage" M.Ed. dissertation, University of Kerala.

Mishra, M (1986). "A critical study of the influence of socio-economic status on academic achievement of higher secondary students in rural and urban area of Kanpur" Ph.D education, Kanpur University.

Narasimaiah, C.V (2000). *Vishkapatnam Jileya hathane thraragathi Vidyarthigal shishanika sadhene mele sambandhitha mano samajika amshagala prabhava ondhu hadyayana,* Unpublished thesis, Mysore University, Mysore.

Prabhuswamy, B.S. 2006. *The social science achievement test for D.Ed. trainees.* Mysore: University of Mysore.

Index

B

C

D

E